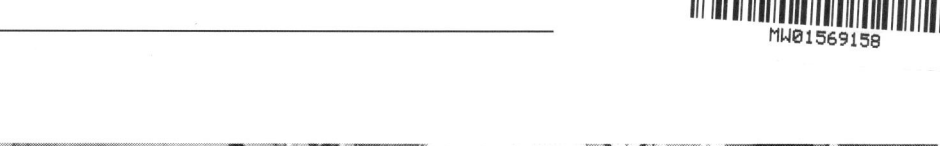

Fiber Optics
For CFOT Certification
The Basics

Created By The FOA
For Use By FOA Approved Schools

Fiber Optic Curriculum © 2013, The Fiber Optic Assn. Inc.

This is a basic fiber optic training program for FOA-Approved Schools to teach classes for the FOA CFOT certification.

The program was developed by Jim Hayes, founder and President of The Fiber Optic Association with inputs from many FOA instructors. It's is based on 30+ years of experience in the business, including starting one of the first fiber optic test equipment companies and training thousands of fiber optic installers.

Instructors:
Using This Fiber Optic PPT Presentation

Please read notes below

Fiber Optic Curriculum © 2013, The Fiber Optic Assn. Inc.

This is a complete training program covering the basics of fiber optics. You may edit it to include in training programs, including removing this slide which is for the instructor only.

Usage of this PPT and other FOA provided training materials is covered by the license agreement.

-The FOA licenses this program to instructors for their use teaching a CFOT course

-It can be edited to use in the course

-Copies with notes should be printed for all students

-The material is subject to the license agreement

-Intellectual property rights and copyright remain the sole property of The Fiber Optic Assn. Inc.

-It may not be resold in any way, either in whole or part of another document or presentation.

-Each slide is annotated.

-This tells the instructor and students what is important about each slide to help with presenting the materials, gives references and further study materials.

-Printing Handouts For Students: Print all slides as "Notes" which provides each slide on a page with the Notes for each slide below the slide, explaining what is meant by the slide.

The FOA CFOT Exam

- Requires field experience or training and demonstrated skills in appropriate tasks - instructors certify that the student has demonstrated those skills!
- Tests knowledge of fiber optics based on:
  - The FOA texts – *The FOA Reference Guides or the FOA Reference website (there is an online CFOT Study Guide)*
  - The *FOA* Installation Tech Bulletin or NECA-301
  - Material reviewed in this presentation

The FOA CFOT certifies those who demonstrate knowledge, skills and abilities appropriate to tasks involving fiber optics. The FOA develops appropriate reference and training curriculum materials to use for teaching or studying fiber optic technology covered in the exam.

It is the job of the instructor to verify that the student has shown the ability and skills to perform typical fiber optic tasks.

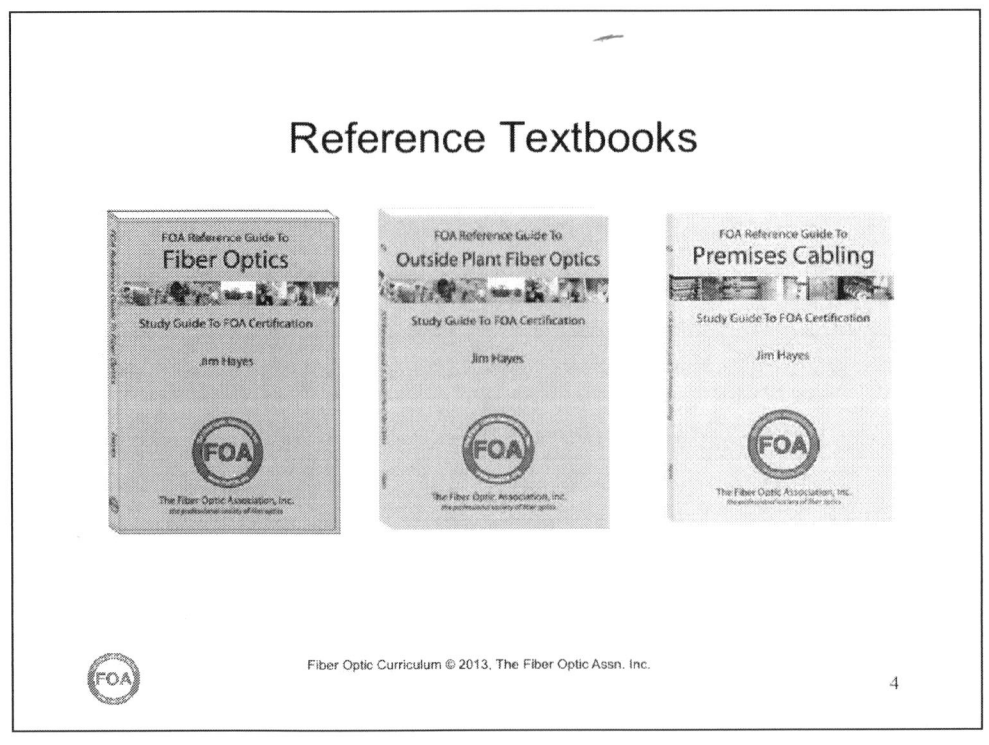

This presentation is based on 25 years of experience in the fiber optic business and much of the material is now available on the web and in printed form in *The FOA Reference Guides to Fiber Optics, Outside Plant Fiber Optics and Premises Cabling*, any of which may be used as a text for the course. References to the proper chapters are given in the notes. The notes give an overview of what the slide means and provide hints to explaining the meaning of the slide.

For the text references, FRG means FOA Reference Guide to Fiber Optics, OSP refers to the OSP book and PC to the Premises Cabling book.

FOA Online Fiber Optic Reference Guide

- Complement to *FOA texts*
- Includes all necessary references for CFOT, CPCT, CFospT
- *Understanding Fiber Optics, The Basics* section has self-test online quizzes, links to other tech pages
- *Premises Cabling* covers fiber, copper and wireless for CPCT
- *Outside Plant* covers OSP installations for CFospT
- Includes online student study guides and instructor teaching guide plus Google Custom Search

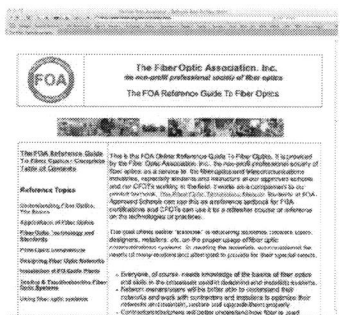

The FOA has created a complete online reference guide for fiber optics aimed at the CFOT and other FOA certifications. The site is at http://www.thefoa.org/tech/ref/. Included in the site are technical pages, including a basic section that includes quizzes on the materials and links to pages with more details. There are also a student guide for studying for the CFOT and an instructor guide to teaching a course based on the website.

FOA YouTube Channel

- About 60 videos covering topics similar to this PPT
- Short - ~ 10 minutes each
- Complete Lecture Series on Fiber Optics and Premises Cabling
- Hands-on fiber and premises cabling installation
- Channel "thefoainc"

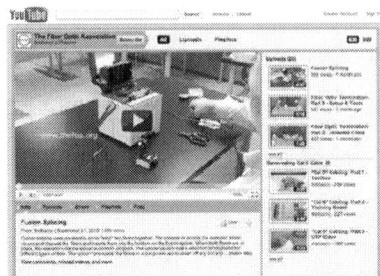

The FOA YouTube Channel "thefoainc" has about 50 short videos on fiber optics and premises cabling. The "Lecture Series on Fiber Optics" covers how fiber is used in communications, fiber optic components, network design, installation and testing. Dozens more videos cover "hands-on" topics like fiber optic cable preparation, splicing, termination and testing as well as how UTP cable used in premises cabling is terminated.

For those wanting to know more about fiber optics or studying for FOA certifications, both basic and advanced, these are good study materials.

Fiber U
www.fiberu.org

- Online learning site
- Self-study "web-based training" programs
- Online tutorials
- Uses technical resources of FOA Guide
- Use for "blended learning"
- Preparation for formal training and certification exams
- Homework for students

 Fiber Optic Curriculum © 2013, The Fiber Optic Assn. Inc.

Fiber University (Fiber U at www.fiberu.org) is a focal point for online learning about fiber optics. It's based on the giant FOA Online Reference Guide and hosts self-study programs and tutorials that can make learning about fiber much easier!

FOA Apps

- Fiber optic self-study program based on FOA Reference Guide
    - iPad only
- FOA LossCalc will calculate fiber optic link loss for design or testing
    - iPad/iPhone/iPod touch
- Look for more

FOA has created two apps for iOS devices, a Fiber optic self-study program based on FOA Reference Guide for iPad only and FOA LossCalc will calculate fiber optic link loss for design or testing on the iPad/iPhone/iPod touch.

Look for more, including for the Android OS.

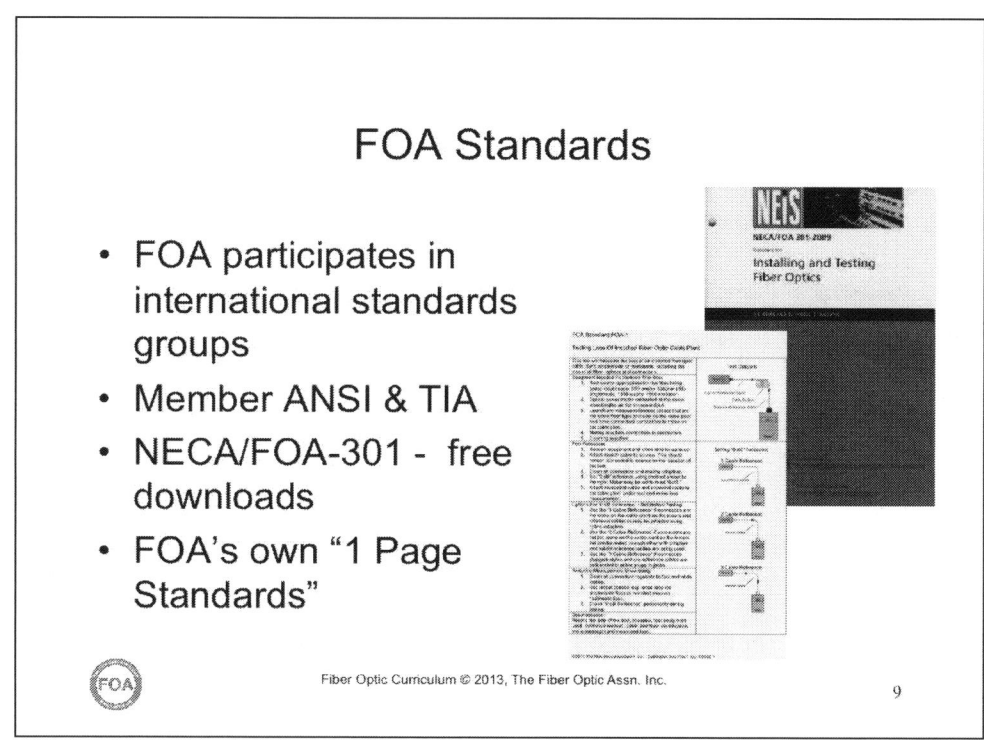

FOA participates in many US and international standards activities with ANSI, TIA, ISO/IEC and NECA plus specialized groups.

Recently we have added our own standards - Standards written BY contractors, designers, installers and users FOR contractors, designers, installers and users. These are based on TIA, ISO/IEC standards but summarized in 1 page and backed by tech info on the FOA website

FOA "1-Page" Standards

- Covers testing and other relevant topics
- Provides complete overview, links to details
- Available as PDF files, free to download
- Use as references for contracting documents

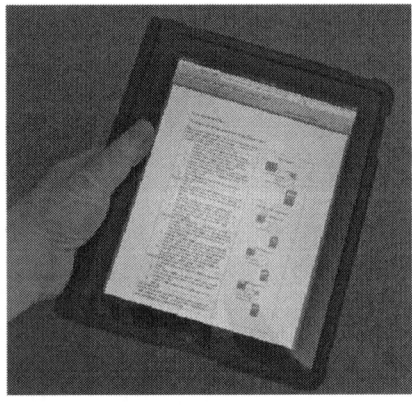

FOA 1 Page Standards

FOA's Standards are concise standards created by FOA with the participation of experts in the field for the most common issues affecting fiber optic network owners, contractors, designers and installers. Each standard summarizes what the reader needs to know in just 1 page. Each of the FOA's Standards will reference other industry standards that are similar in scope and which are used as the basis of the FOA standard, allowing FOA standards to be substituted for them. These FOA standards can be used for reference in project paperwork when the user and contractor need to be certain they agree what is being specified for the project.

Fiber Optic Installation Standard And FOA Installation Tech Bulletin

- *FOA Tech Bulletin on Installation,* FOA Tech Topics
- ANSI/NECA/FOA 301-2009
- Written for installers
- Defines installation in a "neat and workmanlike manner"
- Covers premises and outside plant
- Free downloads for FOA members and students

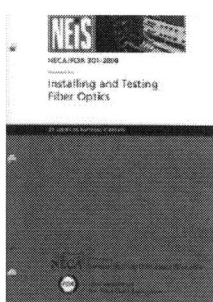

The FOA Installation Tech Bulletin, available free on FOA Tech Topics and the ANSI/NECA/FOA 301 were written for installers to provide a single standard to cover all issues of installation, from safety through installation, termination/splicing and test.

These standards define what is meant by installation in a "neat and workmanlike manner."

NECA-301 is available from NECA at http://www.neca-neis.org/

It covers both premises and outside plant applications.

FOA members and students can get Free downloads – get directions from FOA.

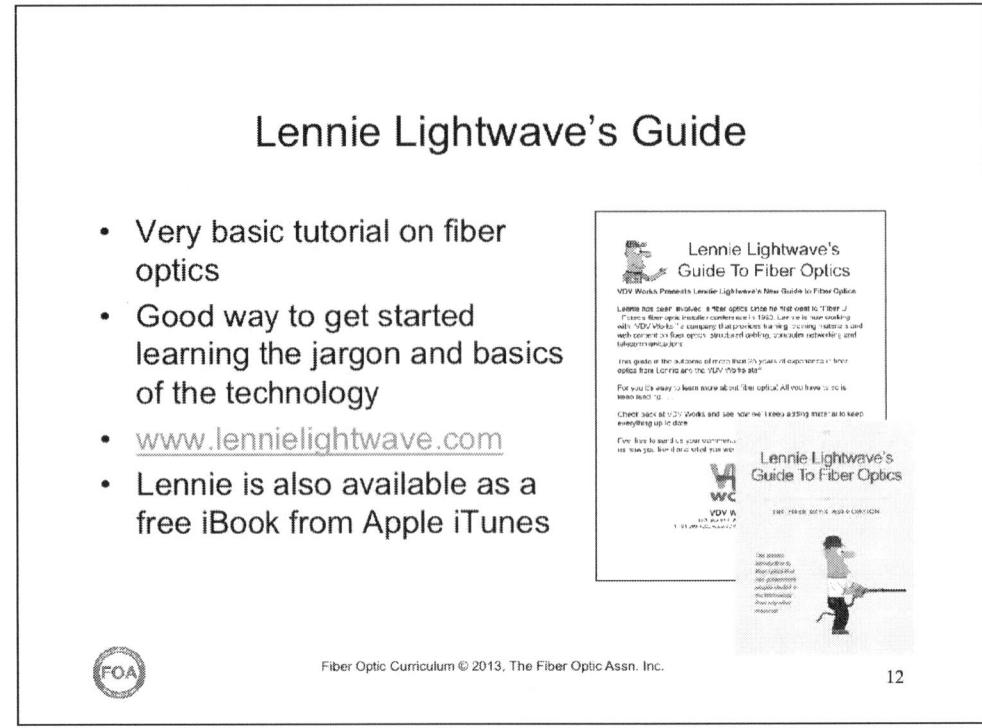

Another good handout for the course is Lennie Lightwave's Guide to Fiber Optics. Lennie has been around since the early 1990s as the beginner's source for technical information on fiber optics.
You can see it on the web at www.LennieLightwave.com and a printable version in PDF format is linked from the site or included in the FOA Starter Kit IIguide.pdf.
If you have an iPad, download the free Lennie iBook.
Also see the "Virtual Hands-On" section of Lennie Lightwave's Guide, FOA Tech Topics:http://www.thefoa.org/tech/index.html and videos on the FOA Website: http://www.thefoa.org/video/FOA_Videos/Termination.html

Learn More: College-Level Textbook

- For those looking for more theory and depth
- Jim Downing's *Fiber Optic Communications*
- Jeff Hecht's *Understanding Fiber Optics*

The FOA Reference Guide to Fiber Optics is aimed at installer training and hands-on labs. Some students want more in-depth knowledge. College-level classroom courses need more theory than The Fiber Optic Technicians Manual includes, so another textbook is needed. We used to recommend Jeff Hecht's Understanding Fiber Optics for an entry-level college text, but it has become very expensive. Delmar has recently published Jim Downing's Fiber Optic Communications which covers similar material but a a much lower cost. The Downing book also includes a lab manual for college labs (not installation training.)

What is "Fiber Optics"?

- Transmitting communications signals over hair thin strands of glass or plastic
- Not a "new" technology
- Concept over a century old
- Used commercially since 1976
- Dominates communications

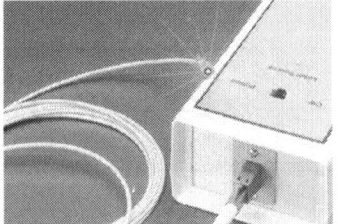

Fiber Optic Curriculum © 2013, The Fiber Optic Assn. Inc.

The first commercial fiber optic installation was for telephone signals in Chicago, installed in 1976. The first long distance networks and computer links were operational in the early 1980s. By 1985, most of today's basic technology was developed and being installed in the fiber optic networks that now handle virtually all long distance telecommunications and provide the backbone for most other communications and data networks.

FRG: Chapter 1, RGPC Chapter 1, FOTM, Chapter 2, DVVC, Chapter 11
FOA Online Fiber Optic Reference Guide, Understanding Fiber Optics, The Basics: Basic Overview

Fiber Optics Has It's Own Jargon

- Core, cladding, dB, multimode, singlemode, etc.
- Fiber has lots of technical terms that one needs to learn to understand the technology.
- Start by learning some of the basic jargon
  - Chapter 2, *FOA Reference Guide to Fiber Optics*
  - Jargon on the *FOA Online Reference Guide*

Fiber has lots of technical terms that one needs to learn to understand the technology. We have provided an explanation of the jargon in the textbook: Chapter 2, FOA Reference Guide to Fiber Optics and Basics/Jargon on the FOA Online Reference Guide

FRG: Chapter 2, RGPC Chapter 2, FOTM, Chapter 2, DVVC, Chapter 11
FOA Online Fiber Optic Reference Guide, Understanding Fiber Optics, The Basics: Jargon

Why Use Fiber Optics?

- Economics
- Speed
- Distance
- Weight/size
- Freedom from interference
- Electrical isolation
- Security
- Fiber is the least expensive, most reliable method for high speed and/or long distance communications

The biggest advantage of optical fiber is the fact it can transport more information longer distances in less time than any other communications medium. In addition, it is unaffected by the interference of electromagnetic radiation which makes it possible to transmit information and data with less noise and less error. Fiber is lighter than copper wires which makes it popular for aircraft and automotive applications. These advantages open up the doors for many other advantages that make the use of optical fiber the most logical choice in data transmission.

FRG: Chapter 1,3, RGPC Chapter 1, FOTM, Chapter 2, DVVC, Chapter 11
FOA Online Fiber Optic Reference Guide, Understanding Fiber Optics, The Basics: Basic Overview

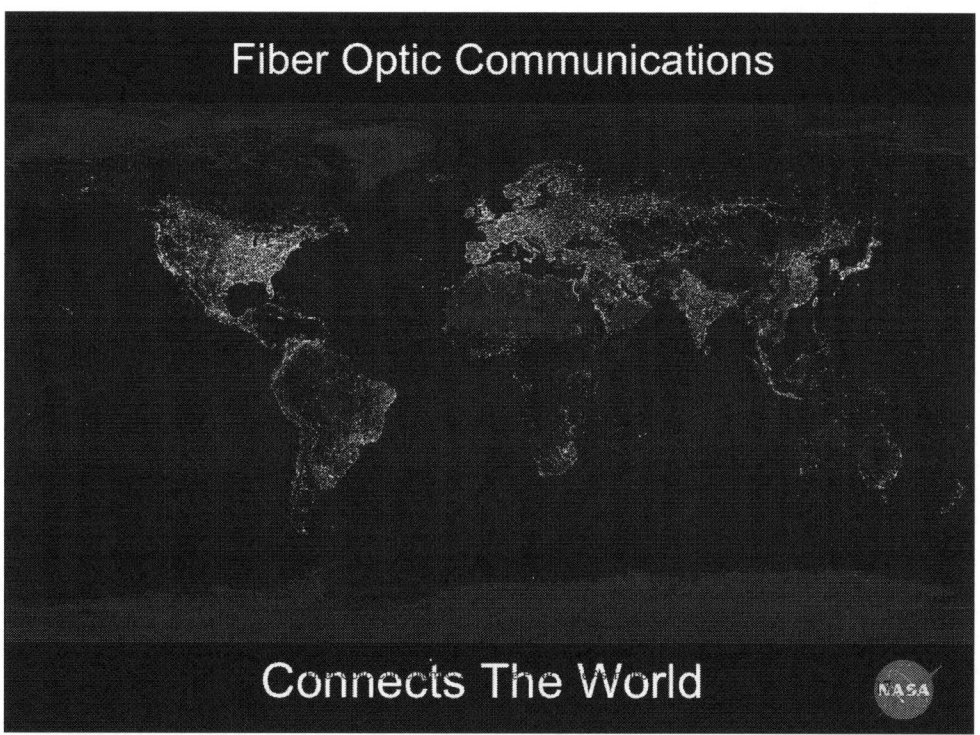

And the power of fiber optic communications connects the world.

This is a NASA composite map of the world at night. The lights show where people live.

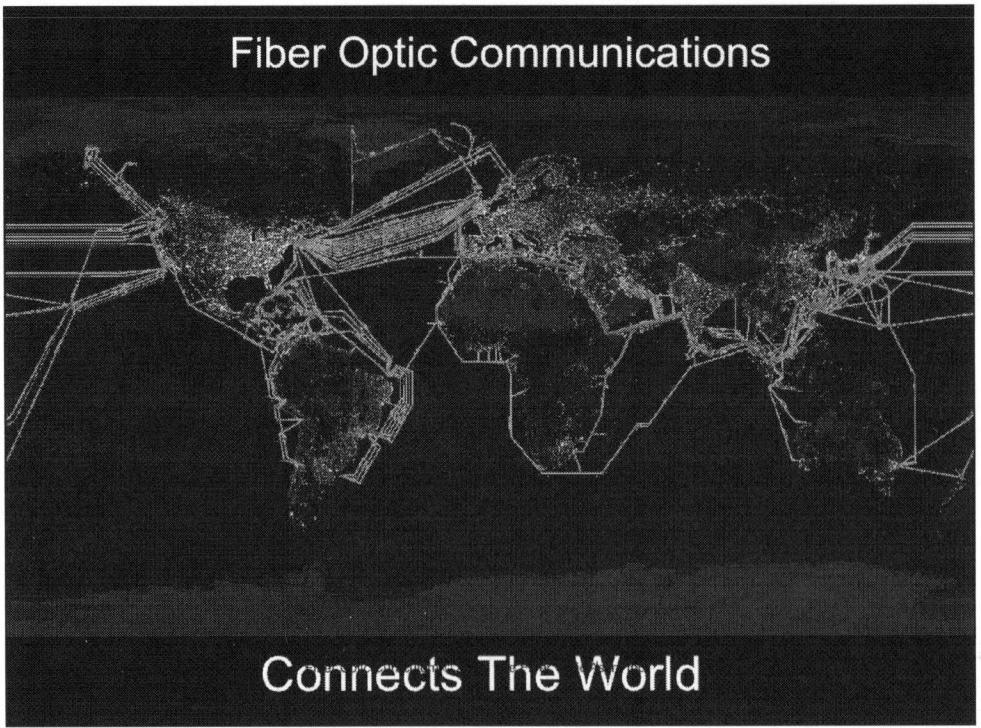

The red lines are all the submarine fiber optic cables that connect the places where people live and provide their communications links to each other.

And the power of fiber optic communications connects the world.

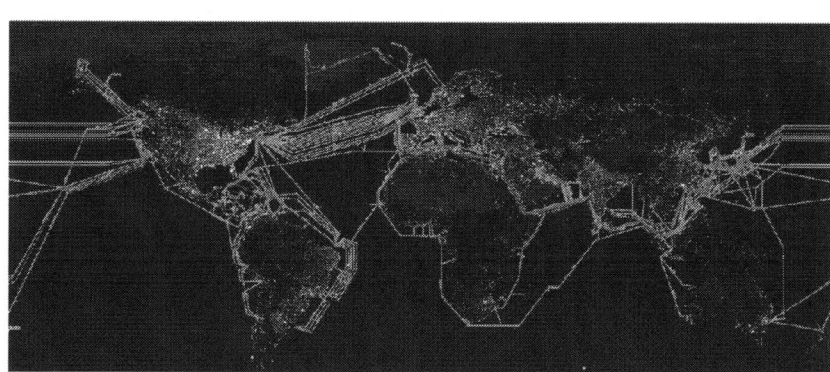

- Fiber optics connects the world under the seas and over the land
- Virtually all communications at some point travels via fiber

All those lines represent fiber optic cables that connect us and give us the ability to communicate. This the the world's communications backbone – telephones, Internet, data, everything,,,

Fiber Optic Applications

- Telecom – telephones, fiber to the home, wireless
- Internet, computer networks and data centers
- CATV - for video, voice and Internet connections
- Utilities - management of power grid, private telecom
- Security - CCTV and intrusion sensors, military
- Entertainment - video and audio
- Intelligent Highways

Lighting too!

These are but a few of the applications of fiber optics, as we concentrate on communications. Fiber optics are also used for lighting, signs, sensors and visual inspection (medicine and non-destructive testing).

FRG: Chapter 1, 3, FOTM, Chapter 2, DVVC, Chapter 11
FOA Online Fiber Optic Reference Guide, Understanding Fiber Optics, The Basics: Basic Overview

Fiber Use Is Growing In:

- Internet Backbone
- Wireless System Backhaul, Antenna Connections
- Smart Grid - Utilities
- Metropolitan Networks
- Security Systems
- Data Centers
- Fiber To The Home (FTTH)
- OLANs
- …and more!

Fiber use is growing in many areas – even wireless, both cellular and municipal WiFi – depends on fiber optics for its communications backbones. One of the newest applications is OLANs using FTTH technology is making inroads into corporate LANs because it's cheaper and more power efficient.

Fiber Growth Is A Result Of:

- Worldwide expansion of telecommunications
- Increased Internet data and video traffic
- Growth in wireless communications
  - Smartphones, iPads, Kindles
- Internet growth, especially video (IPTV)
- More security, surveillance systems
- ...and more new applications

Fiber is the most efficient, cost effective means of communications and is being used to transmit the explosive growth of communications.

Telecom Technology

- Fiber replaces copper or radio links
- All digital, gigabit speeds
- SONET/SDH protocol
- Moving to IP and all-optical protocols
- Fiber To The Home (FTTH) using PONs (passive optical networks)

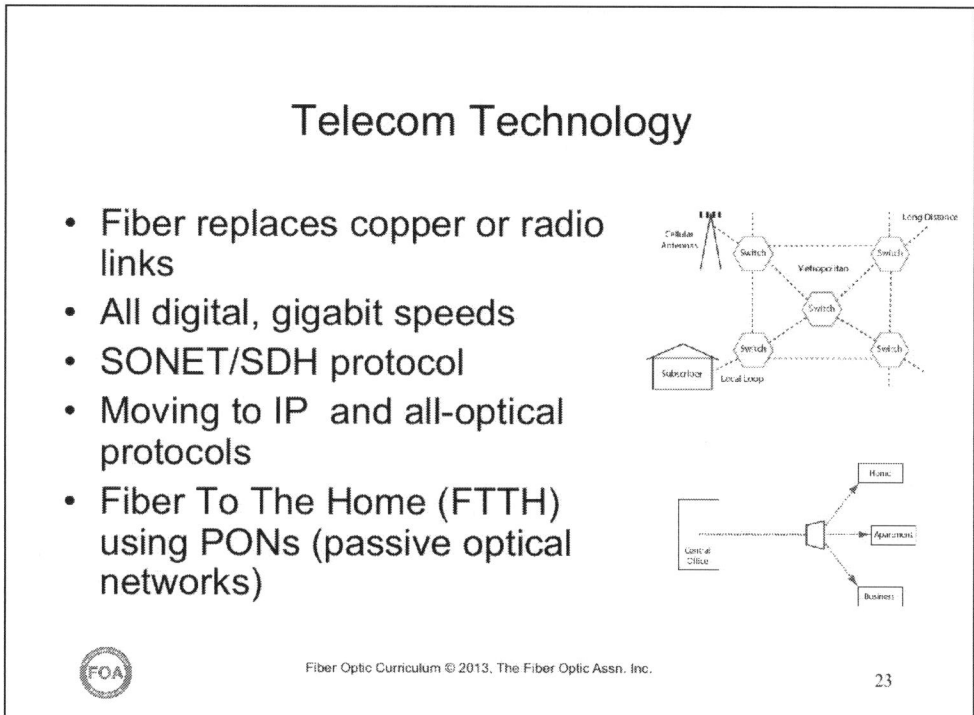

Fiber optics has become widely used in telecommunications because of its enormous bandwidth and distance advantages over copper wires. The application for fiber in telephony is simply connecting switches over fiber optic links.

Telecom systems carry more phone conversations over a single pair of fibers than could be carried over millions of copper pairs. Material costs, installation and splicing labor and reliability are all in fiber's favor - not to mention space considerations. In major cities today, insufficient space exists in current conduit to provide communications needs over copper wire.

While fiber carries over 90% of all long distance communications and 50% of local communications, the penetration of fiber to the curb (FTTC) and fiber to the home (FTTH) has been hindered by a lack of cost effectiveness. These two final frontiers for fiber in the phone systems hinge on fiber becoming less expensive and the customer demand for high bandwidth services impossible over current copper telephone wires.

FRG, Chapter 3, FOTM, Chapter 3, DVVC, Chapter 11
FOA Online Fiber Optic Reference Guide, Understanding Fiber Optics, The Basics: Basic applications and transmission systems

Telecom Technology

- Fiber replaces copper or radio links
- All digital, gigabit speeds
- SONET/SDH protocol
- Moving to IP and all-optical protocols
- Fiber To The Home (FTTH) using PONs (passive optical networks)

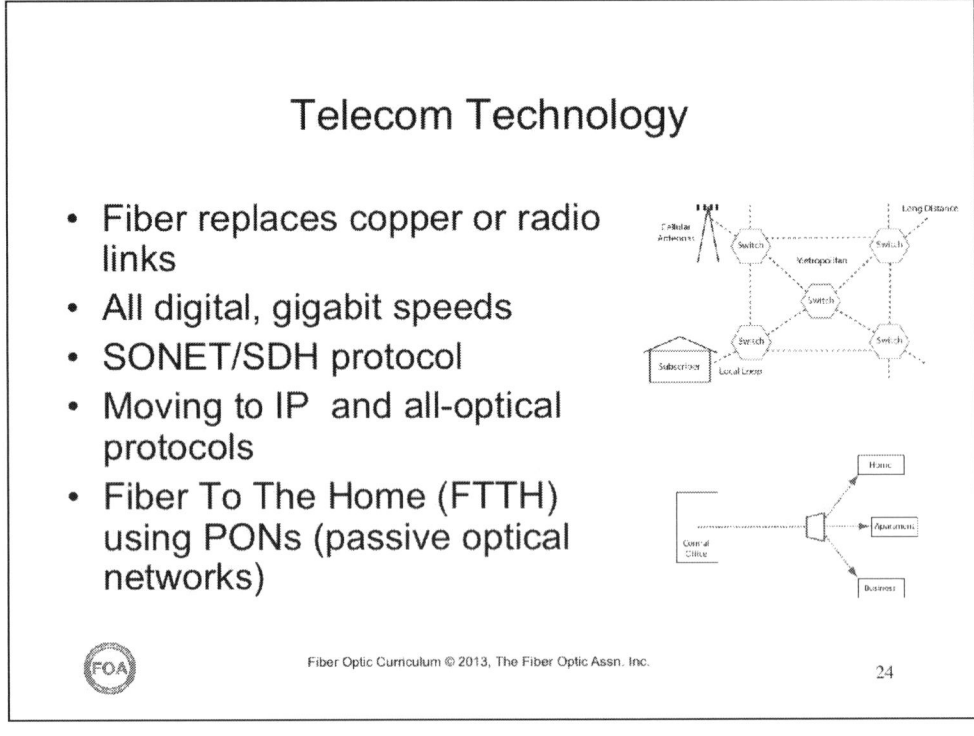

The secret to making FTTH cost effective has been the development of the passive optical network (PON).

The passive optical network (PON) uses optical couplers, both wavelength division multiplexers and simpler splitter/combiners, to allow connection of many customers over one fiber from the CO. Thus a few fibers can support many customers, up to 32 customers on one fiber from the CO to the local splitter.

A PON using wavelength division multiplexing (WDM) can be used two ways: It can provide every customer with a dedicated wavelength, greatly expanding bandwidth to any one customer, but a a much greater cost.

A more popular option is to use WDM to send multiple services, usually voice data and video, as well as upstream signals, over a single fiber. Telecom systems operate at bit rates up to 10 gigabits per second and many links use WDM - wavelength division multiplexing - to put several channels of signals over one fiber.

FRG, Chapter 3, FOTM, Chapter 3, DVVC, Chapter 11
FOA Online Fiber Optic Reference Guide, Understanding Fiber Optics, The Basics: Basic applications and transmission systems

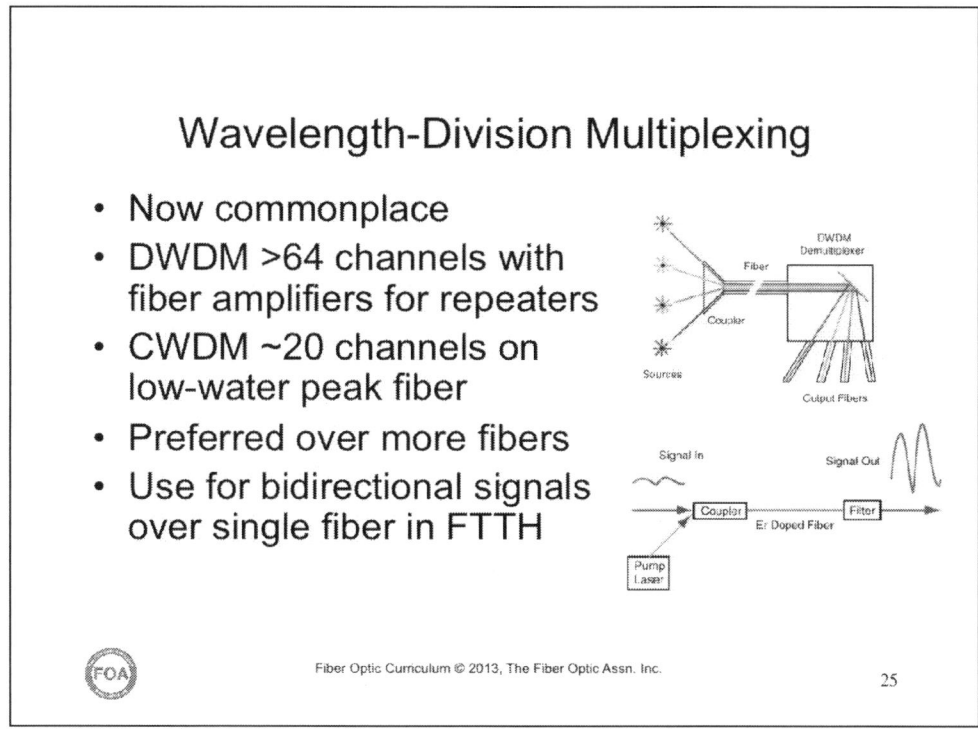

Wavelength-Division Multiplexing

- Now commonplace
- DWDM >64 channels with fiber amplifiers for repeaters
- CWDM ~20 channels on low-water peak fiber
- Preferred over more fibers
- Use for bidirectional signals over single fiber in FTTH

To expand bandwidth, it's now common to add new wavelengths rather than use new fibers.

How Does WDM Work? It is easy to understand WDM. Consider the fact that you can see many different colors of light - red, green, yellow, blue, etc. all at once. The colors are transmitted through the air together and may mix, but they can be easily separated using a simple device like a prism, just like we separate the "white" light from the sun into a spectrum of colors with the prism. The input end of a WDM system is really quite simple. It is a simple coupler that combines all the inputs into one output fiber. These have been available for many years, offering 2, 4, 8, 16, 32 or even 64 inputs. It is the demultiplexer that is the difficult component to make.

The demultiplexer takes the input fiber and collimates the light into a narrow, parallel beam of light. It shines on a grating (a mirror like device that works like a prism, similar to the data side of a CD) which separates the light into the different wavelengths by sending them off at different angles. Optics capture each wavelength and focuses it into a fiber, creating separate outputs for each separate wavelength of light.

Current systems offer from 4 to 64 channels of wavelengths. The higher numbers of wavelengths has lead to the name Dense Wavelength Division Multiplexing or DWDM. The technical requirement is only that the lasers be of very specific wavelengths and the wavelengths are very stable, and the DWDM demultiplexers capable of distinguishing each wavelength without crosstalk.

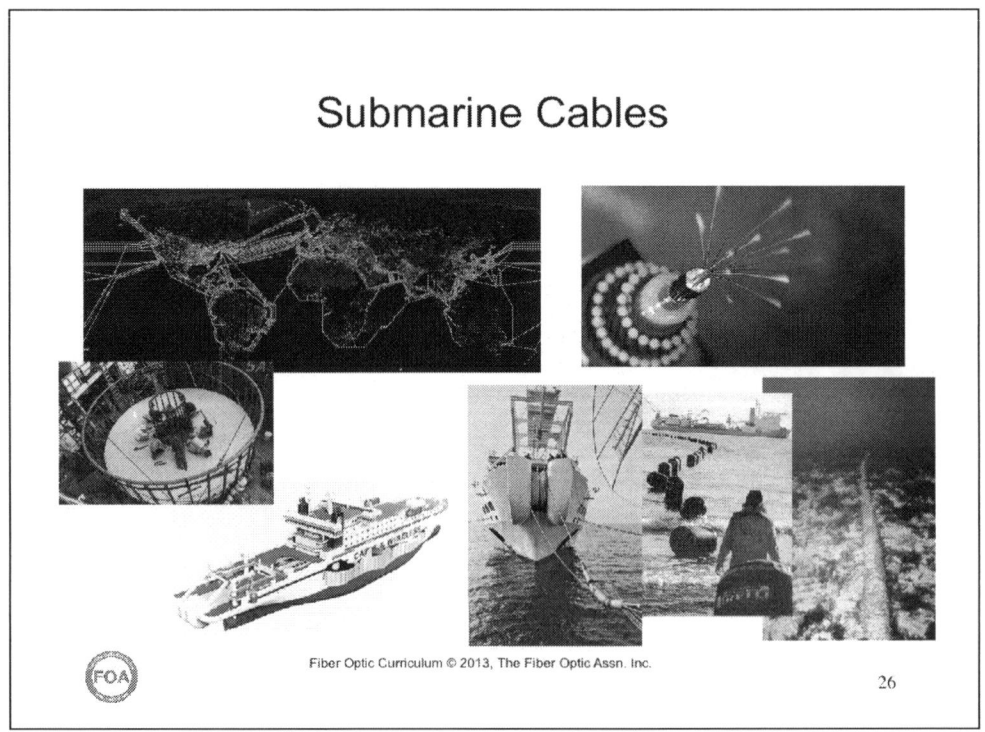

Top: Submarine cable map, actual undersea cable with fibers in the center surrounded by electrical conductors to power repeaters and strength members and covered by a heavy-duty jacket.

Below: Cable being loaded onto ship spool, cable laying ship, deploying a cable – note the repeater in the lower right hand corner, cable landfall and the undersea cable in place.

Fiber optic cables sometimes need to be installed underwater. The best known of these installations are probably the transoceanic cables that provide worldwide telecom and Internet communications. Installing those cables is a very specialized process that requires special cable designs and custom cable-laying ships to pay out the cable over thousands of kilometer runs and place it on the ocean floor at great depths. Those applications, while interesting, are beyond the scope of this book.

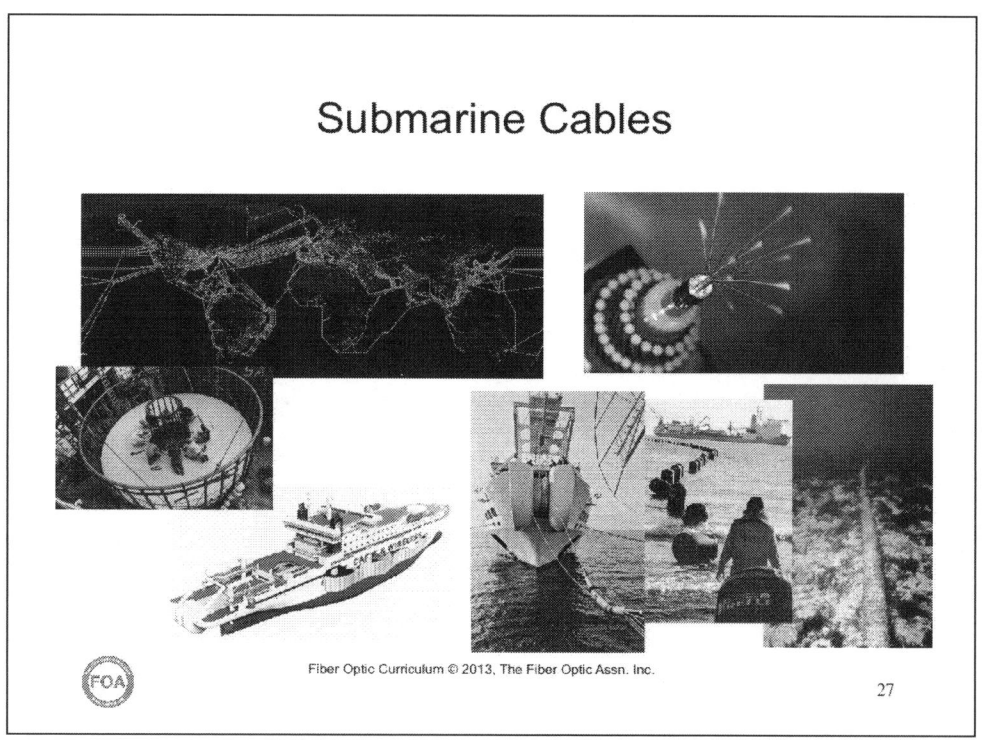

Other underwater installations involve river or lake crossings where it is more cost effective to lay fiber cable under water than detour around the water, place the cable in conduit lashed to bridges or other structures or run the cable aerially. Underwater crossings may require special permits because of the jurisdiction of various environmental groups.When cables are run underwater, there is always danger of the cable being snagged. For relatively shallow water, the cable should, if at all possible, be buried several feet under the bottom of the river or lake. For deeper water, special armored cables with one of more layers of wire armor should be used to prevent damage to the cable if snagged. Due to the specialized splice housings needed for underwater cables, running a single length across the water will be much easier and less costly. Underwater installation brings its own safety hazards also. Experienced divers may be needed to assist in placing the cable and troubleshooting problems.

Fiber to the Home (FTTH)

- For telephone systems, fiber is already used in:
    - Long distance backbones
    - Connecting switches in cities
- New Technology makes it cost effective to connect homes directly with fiber

FTTH has taken off because of the explosion of data use for the Internet and the reduction of cost of installing fiber to the home.

FTTH Economics

- Fiber optic components are getting cheaper
- Passive optical networks cut costs even more
- Fiber is cheaper to maintain than copper
- Fiber offers new services like TV and high speed Internet that increase revenues

Over the last decade, the cost of connecting a subscriber directly on fiber had dropped by about 75-80%, making FTTH more cost effective. This is a combination of component cost reductions and new architectures like PONs – passive optical networks. Plus fiber is much cheaper to maintain than copper, especially aging copper networks typical of most areas. With fiber the new services like IPTV downloaded over the Internet are possible.

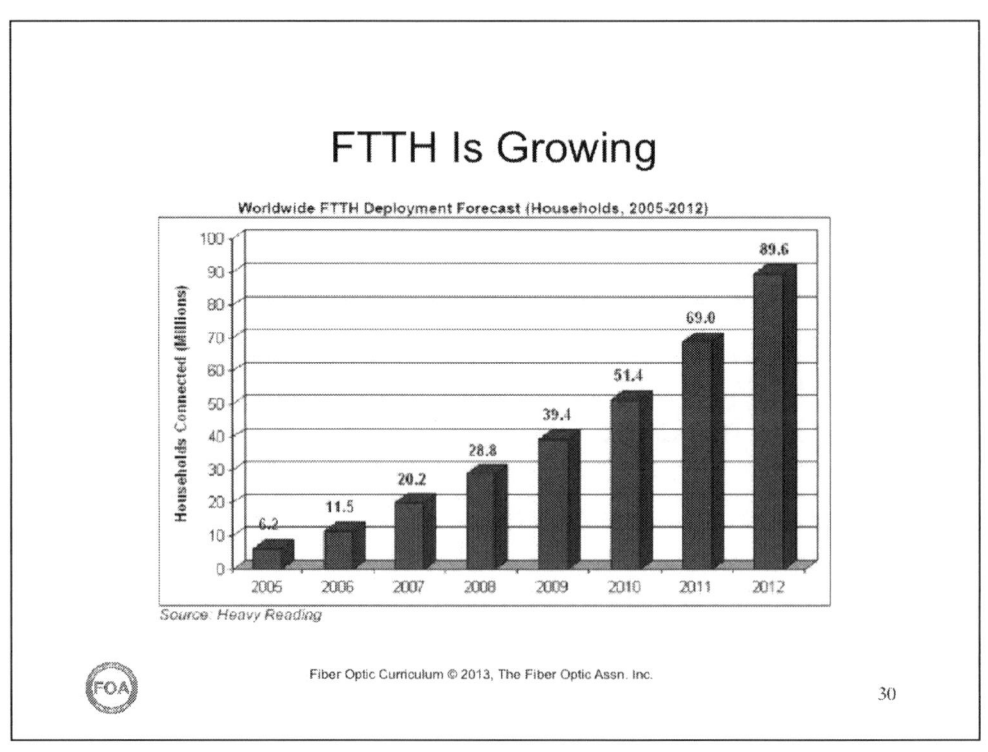

All these factors are making FTTH a fast growing field, not only for telcos but cities and regions and independent operators.

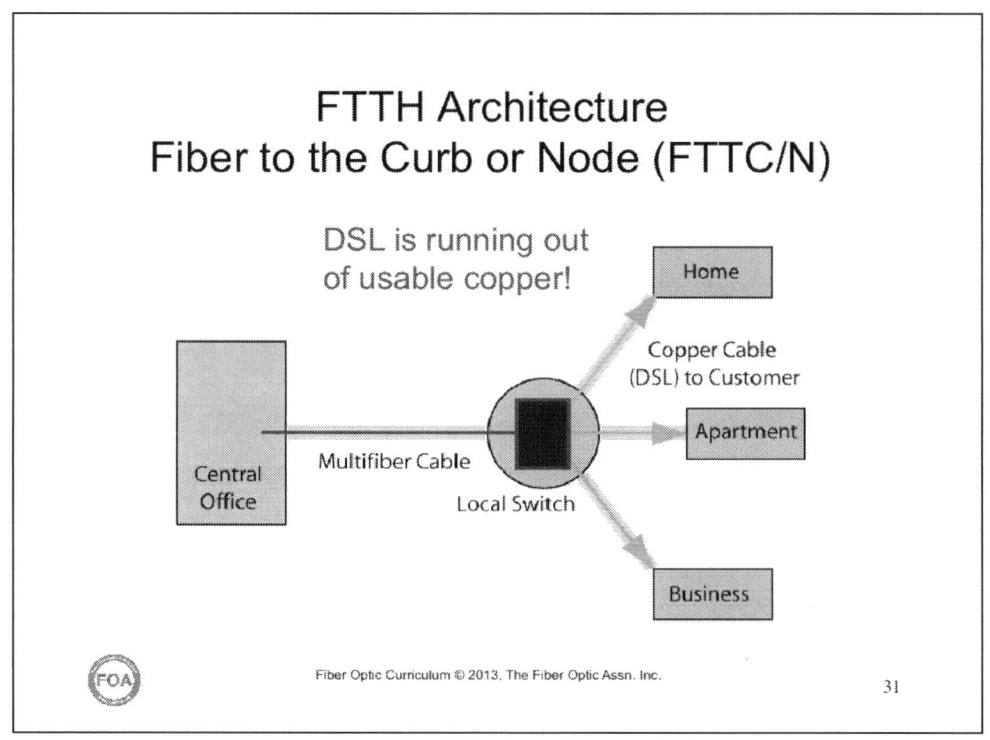

An active star network uses fiber from the central node (CO) to a local active node carrying multiplexed signals to be distributed to all the customers. At the active node, (electronic) switching occurs for each customer and connects to a dedicated optical link to the premises. This may be a more expensive network due to the electronics and powering required, as the node requires uninterruptible local power if support of services like 911 are required, or cheaper for small networks that do not need the size or capability of a PON network. Each system needs to be considered carefully in light of all options.

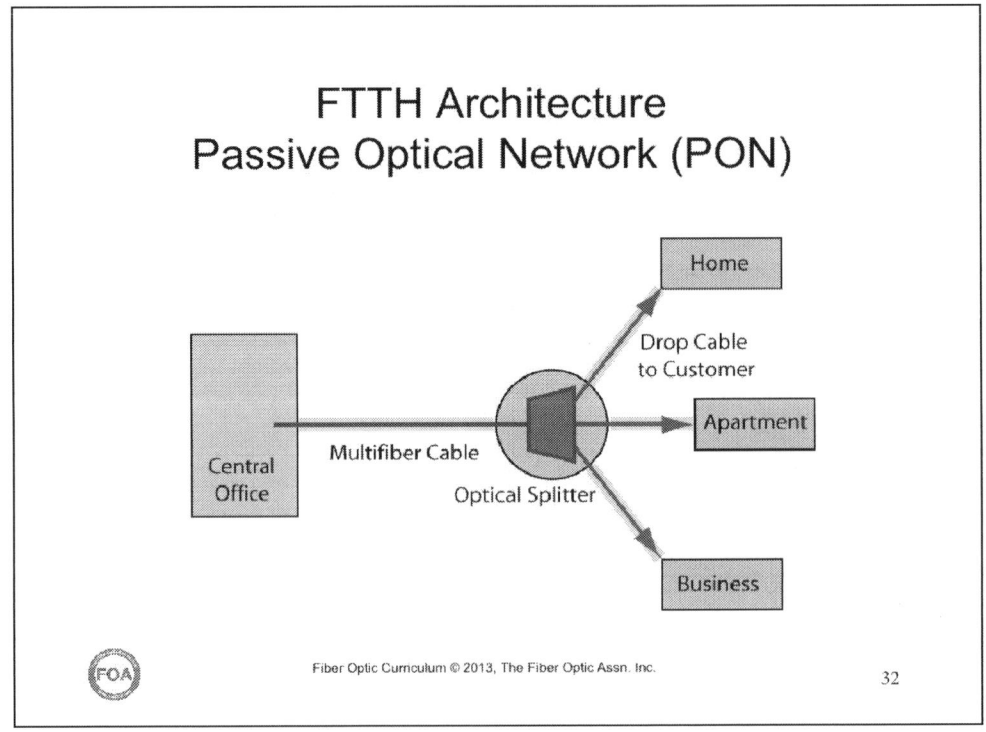

The passive optical network (PON) uses optical couplers, both wavelength division multiplexers and simpler splitter/combiners, to allow connection of many customers over only one fiber from the CO - like broadcasting TV or radio over air waves. Thus a few fibers can support many customers, typically up to 32 customers on one fiber from the CO to the local splitter.

A PON using wavelength division multiplexing (WDM) can be used two ways: It can provide every customer with a dedicated wavelength, greatly expanding bandwidth to any one customer, but a a much greater cost.

A more popular option is to use WDM to send multiple services, usually voice data and video, as well as upstream signals, over a single fiber, as shown in the slides following.

Upstream data from multiple subscribers is time-division multiplexed so each subscriber has a time window to send data back to the system.

Some people refer to this as a P2MP or point-to-multipoint network.

Passive Optical Network (PON) Options

Type	Description	Standard
BPON Broadband PON	ATM and video on HFC	ITU-T G.983
GPON Gigabit PON	IP + ATM or GEM	ITU-T G.984
EPON Ethernet PON	Ethernet 1-10 Gb/s	IEEE-802.3ah

There are several types of PONs being deployed, categorized by their transport protocol, or how the data is encoded and transmitted.

BPON, or broadband PON, uses ATM as the protocol. ATM is widely used for telephone networks and the methods of transporting all data types (voice, Internet, video, etc.) are well known. BPON operates at ATM rates of 155, 622 and 1244 Mb/s. Video is sent to subscribers using analog transmission like hybrid-fiber coax CATV systems.

GPON, or gigabit-capable PON, uses an IP-based protocol and either ATM or GEM (GPON encapsulation method) encoding. Data rates of up to 2.5 Gb/s are specified and it is very flexible in what types of traffic it carries. GPON enables "triple play" (voice-data-video) and is the basis of most planned FTTP applications in the near future.

EPON or Ethernet PON is based on the IEEE standard for Ethernet in the First Mile. It uses packet-based transmission at 1 Gb/s with 10 Gb/s under discussion. EPON is widely deployed in Asia.

Optical Network Terminal

ONT - Optical Network Terminal - optical network terminals generally mount on the outside of the customer premises and provide voice, data and video feed to the home. Larger units are used for businesses and apartments. Sometimes, ONTs are installed indoors and some look similar to a cable modem or router.

ONTs can be connected to the network by splicing or connectors, but connectors are generally favored for their simplification of testing and troubleshooting. Connectors may be spliced on drop cables or prepolished/splice connectors can be used on the cables. Many vendors are developing preterminated cable assemblies with weatherproof connectors as the simplified installation can save costs over field termination.

ONTs contain transmitters and receivers for the optical fiber connections and electronics to drive phone, Internet and TV connections in the home. Thus each ONT needs powering at the home. Powering ONTs is an issue, since customers expect phone service to not be interrupted by power outages, a consequence of over a century of phones being powered from the central office. Now most ONTs are powered from the customer's AC power and include an uninterruptible power supply to maintain service during power outages.

New Products Coming From FTTH

- FTTH required
    - Low cost components
    - Fast and easy Installation
    - Installation indoors in small spaces
- Resulted in development of many new products

FTTH has caused the development of several new technologies to simplify installation and lower cost.

Prefabricated Cabling Systems

- Factory terminated cables used for drop to home
- Weather-resistant closures used on cables, poles or underground
- Saves time and cost

Many FTTH systems now use prefabricated cables for the drop to the house. Crews come into the neighborhood and install the drop closures on poles or in underground vaults and splice the fibers into the backbone fiber network that terminates in the central office or a local PON distribution hub. The tech doing the actual FTTH install merely plugs in the cables between the closure and the optical network terminal and spends the bulk of the time connecting the user to telephone, Internet and TV services.

Prefabricated Cabling Systems

- 2 to 12 fibers per module
- Connectors are sealed
- Fusion splice other end to feeder cable

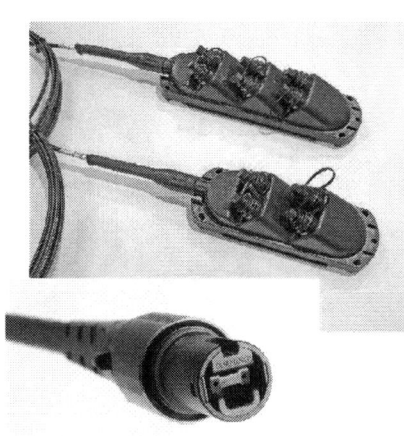

Many FTTH systems now use prefabricated cables for the drop to the house. Crews come into the neighborhood and install the drop closures on poles or in underground vaults and splice the fibers into the backbone fiber network that terminates in the central office or a local PON distribution hub. The tech doing the actual FTTH install merely plugs in the cables between the closure and the optical network terminal and spends the bulk of the time connecting the user to telephone, Internet and TV services.

Bend Insensitive Fiber

- Normal fiber has high loss when bent
- New "bend insensitive fiber" can be bent tightly without loss - or long term harm
- Use indoors to fit fibers in small spaces

Most optical fiber manufacturers are now offering bend-insensitive fibers that can be bent tightly without much loss. This allows them to be used in close spaces like cable trays or run around the edge of a wall in a room.

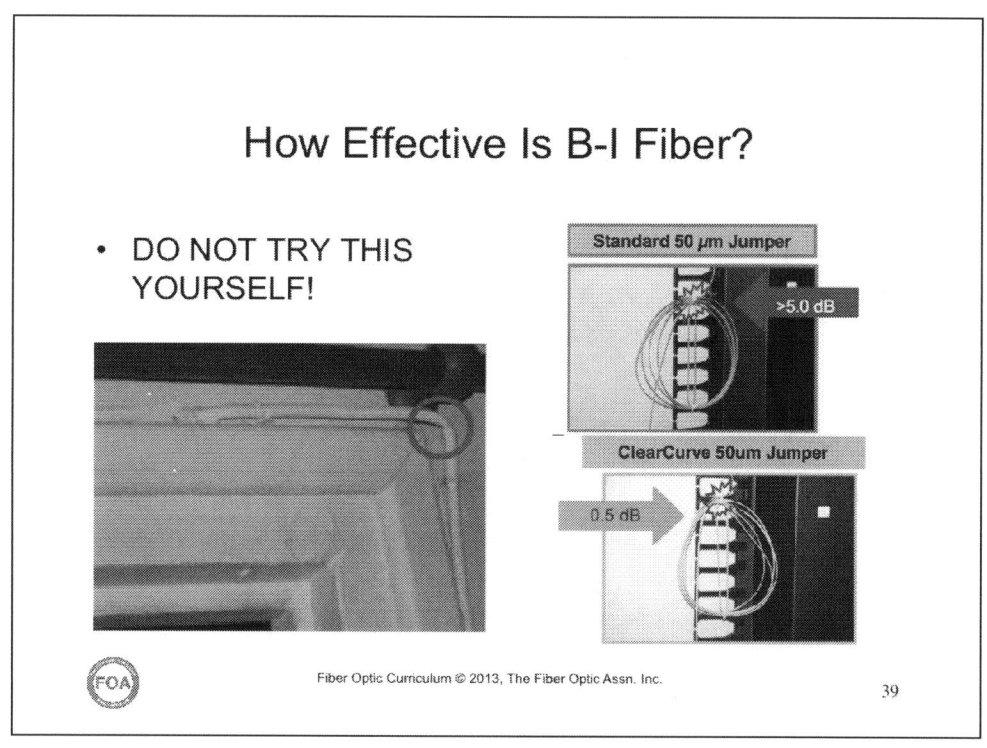

Bend-insensitive fiber simplifies installations because it allows fiber to be installed in tight quarters without stress losses induced in regular fibers. It also allows fibers to be made much smaller diameter also simplifying installation.

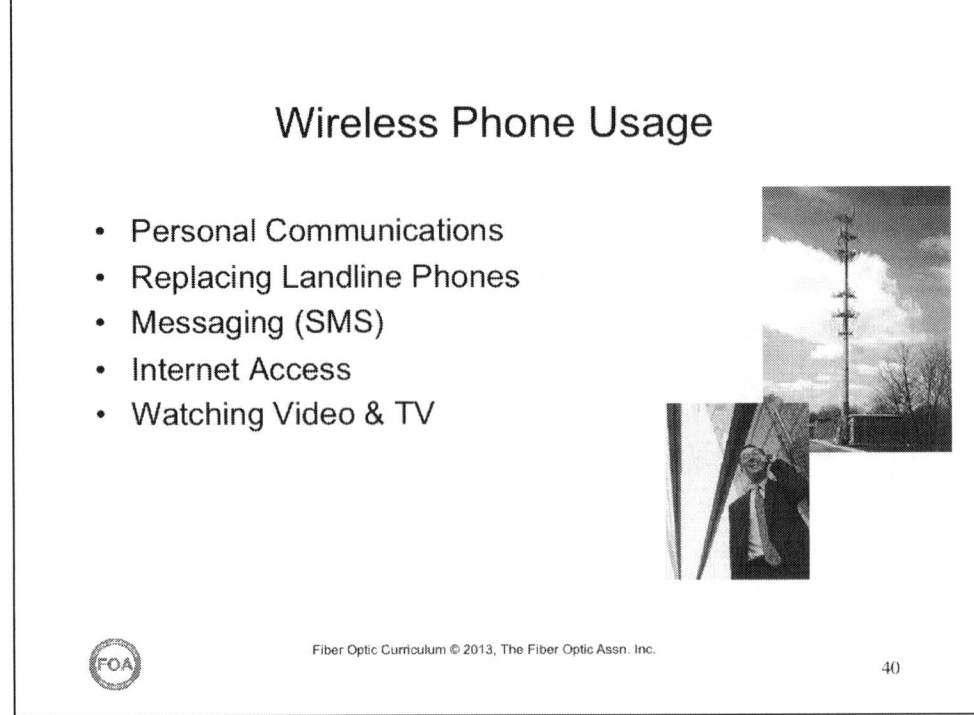

Wireless communications is also booming.

What Can Happen!

- AT&T: wireless network data traffic in the US had grown >8000% - that's 80 times — in 3-1/2 years since the introduction of the first Apple iPhone!
- Here comes the iPad!

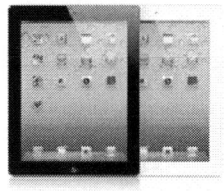

Here is an example of the effects of smartphones on phone networks. Worldwide, smartphones have become the majority of all phones sold and are driving data use to record levels.

Fiber Optics & Wireless Communications

- Cellular antennas
- Wireless LAN antennas (WiFi, WiMax)
- Satellite links
- Connect into worldwide networks on fiber

Most wireless systems like cellular systems are not all wireless - most antennas are connected into the worldwide communications networks via buried fiber optic cables.
Likewise, wireless LANs and metropolitan wireless systems require cabling and fiber provides greater distances from hubs and switches and immunity to noise.

FRG, Chapter 3, FOTM, Chapter 3, DVVC, Chapter 11
FOA Online Fiber Optic Reference Guide, Understanding Fiber Optics, The Basics: Basic applications and transmission systems

Super WiFi/White Space

- WiFi protocols
- Broadcasts on unused analog TV channels
- Lower frequency means longer reach
- Frequency availability may limit to rural areas
- In trials in rural California, Oregon, Houston and London

This new system uses frequency spectrum opened up by the change from analog to digital TV broadcasting.

How Do You Connect Antennas?

- Bandwidth for wireless is scarce
- Must connect to phone systems which are already fiber optics
- So fiber is used for many wireless connections – even up the towers!

Many wireless towers are connected to the phone system using fiber backbones using standard singlemode optical fiber. Expanded 4G and LTE service requires more antennas on the towers. Traditionally the antennas are connected on large coax cables to stations on the ground. Now fiber, usually multimode fiber for the short links, is being used for it's lower bulk and weight, so only a single fiber optic cable and a power cable needs to run up the tower rather than the big bundles of coax shown on the towers on the upper left.

How Do You Connect Antennas?

- Large coax up the tower to antennas is too big and too heavy
- Use small fiber cable, sometimes with power conductors to connect multiple antennas

MF2 Fiber Terminal
RRH
Antenna

Many wireless towers are connected to the phone system using fiber backbones using standard singlemode optical fiber. Expanded 4G and LTE service requires more antennas on the towers. Traditionally the antennas are connected on large coax cables to stations on the ground. Now fiber, usually multimode fiber for the short links, is being used for it's lower bulk and weight, so only a single fiber optic cable and a power cable needs to run up the tower rather than the big bundles of coax shown on the towers on the upper left.

Is This The Antenna Of The Future?

- Alcatel-Lucent has recently shown "lightRadio cube" a small cellular antenna that can be placed anywhere
- Needs only fiber and power connections

Many wireless towers are connected to the phone system using fiber backbones using standard singlemode optical fiber. Expanded 4G and LTE service requires more antennas on the towers. Traditionally the antennas are connected on large coax cables to stations on the ground. Now fiber, usually multimode fiber for the short links, is being used for it's lower bulk and weight, so only a single fiber optic cable and a power cable needs to run up the tower rather than the big bundles of coax shown on the towers on the upper left.

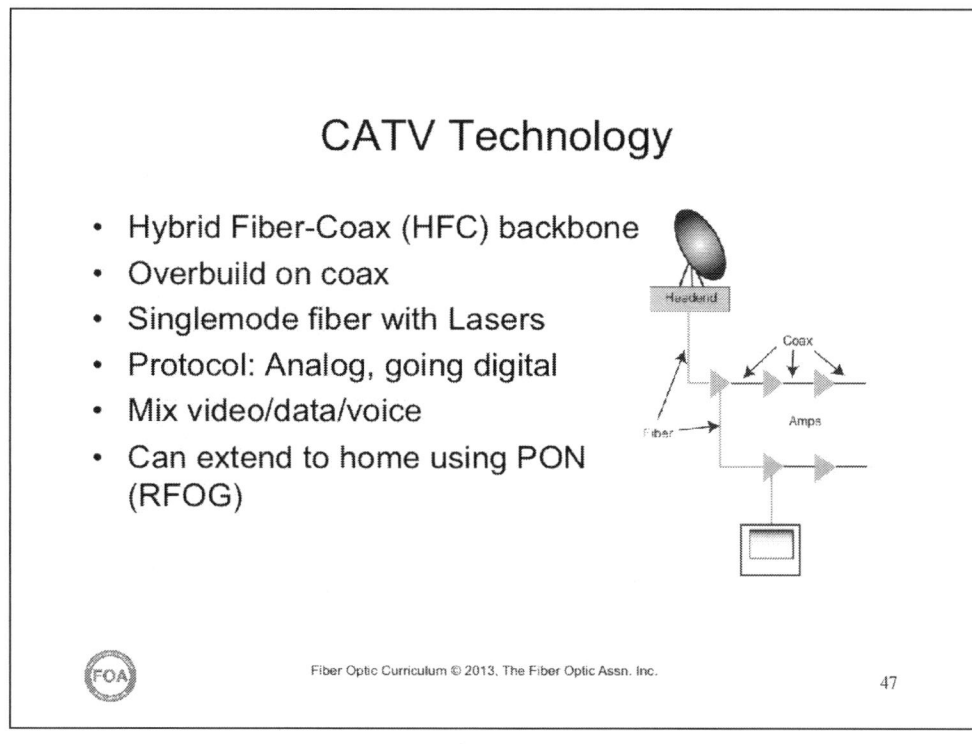

CATV Technology

- Hybrid Fiber-Coax (HFC) backbone
- Overbuild on coax
- Singlemode fiber with Lasers
- Protocol: Analog, going digital
- Mix video/data/voice
- Can extend to home using PON (RFOG)

The reason fiber is used in CATV networks is that the fiber pays for itself in enhanced reliability. The enormous bandwidth requirements of broadcast TV require frequent repeaters. The large number of repeaters used in a broadcast cable network are a big source of failure. And CATV systems' tree and branch architecture means and upstream failure causes failure for all downstream users. Reliability is a big issue, since viewers are a vocal lot if programming is interrupted!

Applications in CATV were slow until the development of the AM analog systems. By simply converting the signal from electrical to optical, the advantages of fiber optics, especially reliability, became cost effective. Now CATV has adopted a network architecture that overbuilds the normal coax network with fiber optic links.

The HFC network lets the CATV provider have a two-way connection to the subscriber that allows them to offer broadband Internet connections at a low cost. The fiber network will also allow easy conversion to digital TV when it's ready.

FRG, Chapter 3, FOTM, Chapter 3, DVVC, Chapter 11
FOA Online Fiber Optic Reference Guide, Understanding Fiber Optics, The Basics: Basic applications and trans. systems

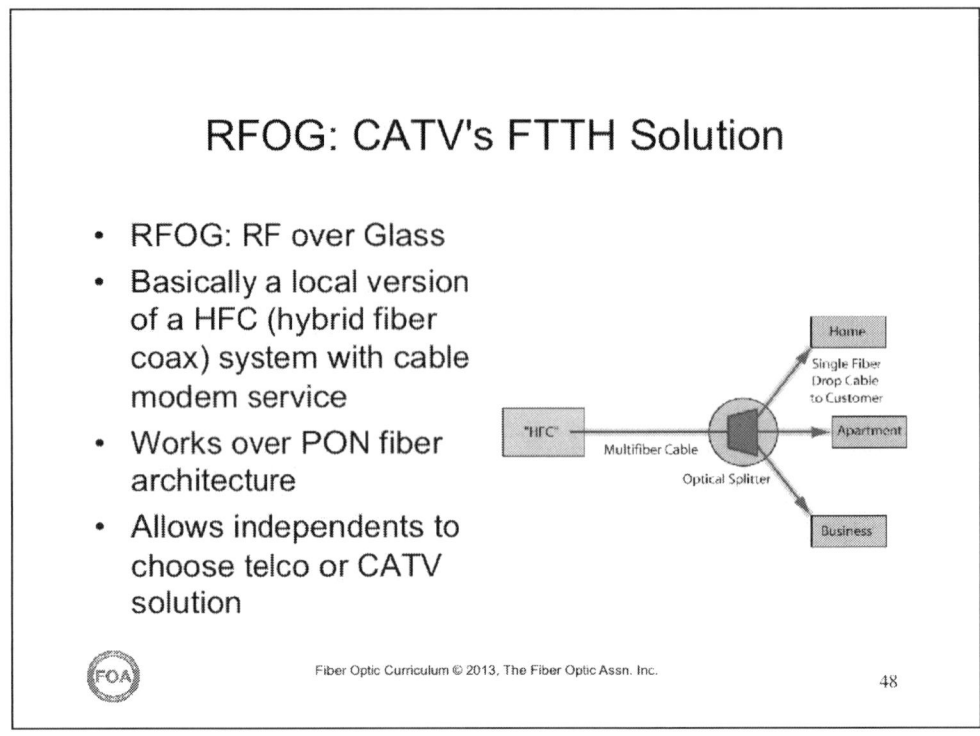

But CATV operators needed something to combat the subscriber's clamoring for fiber to the home, which lead to the development of RFOG, RF over Glass. RFOG is basically nothing more than a HFC/cable modem system built with less expensive components now available thanks to the volume pricing of components used in FTTH. It's designed to operate over a standard telco PON (passive optical network) fiber architecture with short fiber lengths and including the losses of a FTTH PON splitter.

There is one interesting side effect of this approach. Now telcos and CATV companies can deliver the same services over the same cable plant using totally different technologies. But that means that office or apartment building owners, developers or even whole towns that might be considering installing FTTH infrastructure themselves and leasing the fiber to a service provider can have a choice of service providers. One cable network can support either CATV or telco systems – or even someone else for that matter. That opens up a big market for private fiber optic systems.

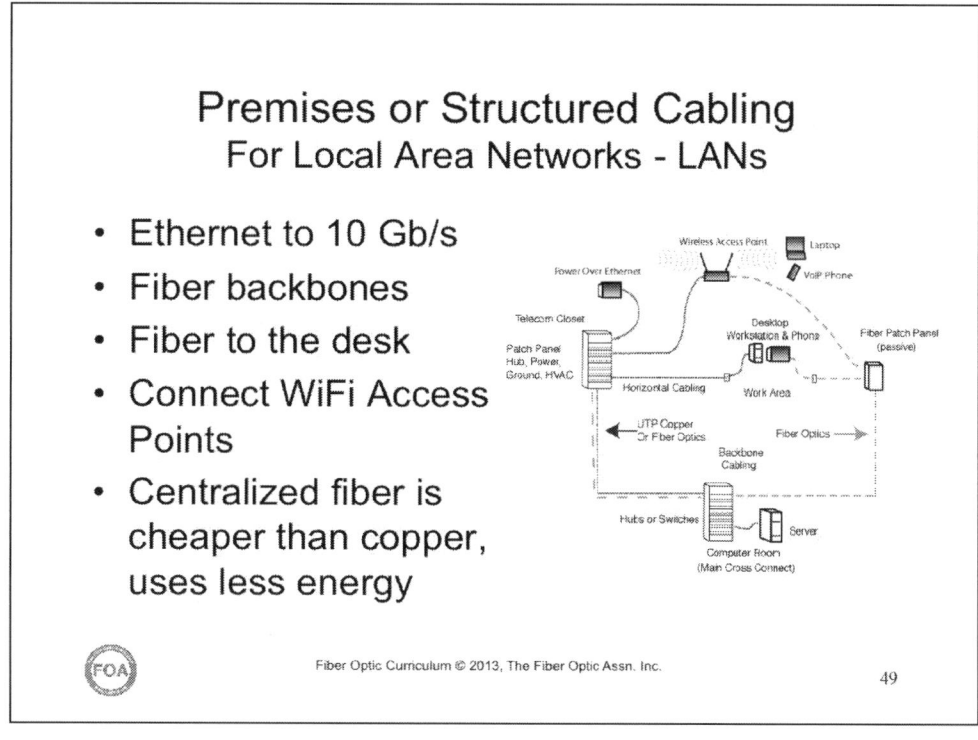

Premises or Structured Cabling
For Local Area Networks - LANs

- Ethernet to 10 Gb/s
- Fiber backbones
- Fiber to the desk
- Connect WiFi Access Points
- Centralized fiber is cheaper than copper, uses less energy

Fiber is widely used in premises or structured cabling, supporting Ethernet to 10 Gb/s and soon 40/100 Gb/s.

Fiber is used for most backbones, some fiber to the desk and to connect WiFi access points, especially 802.11n. Some networks run a separate wireless network for visitors for security, keeping unauthorized users off the corporate network.

A centralized fiber network allows using fiber without telecom rooms near the users, centralizing all the electronics in the computer room. Data centers are another big user of fiber, with connections at 10 Gb/s or higher where fiber is more reliable and consumes much less power.
FRG, Chapter 3, FOTM, Chapter 3, DVVC, Chapter 11
FOA Online Fiber Optic Reference Guide, Understanding Fiber Optics, The Basics: Basic applications and transmission systems and the Premises Cabling Section
More on Premises cabling is in the "Premises Cabling" PPTs

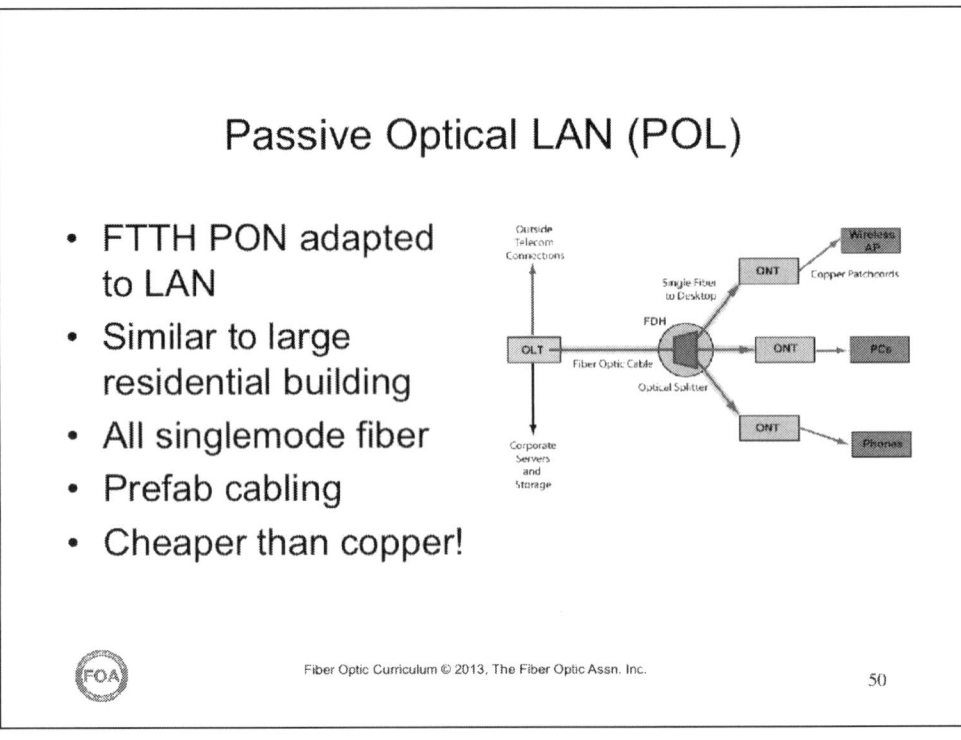

Passive Optical LAN (POL)

- FTTH PON adapted to LAN
- Similar to large residential building
- All singlemode fiber
- Prefab cabling
- Cheaper than copper!

Motorola, one of the largest suppliers of FTTH PON equipment is now offering systems similar to those used in large residential buildings for enterprise LANs in companies. They quote system costs that are much less expensive than installing a fiber optic backbone and copper cabling to the desktop. Because a POL brings to enterprise networks the management and control – plus encryption – of a PON FTTH network, it has become popular with organizations concerned over security and network management.

Data Centers - Internet Servers

- Store and switch data on the Internet
- Massive centers
- Use lots of power, create lots of heat, need lots of cooling
- Connections are critical

Data centers are the fastest growing application for computers used as servers. Connections are now at 10 Gb/s and new systems are becoming available at 40 Gb/s and 100 Gb/sis not far away. Fiber links between these computers and storage devices or routers are quite common as fiber saves power, space and is much easier to install.

Data Centers - Internet Servers

- 10 Gb/s now, 40/100 Gb/s coming soon
- Cabling is a problem
- Fiber is cost effective
- Fiber uses 20% as much power as a Category 6A link

Data centers are the fastest growing application for computers used as servers. Connections are now at 10 Gb/s and new systems are becoming available at 40 Gb/s and 100 Gb/sis not far away. Fiber links between these computers and storage devices or routers are quite common as fiber saves power, space and is much easier to install.

Data Centers – Cable Controversy

- 40/100G: Multimode or singlemode fiber?
- MM uses parallel 10G channels
- SM uses CWDM 10G channels
- Google says SM !

	40G	100G
MM Parallel	8 fibers	20 fibers
SM CWDM	2 fibers	2 fibers

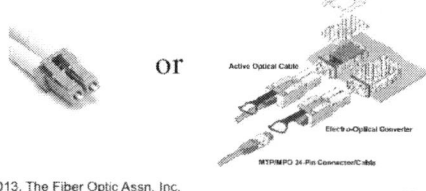

Data centers are the fastest growing application for computers used as servers. Connections are now at 10 Gb/s and new systems are becoming available at 40 Gb/s and 100 Gb/sis not far away. Fiber links between these computers and storage devices or routers are quite common as fiber saves power, space and is much easier to install.

Board Level Interconnects

- Fast computers need fast connections
- Copper uses too much power - fiber is faster and lower power consumption
- Intel promoting use as "Light Peak"

Intel is promoting the use of optical fiber on computer boards. Fiber is faster than board connections and uses less power. New low cost components makes it cost effective.

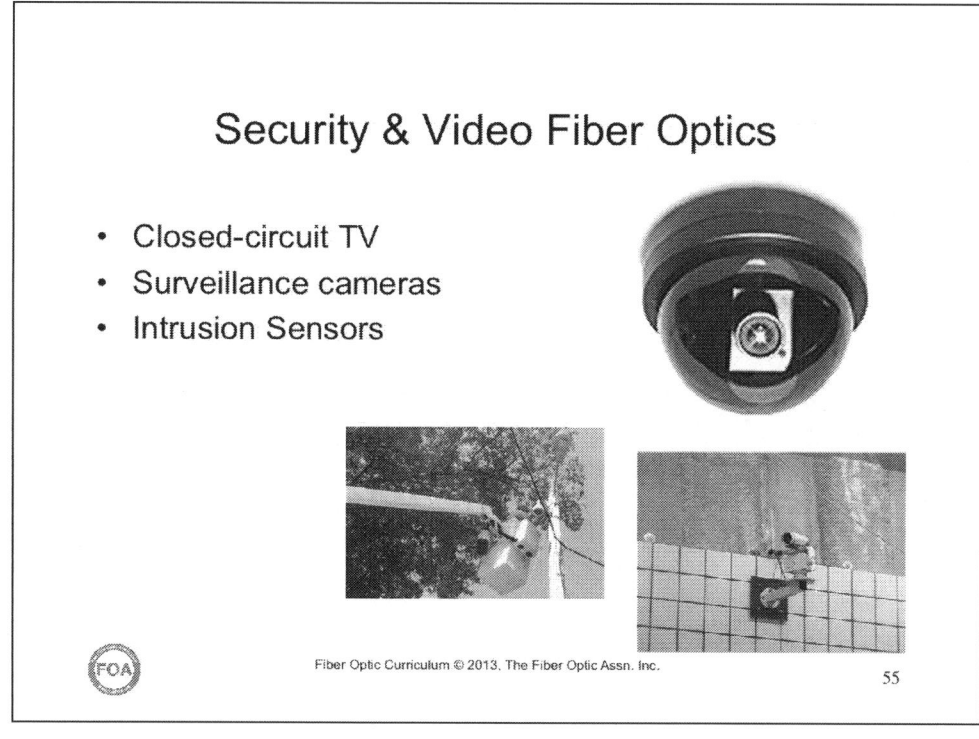

Fiber has found many other uses. Cellular systems are not wireless - most antennas are connected via buried fiber optic cables. Likewise, wireless LANs require cabling and fiber provides greater distances from hubs and switches and immunity to noise. Utilities have used fiber for managing their grids and communications throughout their networks for many years. Recent problems have had many upgrading their systems. Security systems use lots of fiber. CCTV cameras use fiber to extend their reach, for example in large airport terminals, outdoors in power plants or inside and outside big office buildings. Fibers can also be used as sensors, for example sensing intruders on fences or walking across buried fiber sensors. And, of course, fiber is very difficult to "tap," making it popular for secure military and government networks.

FRG, Chapter 3, FOTM, Chapter 3, DVVC, Chapter 11
FOA Online Fiber Optic Reference Guide, Understanding Fiber Optics, The Basics: Basic applications and transmission systems

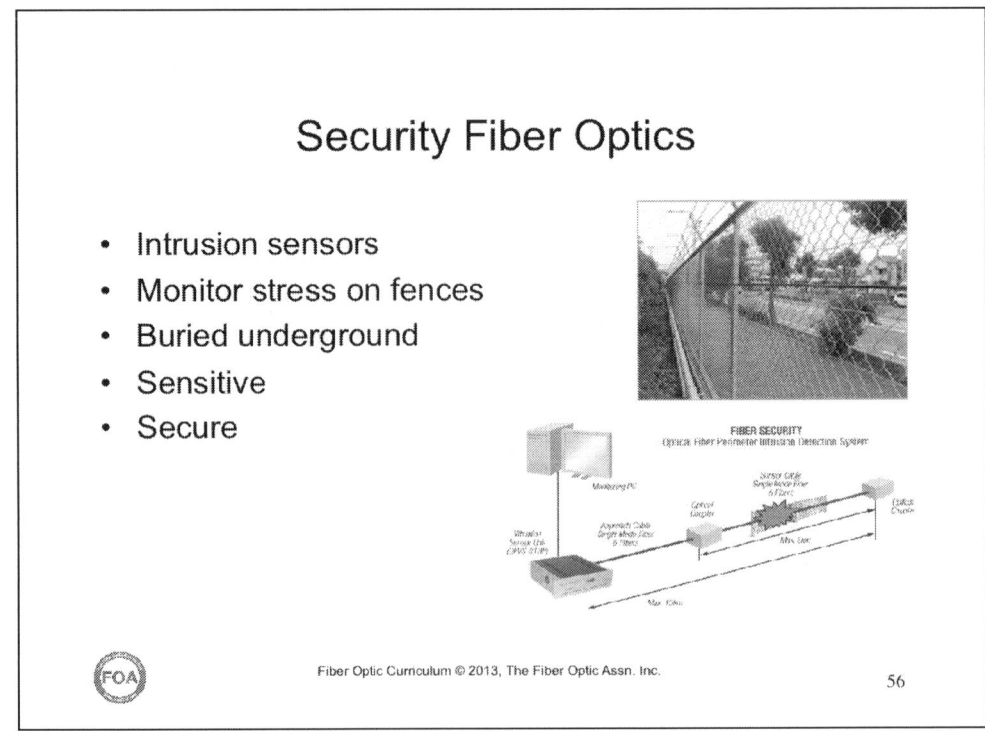

Security systems use lots of fiber. CCTV cameras use fiber to extend their reach, for example in large airport terminals, outdoors in power plants or inside and outside big office buildings.
Fibers can also be used as sensors, for example sensing intruders on fences or walking across buried fiber sensors.

FRG, Chapter 3, FOTM, Chapter 3, DVVC, Chapter 11
FOA Online Fiber Optic Reference Guide, Understanding Fiber Optics, The Basics: Basic applications and transmission systems

Video and Audio On Fiber

- Analog or digital
- Sporting events
- Concert halls
- Large meeting facilities
- Giant display screens in public places

Many video links are available on fiber optics, from remote security cameras to broadcast TV cameras in studios or on location as in the auto race in Long Beach, CA shown. Audio links are used in concert halls, meeting rooms, or any large auditorium with powered speakers.

FRG, Chapter 3, FOTM, Chapter 3, DVVC, Chapter 11
FOA Online Fiber Optic Reference Guide, Understanding Fiber Optics, The Basics: Basic applications and transmission systems

Remote-Piloted Vehicles (RPVs)

- All RPVs use fiber
- Allows longer tethers for greater exploration range
- Used to find Titanic in 1986 (Jason) and revisit last year

Woods Hole Oceanographic Institute started using optical fiber to connect their underwater robots called remote-piloted vehicles in the 1980s. The most spectacular result was the discovery of the Titanic by Dr. Robert Ballard who developed the technology with Jason, shown in the picture here looking into the window of a stateroom on the Titanic. Using fiber allowed the tether cables to be ten times longer than with copper and produce better signals! Now all RPVs use fiber tethers.

Industrial Applications

- Fiber is used in many industrial applications
- Immune to electrical noise
- More flexible than copper
- Withstand high temperature

The electrical noise common to industrial environments makes it difficult to use copper data cables. But fiber is immune to electromagnetic interference and more flexible and withstands higher heat also. Industrial robots have fibers running along the arm. The machines are connected to a network, almost always on fiber.

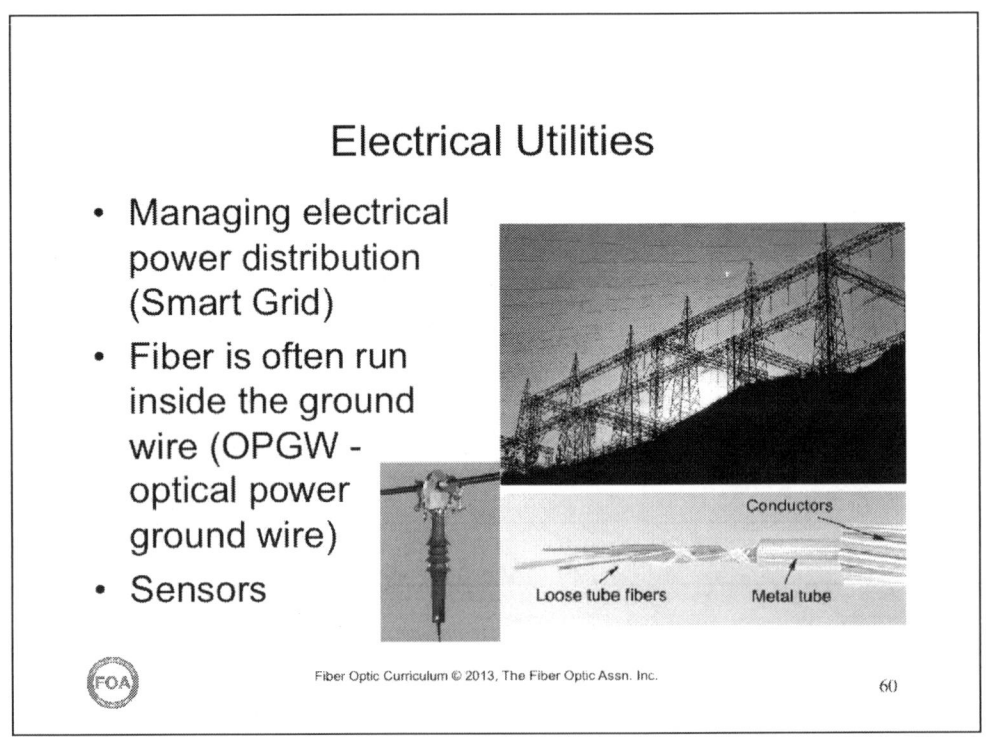

Electrical utilities have been using fiber for many years for communications and to control their electrical distribution systems. Many use optical power ground wire (OPGW) that has fiber running inside of an electrical conductor. Fiber optic sensors are also used to monitor very high voltages and currents

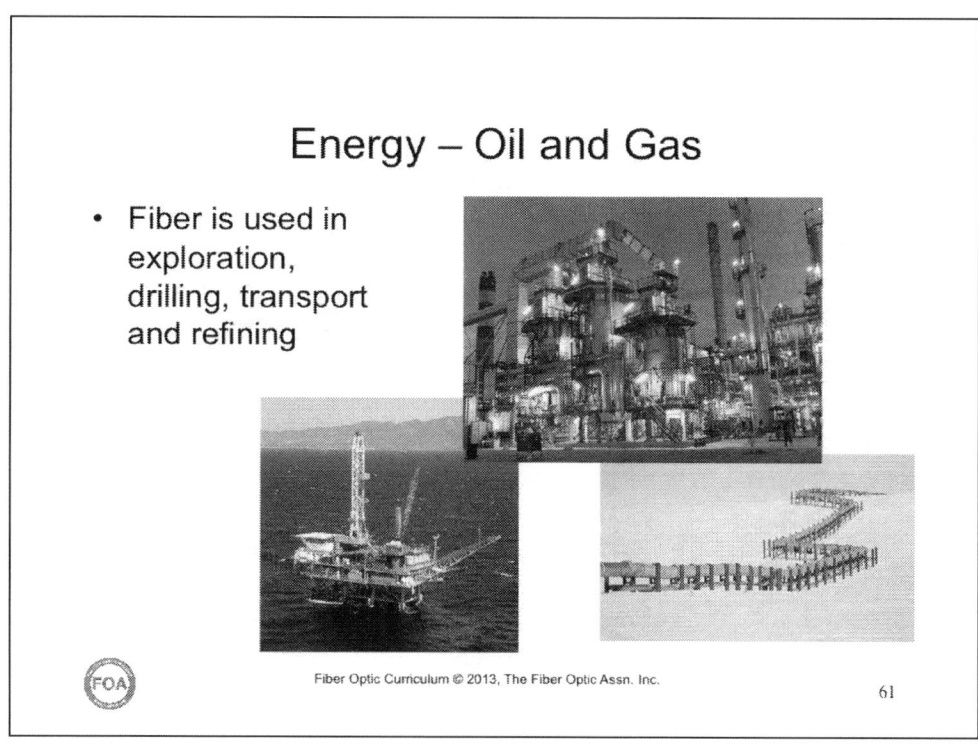

Fiber optics have been used for decades in the energy business. In oil, fiber is used in exploration as super-sensitive sensors to gather geological data and monitor drilling. Fiber is widely used on drilling platforms and in refineries for communications, monitoring and control. Fiber is also used on pipelines to monitor flow and problems as well as communications.

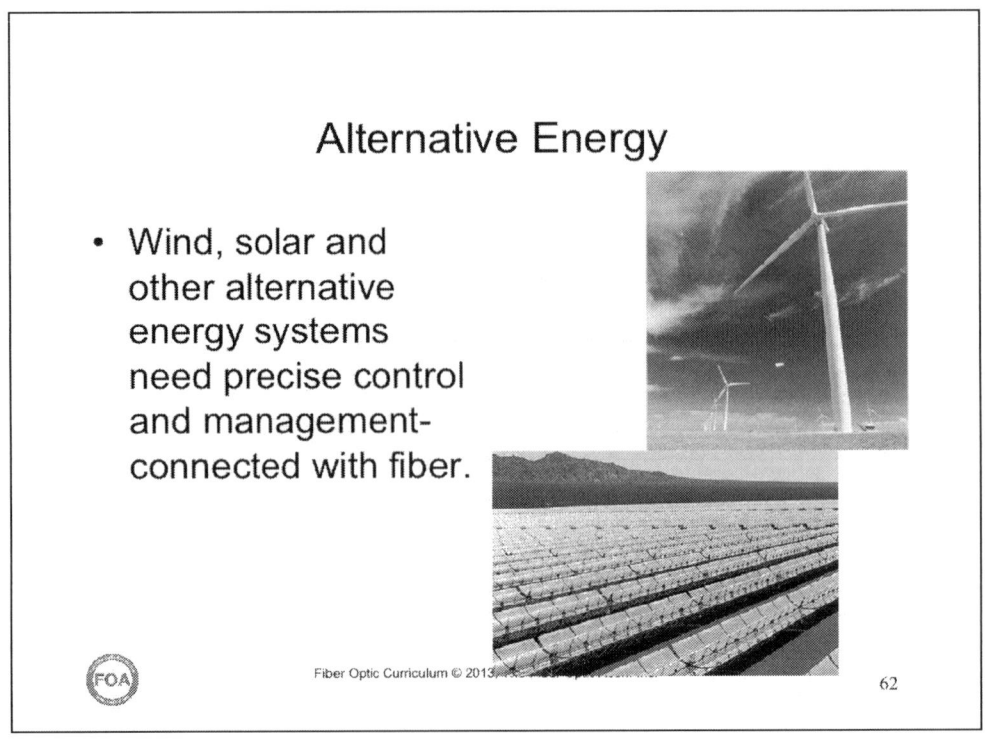

Alternative energy production requires precise control and management to create electrical power compatible to the current grid. Wind and solar systems must be controlled to maximize outputs and control the processes. Solar using heat to generate steam, as well as those involving photovoltaic conversion, have reflectors that follow the sun, maximizing outputs. Windmills, of course, must fact into the wind and control the blades according to wind speeds. All this works on computer systems controlled by fiber. One solar facility in the Mojave has over 750 MILES of fiber!

Metropolitan Networks

- Supports CCTV, traffic control as well as city communications
- Pull into ducts or use microtrenching (shown)
- May be good application for air-blown fiber (shown)

Fiber Optic Curriculum © 2013, The Fiber Optic Assn. Inc.

Many networks are installed in cities. Some are owned by the cities to connect their offices, public services, emergency services, schools and libraries, etc. Some even lease fibers to high-tech companies. New techniques like microtrenching, shown here, is often used to prevent the disruption common to digging up streets to bury conduit or cables.

Data Links & Other Networks

- Industrial: RS232, 422
- Fibre Channel (Data Centers)
- IEEE 1394 (Fire Wire), Toslink (Consumer)
- Automotive: MOST, Flexray (POF)
- Active Optical Cables

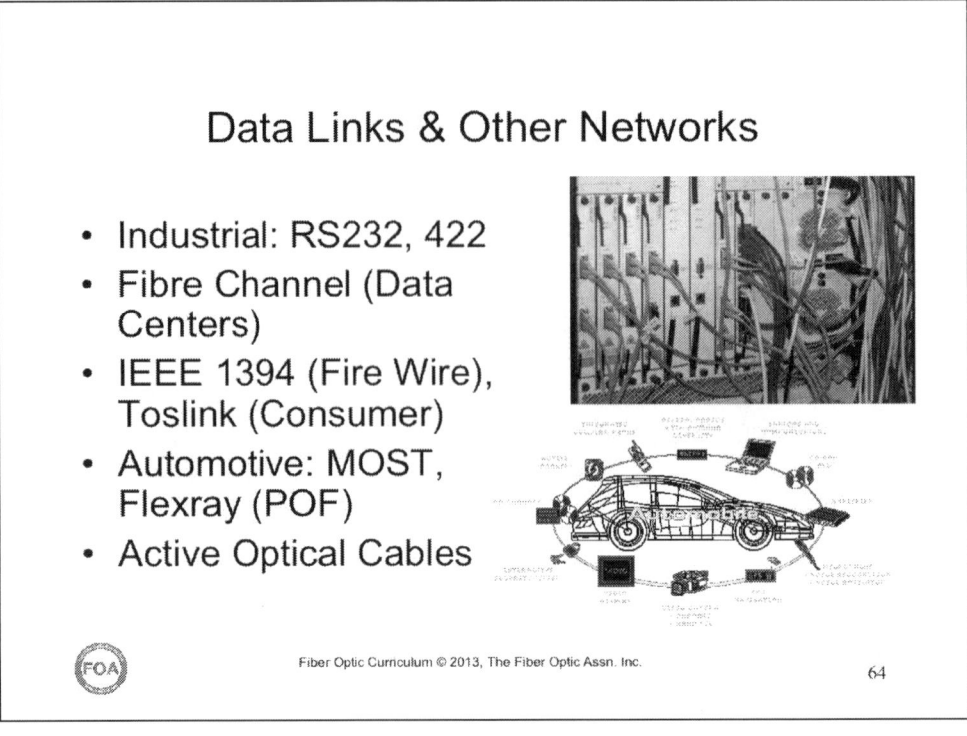

Most data links are used to connect two devices point-to-point and lack the protocols of a network. Most of these links offer fiber optics as an option - and some are only fiber. RS232 and RS422 are industrial links that have been around for many years. They have been available on fiber since fiber got started. Fibre Channel is a high speed link connecting computers to peripherals like disk drives and printers. HIPPI is a similar (and fairly obsolete) link. Fire Wire and Toslink used in consumer applications like digital audio. Most and Flexray are automotive networks, where fiber's lighter weight and immunity to electrical noise make it a better choice than copper. Active optical links are being designed into the next generation of PCs to replace USB and FireWire
FRG, Chapter 3, FOTM, Chapter 3, DVVC, Chapter 11
FOA Online Fiber Optic Reference Guide, Understanding Fiber Optics, The Basics: Basic applications and transmission systems

Other Applications of Fiber Optics

- Building Management
- Traffic Control
- Process Control
- Sensors
  - High voltage/current
  - Chemicals
  - Hazardous environments

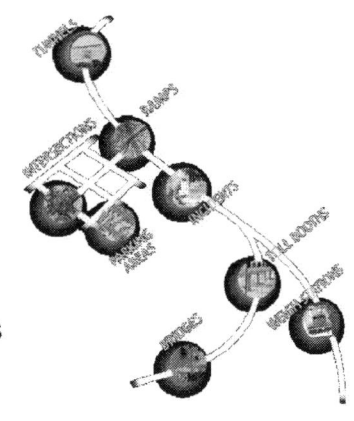

Building management systems can use fiber in place of copper cable for longer distances and greater security.
Industrial networks favor fiber for process control applications due to its distance capability and immunity to electrical noise.
Fiber optic sensors are available for a number of applications, including measuring high voltages and currents as in power grids, dangerous chemicals and can operate in hazardous environments since they are intrinsically safe.
FRG, Chapter 3, FOTM, Chapter 3, DVVC, Chapter 11
FOA Online Fiber Optic Reference Guide, Understanding Fiber Optics, The Basics: Basic applications and transmission systems

Fiber Optic Data Links

- Transmit over two fibers for full duplex
- Transceivers convert to/from electrical signals
- LEDs, F-P lasers or VCSELs as transmitters
- Photodetectors receive signals from fiber

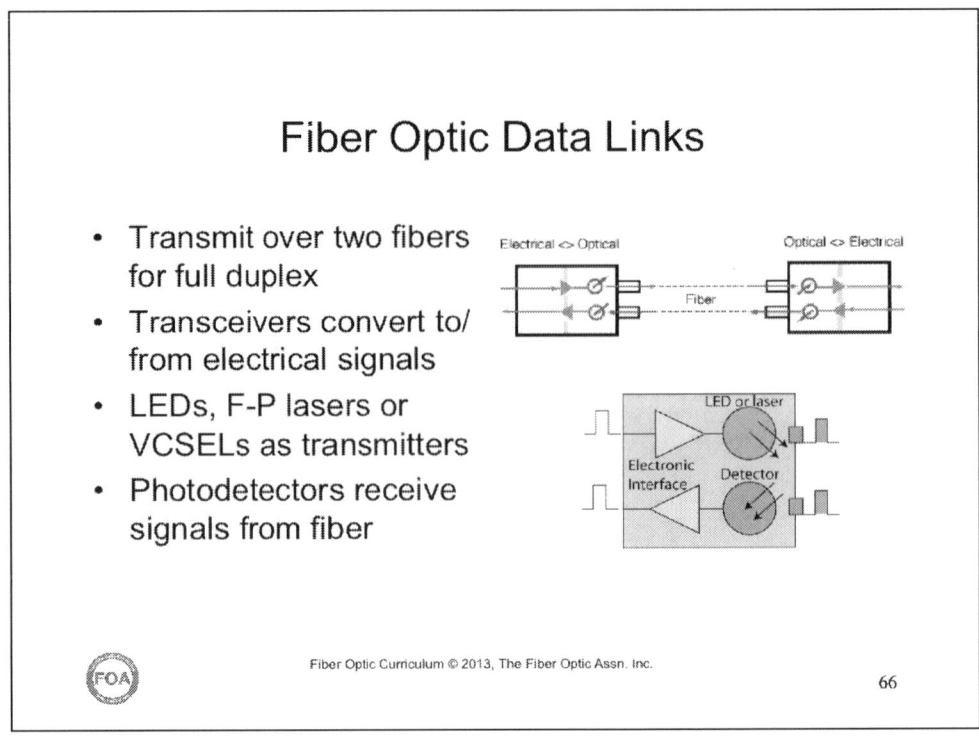

Fiber optic transmission systems all consist of a transmitter which takes an electrical input and converts it to an optical output from a laser diode, VCSEL or LED. The light from the transmitter is coupled into the fiber with a connector and is transmitted through the fiber optic cable plant. The light is ultimately coupled to a receiver where a detector converts the light into an electrical signal which is then conditioned properly for use by the receiving equipment. Most links use two fibers transmitting in opposite directions for full duplex operation. FTTx PON systems use one fiber bidirectionally, using wavelength division multiplexing. Just as with copper wire or radio transmission, the performance of the fiber optic data link can be determined by how well the reconverted electrical signal out of the receiver matches the input to the transmitter.

FRG, Chapter 4, RGPC Chapter 3,5, FOTM, Chapter 2, DVVC, Chapter 11
FOA Online Fiber Optic Reference Guide, Applications of Fiber Optics, Communications: Fiber Optic Datalinks

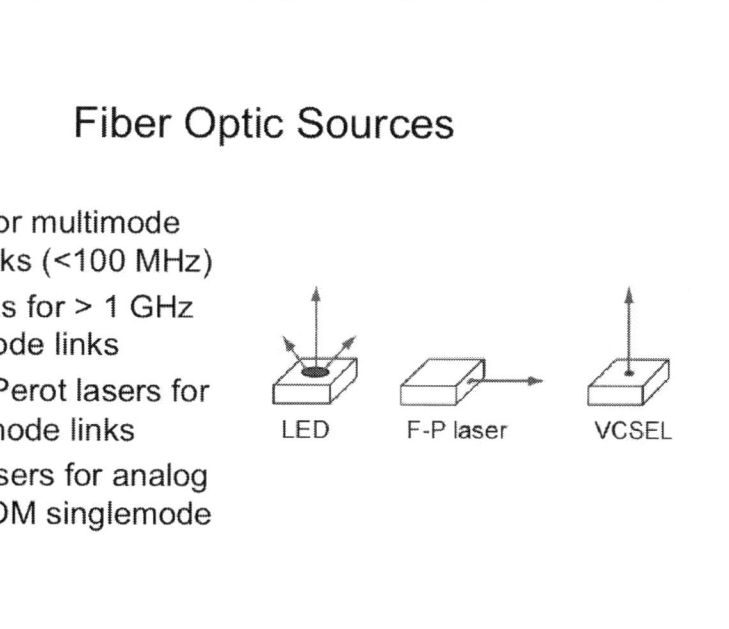

Fiber Optic Sources

- LEDs for multimode fiber links (<100 MHz)
- VCSELs for > 1 GHz multimode links
- Fabry-Perot lasers for singlemode links
- DFB lasers for analog or DWDM singlemode

Four types of sources are commonly used, LEDs, fabry-perot (FP) lasers, distributed feedback (DFB) lasers and vertical cavity surface-emitting lasers (VCSELs). All convert electrical signals into optical signals, but are otherwise quite different devices. All three are tiny semiconductor devices (chips). LEDs and VCSELs are fabricated on semiconductor wafers such that they emit light from the surface of the chip, while f-p lasers emit from the side of the chip from a laser cavity created in the middle of the chip.

LEDs have much lower power outputs than lasers and their larger, diverging light output pattern makes them harder to couple into fibers, limiting them to use with multimode fibers. Laser have smaller tighter light outputs and are easily coupled to singlemode fibers, making them ideal for long distance high speed links. LEDs have much less bandwidth than lasers and are limited to systems operating up to about 250 MHz or around 200 Mb/s. Lasers have very high bandwidth capability, most being useful to well over 10 GHz or 10 Gb/s. because of their fabrication methods, LEDs and VCSELs are cheap to make. Lasers are more expensive because creating the laser cavity inside the device is more difficult, the chip must be separated from the semiconductor wafer and each end coated before the laser can even be tested to see if its good.

FOA Online Fiber Optic Reference Guide, Applications of Fiber Optics, Communications: Fiber Optic Transceivers

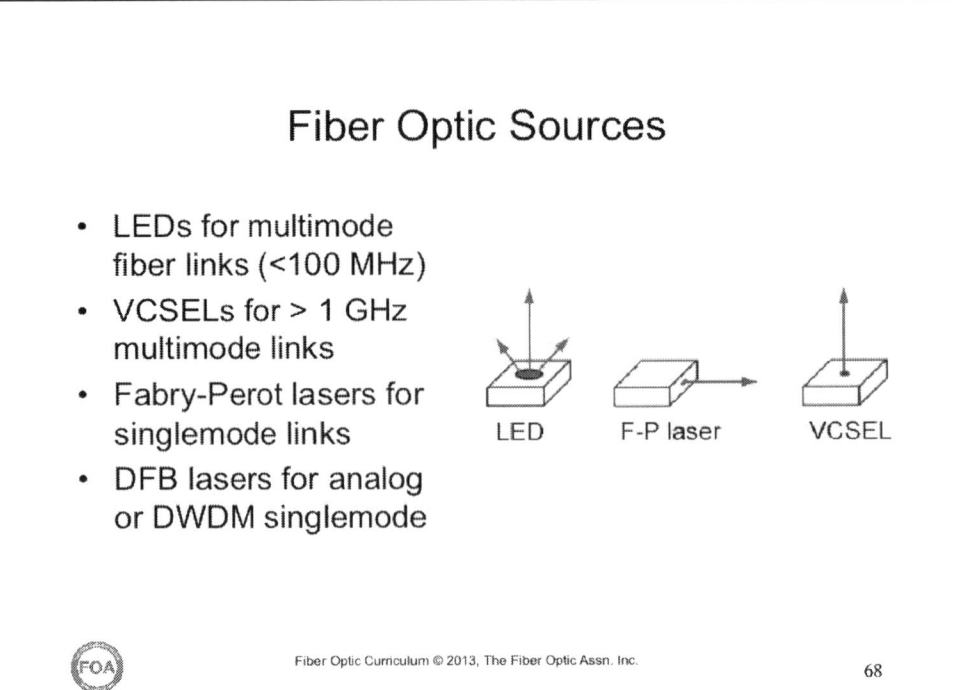

LEDs have a limited bandwidth while all types of lasers are very fast. Another big difference between LEDs and both types of lasers is the spectral output. LEDs have a very broad spectral output which causes them to suffer chromatic dispersion in fiber, while lasers have a narrow spectral output that suffers very little chromatic dispersion. DFB lasers, which are used in long distance and DWDM systems, have the narrowest spectral width which minimizes chromatic dispersion on the longest links. DFB lasers are also highly linear (that is the light output directly follows the electrical input) so they can be used as sources in AM CATV systems.

FRG, Chapter 4

FOA Online Fiber Optic Reference Guide, Applications of Fiber Optics, Communications: Fiber Optic Transceivers

Fiber Optic Link Sources

Fiber	Length	Data Rate	Source
Multimode	Short	<100 MB/s	850nm LED
	Long	~100 MB/s	1300 LED
	Short	>1 GB/s	850 VCSEL
	Long	>1 GB/s	1300 Laser
Singlemode	Short	To 10 GB/s	1300 Laser
	Long	~100 GB/s	1550 Laser

The type of source used in a network depends on the speed of the network and the distance it must operate over.

LEDs are useful to only several hundred megabits per second, so they are used in slower systems. Lasers can be used up to 10 gigabits per second or more, so they are the source of choice in high speed networks.

Since the loss of the fiber goes down with longer wavelengths, long distance links tend to use the longest wavelength sources.

FRG, Chapter 4, FOTM, Chapter 2, DVVC, Chapter 11
FOA Online Fiber Optic Reference Guide, Applications of Fiber Optics, Communications: Fiber Optic Datalinks

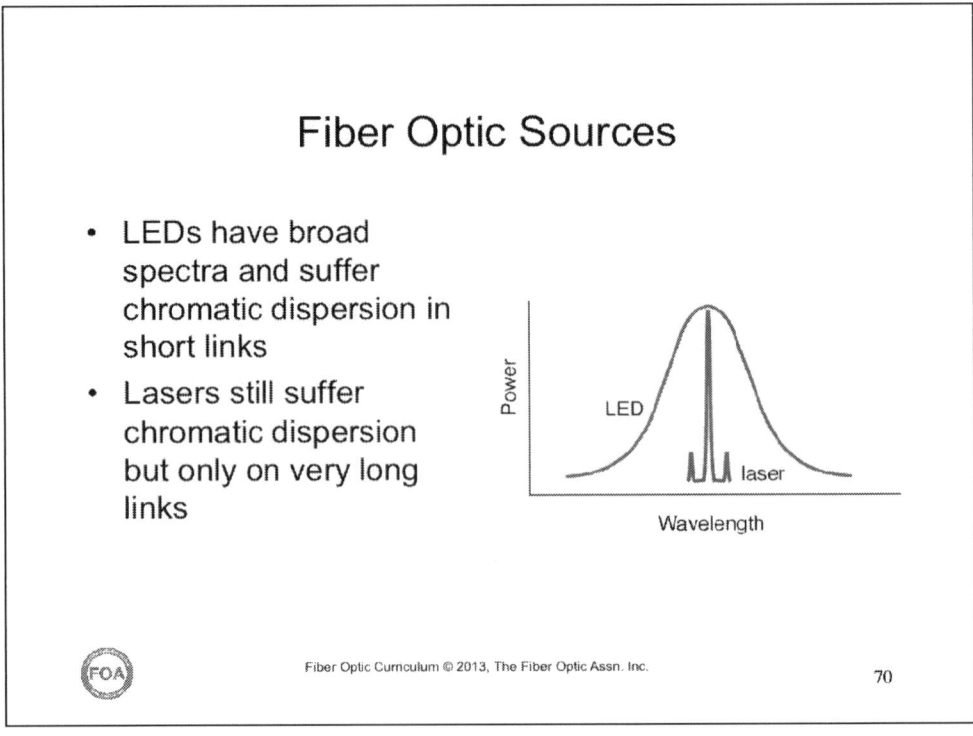

Another big difference between LEDs and both types of lasers is the spectral output. LEDs have a very broad spectral output which causes them to suffer chromatic dispersion in fiber, while lasers have a narrow spectral output that suffers very little chromatic dispersion. DFB lasers, which are used in long distance and DWDM systems, have the narrowest spectral width which minimizes chromatic dispersion on the longest links.

FRG, Chapter 4
FOA Online Fiber Optic Reference Guide, Applications of Fiber Optics, Communications: Fiber Optic Transceivers

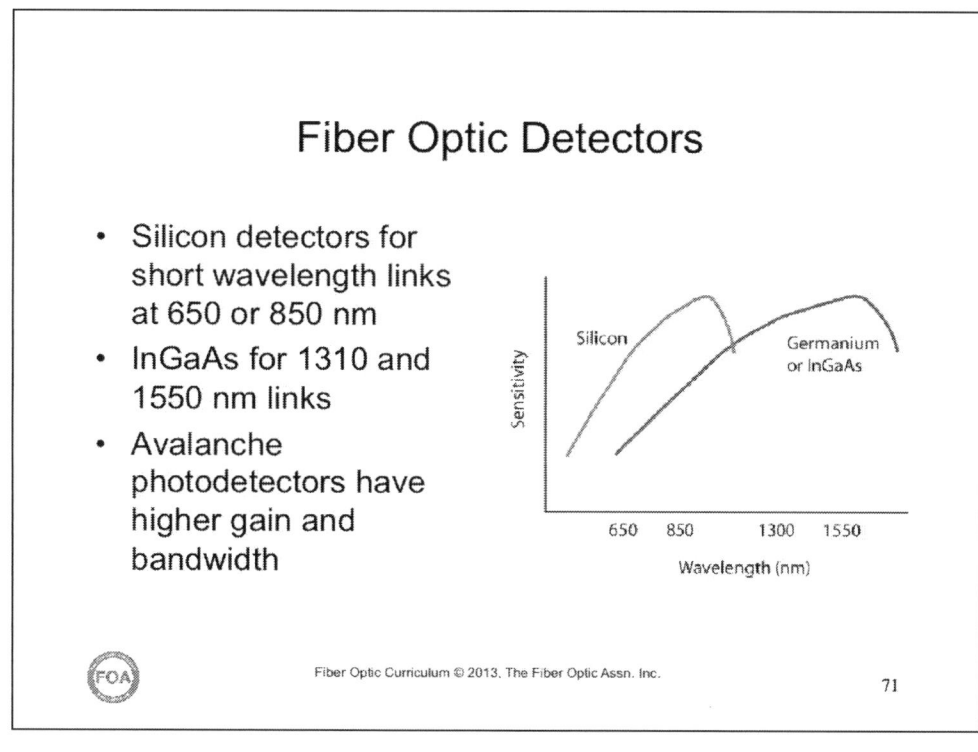

Receivers use semiconductor detectors (photodiodes or photodetectors) to convert optical signals to electrical signals. Silicon photodiodes are used for short wavelength links (650 for POF and 850 for glass MM fiber). Long wavelength systems usually use InGaAs (indium gallium arsenide) detectors as they have lower noise than germanium which allows for more sensitive receivers.

Very high speed systems sometimes use avalanche photodiodes (APDs) that are biased at high voltage to create gain in the photodiode. These devices are more expensive and more complicated to use but offer significant gains in performance.

FRG, Chapter 4

FOA Online Fiber Optic Reference Guide, Applications of Fiber Optics, Communications: Fiber Optic Transceivers

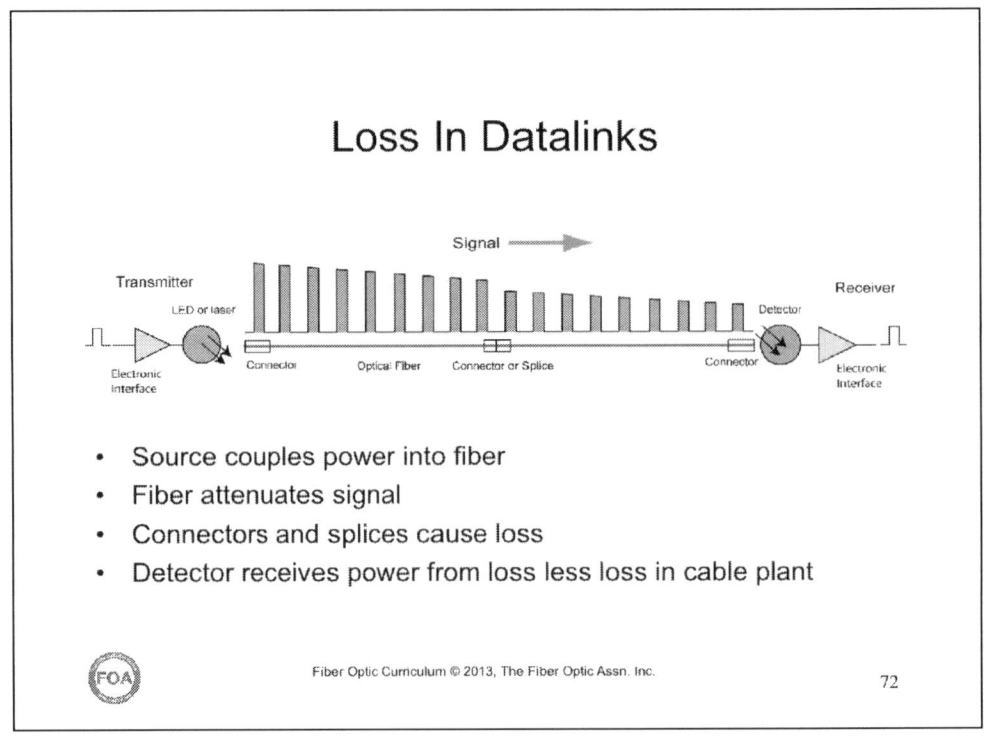

A fiber optic datalink works by transmitting from the transmitter to the receiver. The source in the transmitter couples power into the fiber which is then diminished by the attenuation of the optical fiber and losses from connectors and splices in the link.

FRG, Chapter 4, RGPC Chapter 3, FOTM, Chapter2, 10, DVVC, Chapter 11

FOA Online Fiber Optic Reference Guide, Applications of Fiber Optics, Communications: Fiber Optic Datalinks

Fiber Optic Datalinks

- Operating range receiver power
- High enough for good signal-to-noise level or low Bit Error Rate (BER)
- Low enough to not overload receiver

The ability of any fiber optic system to transmit data ultimately depends on the optical power at the receiver as shown above, which shows the data link bit error rate as a function of optical power at the receiver. (BER is the inverse of signal-to-noise ratio, e.g. high BER means poor signal to noise ratio.) Either too little or too much power will cause high bit error rates. Too much power, and the receiver amplifier saturates, too little and noise becomes a problem as it interferes with the signal.

This receiver power depends on two basic factors: how much power is launched into the fiber by the transmitter and how much is lost by attenuation in the optical fiber cable plant that connects the transmitter and receiver. The optical power budget of the link is determined by two factors, the sensitivity of the receiver, which is determined in the bit error rate curve above and the output power of the transmitter into the fiber. The minimum power level that produces an acceptable bit error rate determines the sensitivity the receiver. The power from the transmitter coupled into the optical fiber determines the transmitted power. The difference between these two power levels determines the loss margin (loss budget or power budget) of the link.

FRG, Chapter 4, RGPC Chapter 3, FOA Online Fiber Optic Reference Guide, Applications of Fiber Optics, Communications:
Fiber Optic Datalinks

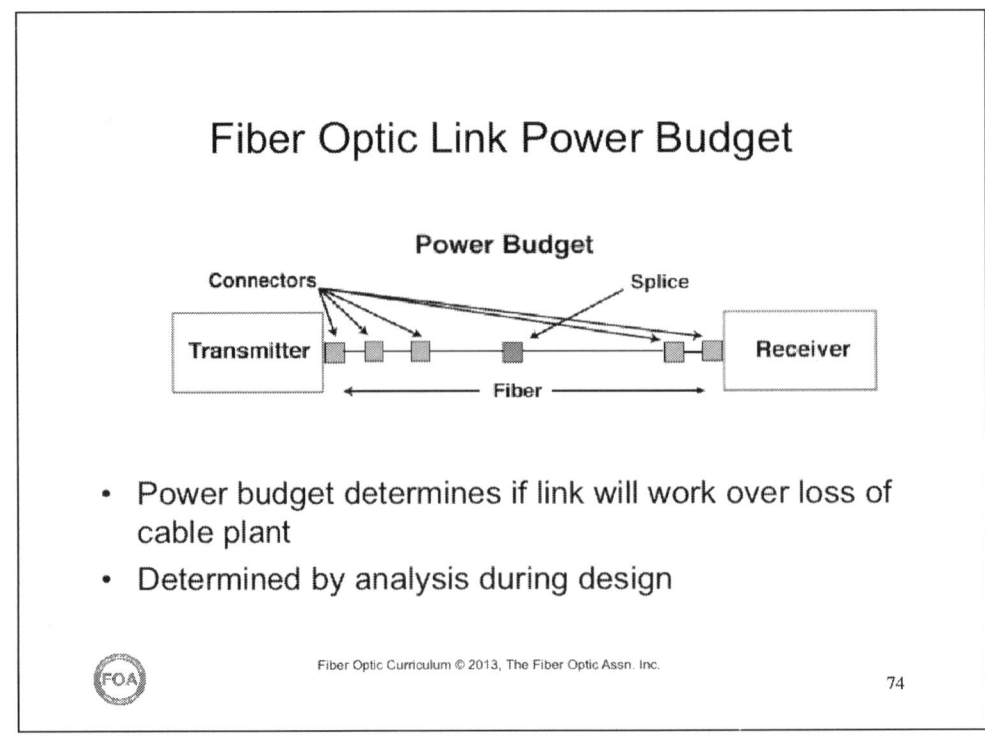

After a fiber optic cable plant is installed, it may be used with a number of different types of fiber optic networks. Computer networks, telephone signals, video links, and even audio can be sent on the installed fibers. Each network type has a requirement for the performance of the fiber optic cable link. Most simply specify the maximum loss in the link that can be tolerated, a function of component specifications and installation quality. Others also specify the bandwidth performance of the fiber which is determined by the specifications of the fiber chosen. Every fiber optic link has a maximum loss of a cable plant over which it can work. That loss is determined by the output power of the transmitter coupled into the fiber and the sensitivity of the receiver, all expressed in dB.. The loss of the fiber optic cable it uses must be less than 1that maximum loss for proper operation.

The drawings here illustrate the example in the textbook in Chapter 10. The transmitter couples a certain amount of power into the fiber in the cable plant. As the light is transmitted down the fiber, it is attenuated by the attenuation of the fiber and the loss in connectors and splices. In this link, the cable plant has 5 connections and a splice, plus the length of the fiber to cause loss.

FRG, Chapter 4, 9, RGPC Chapter 5, The Fiber Optic Association - Tech Topics, Cable Plant Link Loss Budget Analysis

Fiber Optic Link Power Budget

Power Budget

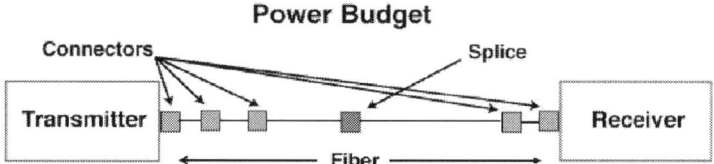

- Power budget determines if link will work over loss of cable plant
- Determined by analysis during design

Fiber Optic Curriculum © 2013, The Fiber Optic Assn. Inc.

While every link installed must meet some maximum loss to allow operation of the network intended to use it, different networks may have different link margins. Therefore we use a different approach. The loss of the link is considered acceptable if it is less than standard maximum values calculated from the characteristics of the link installation. What causes the losses in the fiber optic cable? First the fiber itself. The next loss factor is terminations. Splices are common in singlemode but rare in multimode networks Singlemode fiber is usually spliced with a fusion splicer which welds the two fibers together in an electric arc, with much lower losses. The final loss factor is stress in installation. Fiber optic cable pulled with too much tension may be damaged. Each time you make a bend with a fiber optic cable, you put some stress in the fiber which can cause loss. Even cable ties tightened on the cable can cause loss. Stress loss should be zero!

The drawings here illustrate the example in the textbook in Chapter 10. FRG, Chapter 4, 9, RGPC Chapter 5, FOTM, Chapter 10, DVVC, Chapter 11

The Fiber Optic Association - Tech Topics, Cable Plant Link Loss Budget Analysis

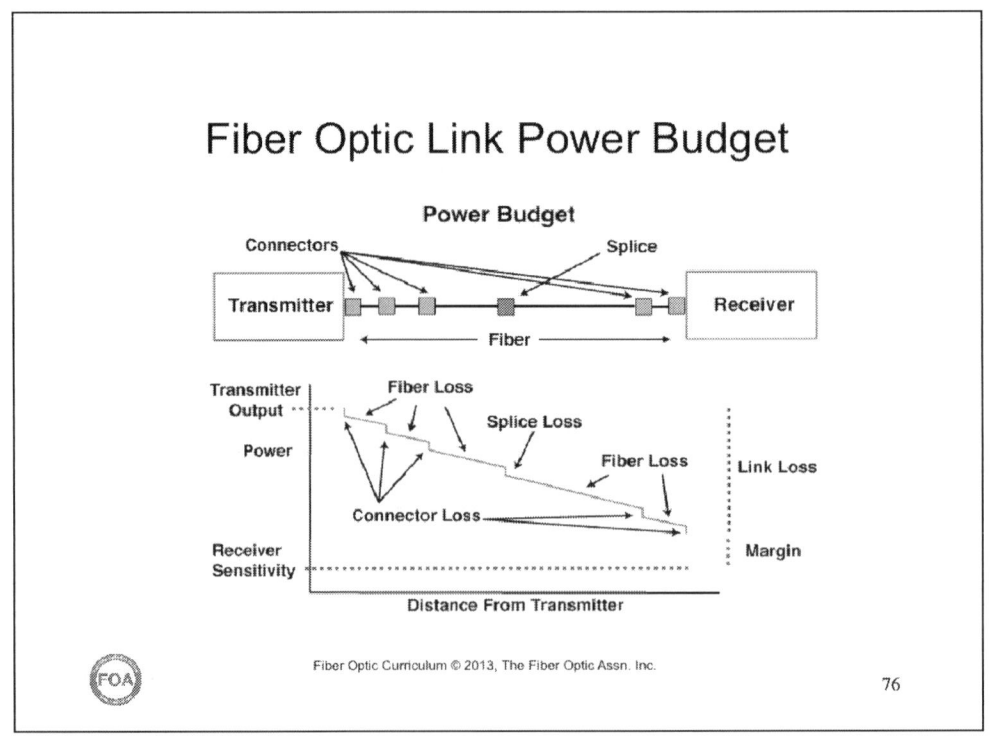

The drawings here illustrate the example in the textbook The graph below the link diagram shows the actual amount of light in the fiber along the length, directly corresponding to the link diagram above it. This diagram looks like an OTDR plot, since it is similar to what the OTDR measures. If you are not familiar with OTDRs, we will cover them in the testing sections. But look at the diagram closely. The power goes down as the light goes down the fiber, reduced by the attenuation of the fiber and the losses in connectors and splices. By convention, we include the loss of the connectors on the end of the cable plant, since when we test connectors, we do so by mating them to another reference connector. The power level starts at the transmitter output, coupled into the fiber, shown at the top of the X-axis of the graph. After the loss of the cable plant, it is reduced by the amount of the loss. In order for the link to work properly, the power at the receiver must be higher than the receiver sensitivity, shown at the bottom of the X-axis of the graph. The amount by which the receiver power exceeds the receiver sensitivity is the margin of the link.

FRG, Chapter 4, 9, RGPC Chapter 5, FOTM, Chapter 10, DVVC, Chapter 11

The Fiber Optic Association - Tech Topics, Cable Plant Link Loss Budget Analysis

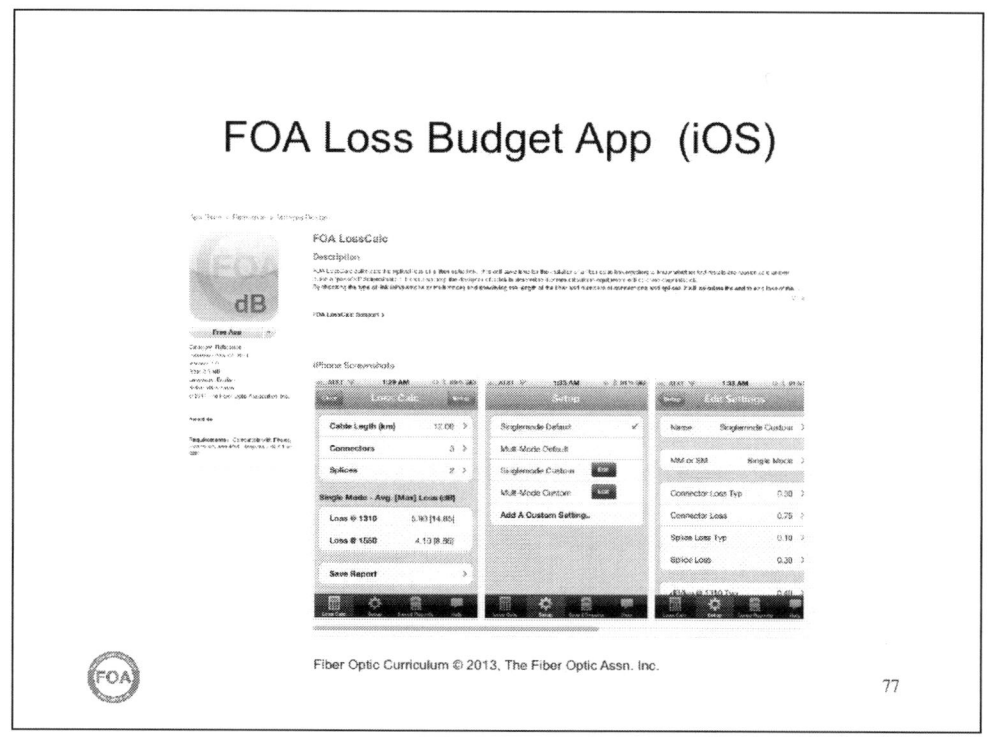

FOA LossCalc estimates the optical loss of a fiber optic link. This will save time for the installer of a fiber optic link needing to know whether test results are reasonable and/or make a "pass/fail" determination. It can also help the designer of a link to determine if communications equipment will operate over this link. By choosing the type of link (singlemode or multimode) and specifying the length of the fiber and numbers of connections and splices, it will calculate the end to end loss of the link. The app has default specifications for singlemode and multimode links or the user may create custom setups with specifications appropriate for any application. http://itunes.apple.com/us/app/foa-losscalc/id476262894?mt=8&ls=1

Fiber Optic Components

- <u>Fiber</u> transmits the signal as light
- <u>Cable</u> protects fibers in the application environment
- <u>Connectors</u> join fibers or connect to active devices so they can be disconnected for rerouting, testing, etc.
- <u>Splices</u> join two fibers permanently
- <u>Hardware</u> provides the mounting, protection, etc. for connectors or splices
- <u>Test equipment</u> checks performance

Now let's take a look at the components of a fiber optic system. We'll examine each of these in detail and look at their installation.

FRG, Chapters 5-7, RGPC Chapter 5, FOTM, Chapter 4-7, DVVC, Chapter 12-13
FOA Online Fiber Optic Reference Guide, Understanding Fiber Optics, The Basics
Most fiber optic components, including "Cables,"
"Termination" (Connectors and Splices) have their own PPTs that include information on the components and how they are installed.

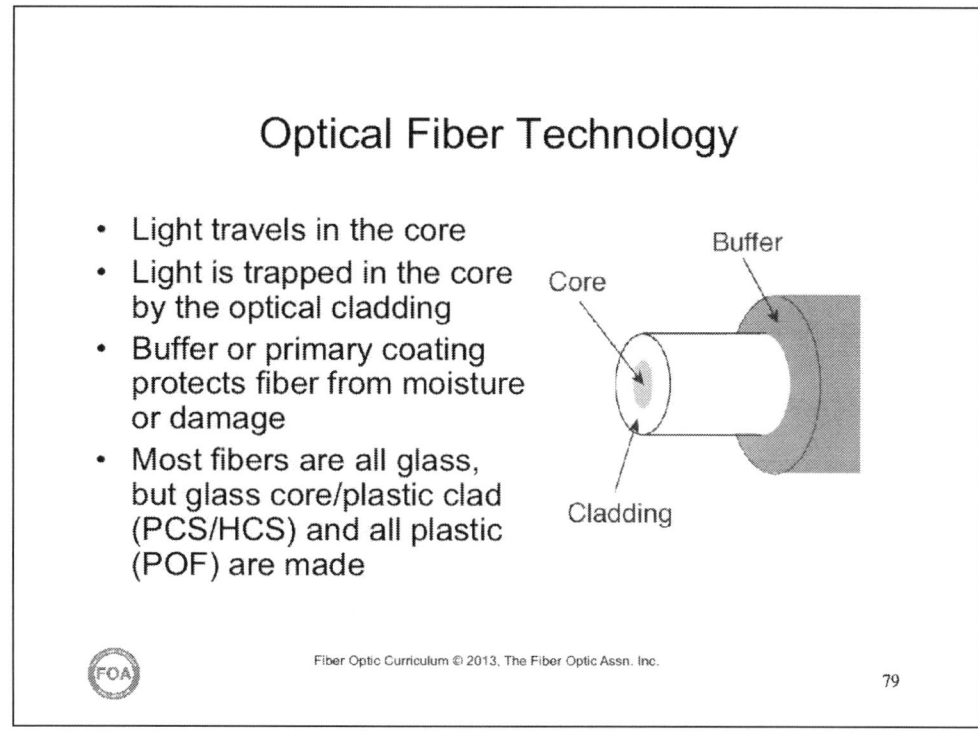

Optical fiber is comprised of a light carrying core surrounded by a cladding which traps the light in the core by the principle of total internal reflection. Most optical fibers are made of glass, although some are made of plastic. The core and cladding are usually fused silica glass which is covered by a plastic coating called the buffer which protects the glass fiber from physical damage and moisture. Most fibers are all glass, but glass core/plastic clad (PCS - plastic clad silica and HCS - hard clad silica) and all plastic (POF - plastic optical fiber) are made. Glass optical fibers are the most common type used in communication applications.

FRG Chapter 5, RGPC Chapter 5, FOTM, Chapter 2, DVVC, Chapter 11
FOA Online Fiber Optic Reference Guide, Understanding Fiber Optics, Optical Fiber

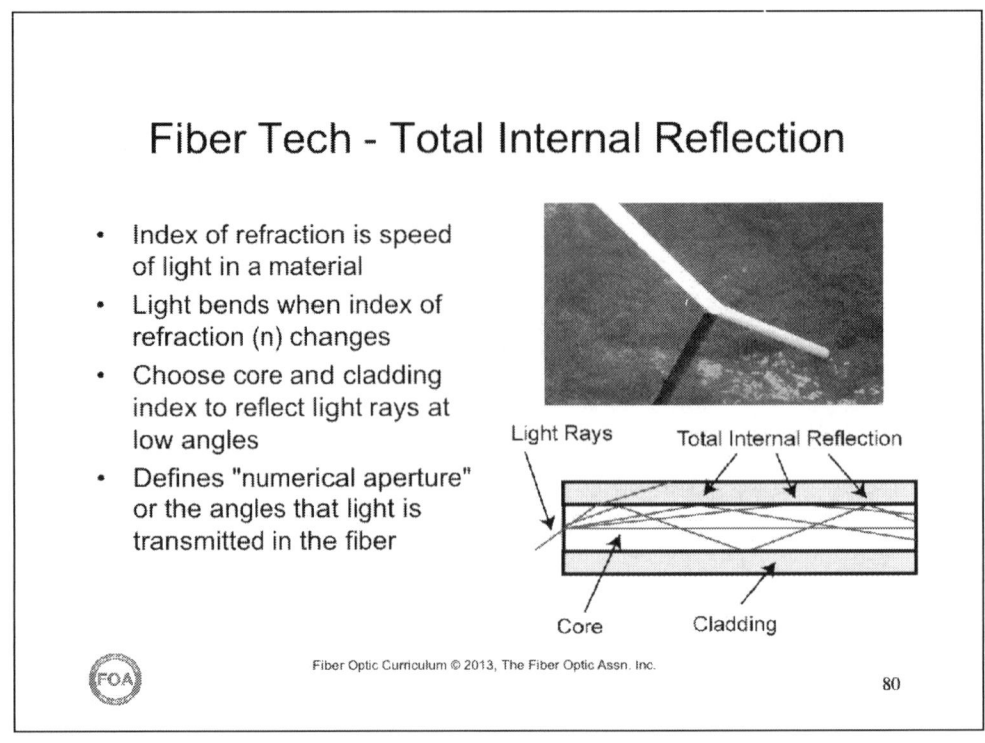

The index of refraction of a material is a property defined by the speed of light in the material. Glass has an index of refraction of about 1.4-1.5, meaning light travels 2/3 as fast in glass as in a vacuum. Whenever light crosses a boundary with materials of different index of refraction, the speed of light changes and the light is refracted or bent. We can see this by looking at a stick stuck in the water as in the photo above. By making the core of the fiber of a material with a slightly higher refractive index, we can cause the light in the core to be totally reflected at the boundary of the cladding for all light that strikes at greater than a critical angle determined by the difference in the composition of the materials used in the core and cladding.

Many students are curious how fiber is made. Good explanations are available in the FOTM, on the Fiber Optic Association website under "Tech Topics" and from most fiber manufacturers.

FRG Chapter 5, FOTM, Chapter 2, DVVC, Chapter 11
FOA Online Fiber Optic Reference Guide, Understanding Fiber Optics, Optical Fiber

Fiber Types

- Defined by core size and material composition
- Multimode has large core that transmits multiple modes or rays of light
- Singlemode has small core that transmits only one modes of light
- Step index fibers have core of same index of refraction so modes travel in straight lines
- Graded index fiber has core that guides modes to reduce dispersion

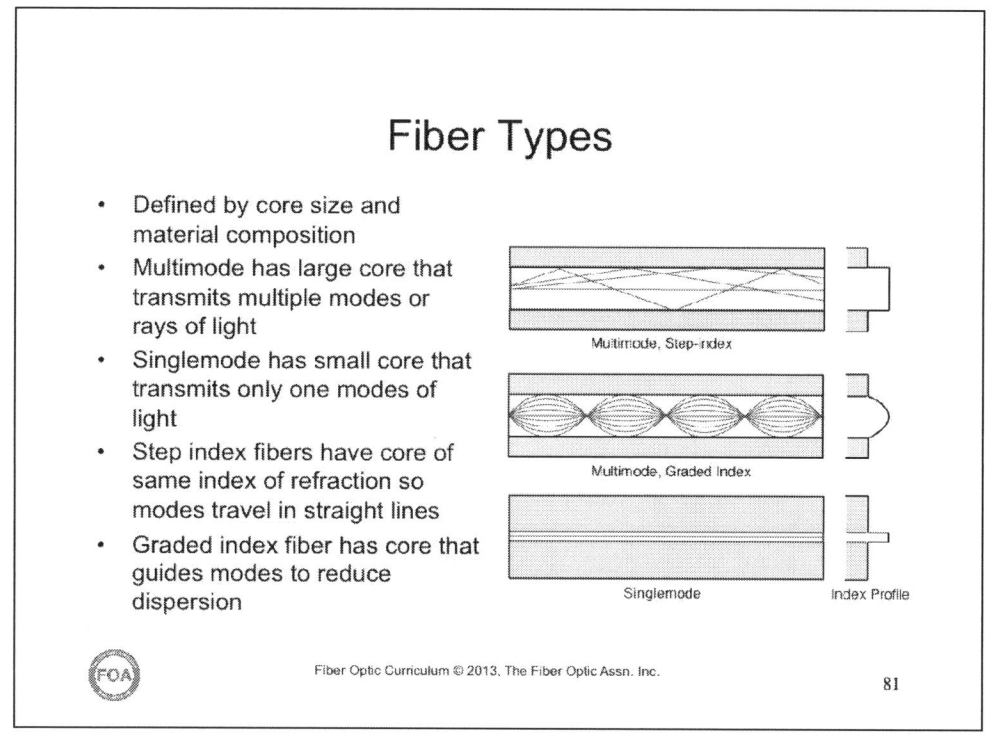

Optical fiber has two basic types, multimode and singlemode. Multimode fiber means that light can travel many different paths (called modes) through the core of the fiber, which enter and leave the fiber at various angles. The highest angle that light is accepted into the core of the fiber defines the numerical aperture (NA) .Two types of multimode fiber exist, distinguished by the index profile of their cores and how light travels in them. Step index multimode fiber has a core composed of one type of glass. Light traveling in the fiber travels in straight lines, reflecting off the core/cladding interface. The numerical aperture is determined by the differences in the indices of refraction of the core and cladding and can be calculated by Snell's law. Since each mode or angle of light travels a different path link, a pulse of light is dispersed while traveling through the fiber, limiting the bandwidth of step index fiber. In graded index multimode fiber, the core is composed of many different layers of glass, chosen with indices of refraction to produce an index profile approximating a parabola. Since the light travels faster in lower index of refraction glass, the light will travel faster as it approaches the outside of the core. Likewise, the light traveling closest to the core center will travel the slowest. A properly constructed index profile will compensate for the different path lengths of each mode, increasing the bandwidth capacity of the fiber by as much as 100 times that of step index fiber. Singlemode fiber just shrinks the core size to a dimension about 6 times the wavelength of the fiber, causing all the light to travel in only one mode. Thus modal dispersion disappears and the bandwidth of the fiber increases by at least another factor of 100 over graded index fiber.

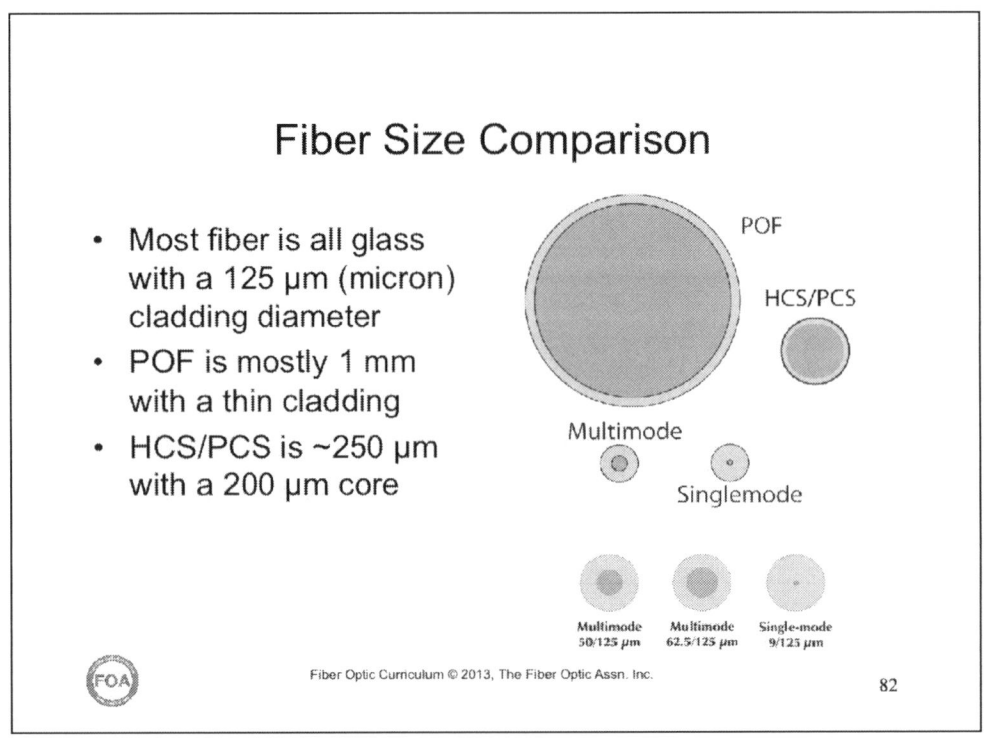

Besides fibers made from pure glass, there are plastic optical fibers (POF) and hard-clad silica (HCS) or plastic-clad silica (PCS) fibers available. POF is all plastic, mostly step index with a 1 mm outer diameter, although some graded-index POF of smaller size is becoming available. POF is used in consumer electronics, automobiles and industrial controls. HCS or PCS fibers use a step-index glass core and a plastic cladding. Both are used in industrial networks where flexibility and ruggedness are important.

Unless specifically called out, we will concentrate on all-glass fibers in our presentation. Below are the three most widely used fiber types, all made from pure glass: Multimode fiber with core/cladding sizes of 50/125 and 62.5/125 microns. 50/125 is often referred to as "laser rated" fiber for it's higher bandwidth capacity with laser sources (and two versions are available with different bandwidth ratings, OM2 with 500 MHz-km bandwidth for 850 nm VCSEL sources and OM3 with bandwidth of 2000 MHz-km at 850 nm.) 62.5/125 (OM1) is often called "FDDI fiber" since it was the standard for that network introduced in 1990.

Illustrate: VFL with SM and MM fiber

FRG Chapter 5, RGPC Chapter 5, FOA Online Fiber Optic Reference Guide, Understanding Fiber Optics, Optical Fiber

Fiber Attenuation - Glass Fibers

- Caused by two factors, both wavelength sensitive
- Scattering decreases quickly at longer wavelengths
- Absorption occurs at specific wavelengths, most water (OH+)
- Systems mainly use longer wavelengths for lower loss but between absorption peaks
- POF has lowest attenuation at ~550 nm, material absorption high above 600 nm

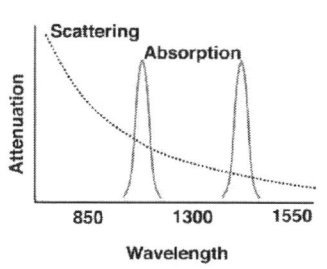

The attenuation of the optical fiber is a result of the combination of two factors, absorption and scattering. The absorption is caused by the absorption of the light and conversion to heat by molecules in the glass. Primary absorbers are residual OH+ and dopants used to modify the refractive index of the glass. This absorption occurs at discrete wavelengths, determined by the elements absorbing the light. The OH+ absorption is predominant, and occurs most strongly around 1000 nm, 1400 nm and above 1600 nm. The largest cause of attenuation is scattering. Scattering occurs when light collides with individual atoms in the glass and is anisotropic. Light that is scattered at angles outside the numerical aperture of the fiber will be absorbed into the cladding or transmitted back toward the source Scattering is also a function of wavelength, proportional to the inverse fourth power of the wavelength of the light. Thus if you double the wavelength of the light, you reduce the scattering losses by 2^4 or 16 times. Therefore , for long distance transmission, it is advantageous to use the longest practical wavelength for minimal attenuation and maximum distance between repeaters. Together, absorption and scattering produce the attenuation curve for a typical glass optical fiber shown.
FRG Chapter 5, FOTM, Chapter 2, DVVC, Chapter 11
FOA Online Fiber Optic Reference Guide, Understanding Fiber Optics, Optical Fiber

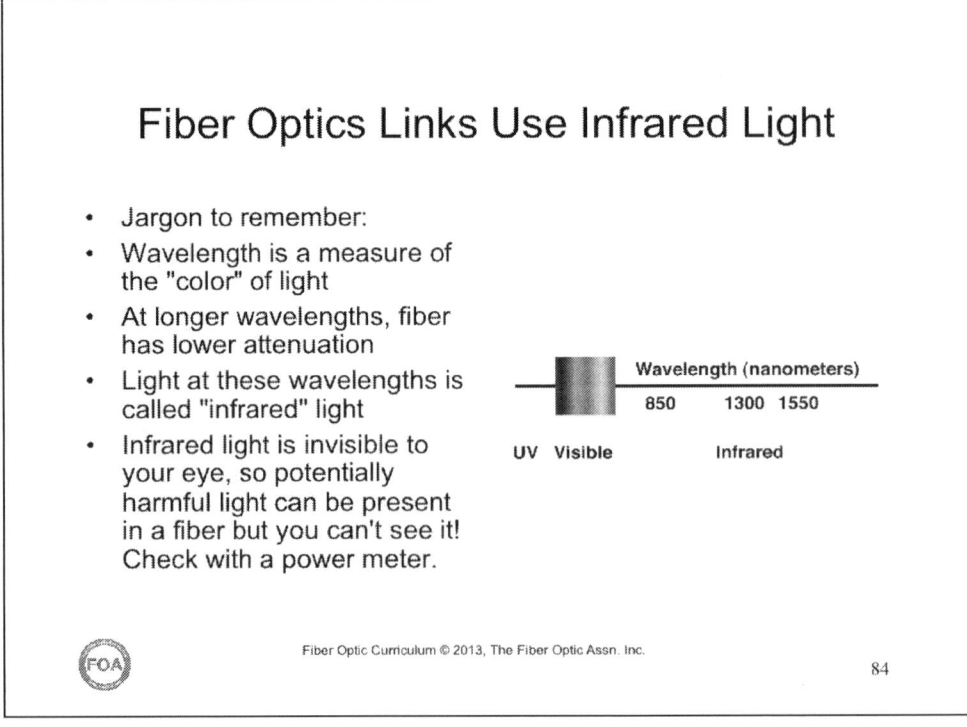

Here is some fiber optic jargon to remember:

Wavelength is a measure of the "color" of light. Visible light is about 500-600 nm wavelength. Beyond that we call it "infrared" light.

At longer (infrared) wavelengths, fiber has lower attenuation, so most systems transmit in that region.

Safety note: Infrared light is invisible to your eye, so potentially harmful light can be present in a fiber but you can't see it! Check with a power meter.

FRG Chapter 2, 5, FOTM, Chapter 2, DVVC, Chapter 11

FOA Online Fiber Optic Reference Guide, Understanding Fiber Optics, Optical Fiber

Fiber Attenuation-Typical Specs

Fiber Type @ Wavelength	850 nm	1300 nm	1550 nm
Multimode	3 dB/km (3.5)	1 dB/km (1.5)	NA
Singlemode	NA	0.4 dB/km (1/0.5)	0.25 dB/km (1/0.5)

(TIA 568 Specs in parentheses)

Fiber Optic Curriculum © 2013, The Fiber Optic Assn. Inc.

More detailed fiber specifications can be found in the textbook or on the Reference website or from manufacturers websites or datasheets
The specifications in parentheses are from TIA-568 which are more conservative than typical specs. The two specs for singlemode are for indoors (1 dB/km) and outdoor (0.5 dB/km).
These are the wavelengths of light generally used for testing fibers for loss.

FRG Chapter 5, RGPC Chapter 5, FOTM, Chapter 2, DVVC, Chapter 11
FOA Online Fiber Optic Reference Guide, Understanding Fiber Optics, Optical Fiber

Spectral Attenuation

- Some coarse wavelength division multiplexing systems (CWDM) use wavelengths from 1260 to 1675 nm
- Requires low water peak fiber
- May be tested over whole range
- Uses broad sources to cover wavelength range

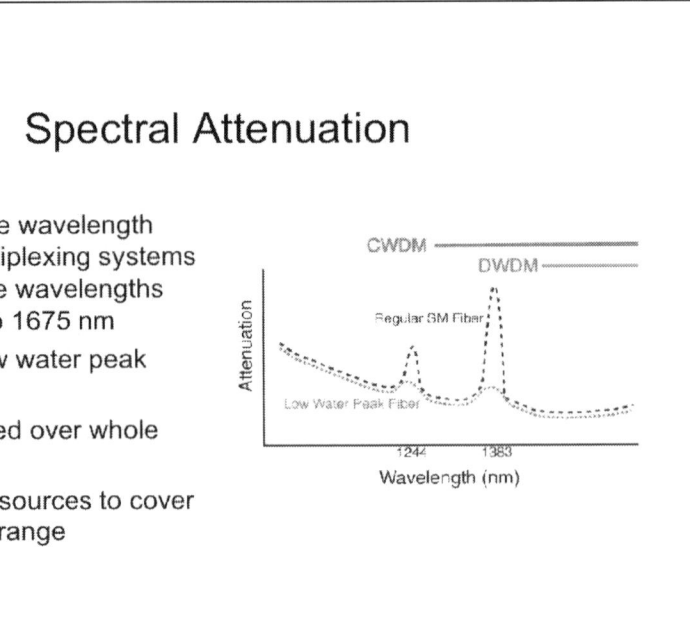

With the development of low water peak fibers, the possibility of transmission from 1260 to 1675 nm has been considered. This results from careful manufacturing of the fiber to reduce the water in the fiber (in the form of OH- ions) that causes higher spectral attenuation at around 1244 and 1383 nm. Systems using coarse wavelength division multiplexing (CWDM) use lasers at 20 nm increments over this range. Since one may want to use available fibers †of unknown spectral attenuation for CWDM which uses lasers from 1260 to 1670 nm in 20 nm windows, it becomes necessary to test for spectral attenuation to verify the usability. At the water peaks, legacy fibers may have attenuation coefficients around 2 dB/km while low water peak fibers may be as low as 0.4 dB/km. Testing spectral attenuation is done per TIA/EIA-455-61 or IEC 61300-3-7 with broadband sources like LEDs and a spectrum analyzer on the receiving end of the fiber. Calibration is done with a short fiber length, the the instrument calculates the spectral attenuation on a long length being tested. The measurement of spectral attenuation uses instruments similar to those used for CD testing by the phase shift method, so some instruments do both measurements at one time.

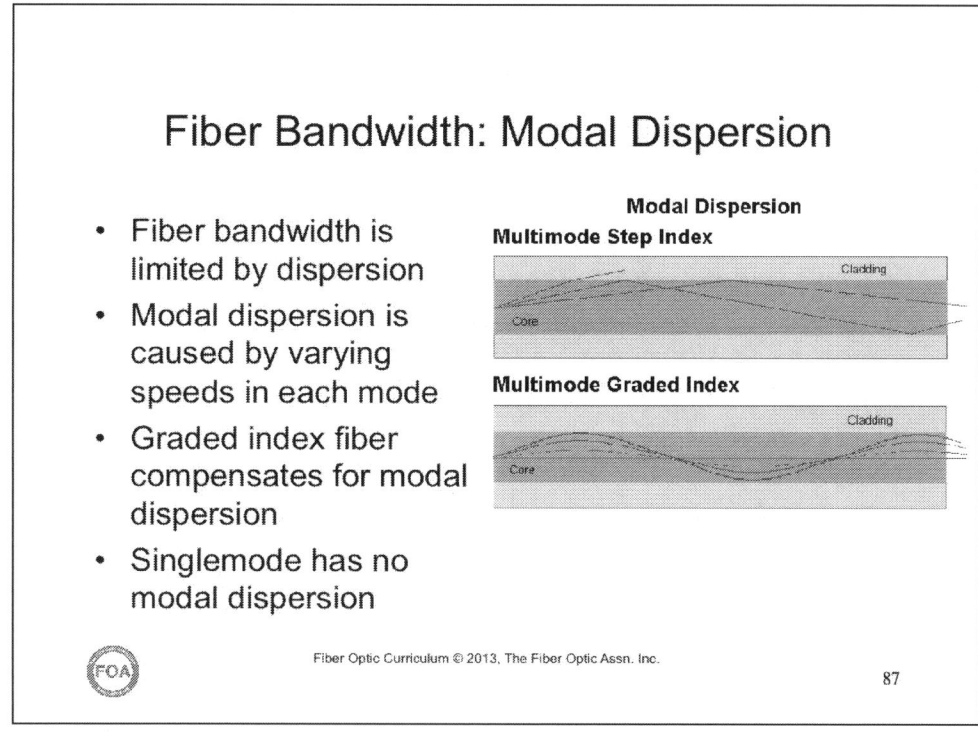

Fiber Bandwidth: Modal Dispersion

- Fiber bandwidth is limited by dispersion
- Modal dispersion is caused by varying speeds in each mode
- Graded index fiber compensates for modal dispersion
- Singlemode has no modal dispersion

Fiber's information transmission capacity is limited by two separate components of dispersion: modal and chromatic dispersion. First modal dispersion:

Step index multimode fiber has a core composed of only one type of glass. Light traveling in the fiber travels in straight lines, reflecting off the core/cladding interface. Since each mode or angle of light travels a different path link, a pulse of light is dispersed while traveling through the fiber, limiting the bandwidth of step index fiber. In graded index multimode fiber, the core is composed of many different layers of glass, chosen with indices of refraction to produce an index profile approximating a parabola. Since the light travels faster in lower index of refraction glass, the light will travel faster as it approaches the outside of the core. Likewise, the light traveling closest to the core center will travel the slowest. A properly constructed index profile will compensate for the different path lengths of each mode, increasing the bandwidth capacity of the fiber by as much as 100 times that of step index fiber. Singlemode fiber just shrinks the core size to a dimension about 6 times the wavelength of the fiber, causing all the light to travel in only one mode. Thus modal dispersion disappears and the bandwidth of the fiber increases by at least another factor of 100 over graded index fiber.

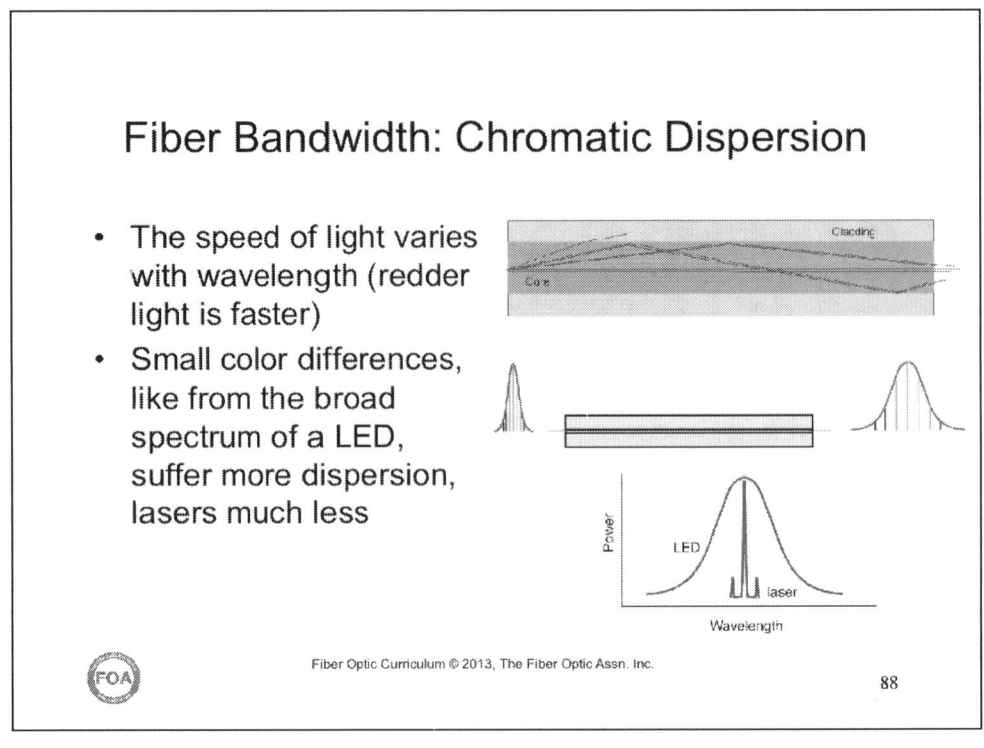

The second factor in fiber bandwidth is chromatic dispersion. Remember a prism spreads out the spectrum of incident light since the light travels at different speeds according to its color and is therefore refracted at different angles. The usual way of stating this is the index of refraction of the glass is wavelength dependent. Thus a carefully manufactured graded index multimode fiber can only be optimized for a single wavelength, usually near 1300 nm, and light of other colors will suffer from chromatic dispersion. Even light in the same mode will be dispersed if it is of different wavelengths. Chromatic dispersion is a bigger problem with LEDs, which have broad spectral outputs (their output light is comprised of many wavelengths of light), unlike lasers which concentrate most of their light in a narrow spectral range. Chromatic dispersion occurs with LEDs because much of the power is away from the zero dispersion wavelength of the fiber. High speed systems, based on broad output LEDs, suffer intense chromatic dispersion, about equal to the modal dispersion.

FRG Chapter 5, RGPC Chapter 5, FOTM, Chapter 2, DVVC, Chapter 11
FOA Online Fiber Optic Reference Guide, Understanding Fiber Optics, Optical Fiber

Fiber Bandwidth: Polarization Mode Dispersion (PMD)

- Affects long singlemode fibers
- The speed of light varies with polarization
- Depends on fiber ovality, wavelength and stress on fiber
- Can vary with temperature or even wind on aerial cable
- Small effect but can be important on long fibers at 40-100 Gb/s

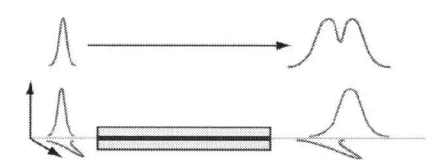

Another factor in fiber bandwidth is polarization mode dispersion. Polarization mode dispersion (PMD) is a bit more complex. Polarization is a phenomenon of light traveling in a medium as a wave with components at right angles. Some materials, like a glass optical fiber, have a different index of refraction for each of those components of the light wave, which is called birefringence. And a different index of refraction means light travels at a different speed, so in the simplest visualization, PMD in fiber looks like the drawing below, where each component of the polarized light travels at a different speed, causing dispersion. The magnitude of PMD in a fier is expressed as this difference, which is known as the differential group delay (DGD) and called Δτ (delta Tau). PMD is generally tested for fibers during manufacture or when being cabled. In the field, it is common to test PMD on newly installed fibers which are intended for operation at high speeds, generally above 2.5 Gb/s or when upgrading fibers installed some time in the past. Since PMD varies over time, a single test becomes an average and tests at a later time may be done for comparison.There are a number of commonly used test methods for PMD, some of which are limited to the manufacturing environment, while others can be used in the field. Essentially, all the test instruments have a source which can vary the polarization of the test signal and a measurement unit that can analyze polarization changes.

Multimode Fiber Bandwidth Grades

Fiber Type	Bandwidth at 850 nm (MHz-km)	Bandwidth at 1300 nm (MHz-km)
62.5/125 (FDDI or OM1)	160	500
50/125 (OM2)	500	500
50/125 (OM3, laser-rated)	2000	500
50/125 (OM4, laser-rated	3600	500

For almost fifteen years, one had only two choices if you were installing fiber. The de facto-standard multimode fiber had a core/cladding size of 62.5/125 microns and was rated for use with FDDI (Fiber Distributed Data Interface) or Fast Ethernet, both 100 Mb/s networks that used inexpensive LED sources as transmitters. Longer distances or higher speeds called for singlemode fiber with a small 8 micron core that required expensive laser sources. Fiber manufacturers had not put any real engineering effort into multimode fiber in fifteen years because 62.5/125 fiber met the industry's needs. But with the advent of Gigabit Ethernet (GbE), calls for longer distances on multimode fiber sent them back to the labs. And what they came up with was a brand new twenty-year old fiber - 50/125! GbE uses a 850 nm laser for a source, so the fiber manufacturers revived a fiber that dated back to the "prehistoric era" of fiber - 1980 - when long distance telecom networks used newly-developed 850 nm lasers with a fiber that had a 50 micron core optimized for use with lasers. Now manufacturers have improved the performance of this 50/125 fiber even more, to allow use with 10 Gigabit Ethernet and Fibre Channel.

FRG Chapter 5, RGPC Chapter 5, FOA Online Fiber Optic Reference Guide, Understanding Fiber Optics, Optical Fiber

SM Fiber Types

Fiber Type (TIA/IEC/ITU)	Description
OS1/B1.1/G.652	Standard SM fiber for 1310nm
OS2/B1.2/G.652	Low water peak fiber
---/B2/G.653	Dispersion-shifted fiber
---/B1.2/G.654	Cutoff-shifted fiber
---/B4/G.654	Non-zero dispersion-shifted fiber
---/---/G.655	Non-zero dispersion-shifted fiber
---/---/G.657	Bend-insensitive fiber

Singlemode fiber have several versions depending on the application. OS1/OS2 are TIA specs for premises/campus applications. Low water peak fiber is used for CWDM – coarse wavelength division multiplexing. The other types are used for long links and DWDM-dense wavelength division multiplexing.

ITU G.653   Covers single-mode dispersion-shifted optical fiber. Dispersion is minimized in the 1,550-nm wavelength range. At this range attenuation is also minimized, so longer distance cables are possible.

ITU G.654: Covers single-mode fibre which has the zero-dispersion wavelength around 1300 m wavelength which is cut-off shifted and loss minimized at a wavelength around 1550 nm and which is optimized for use in the 1500-1600 nm region.

 ITU G.655   Covers single-mode NZ-DSF (nonzero dispersion-shifted) fiber) , which takes advantage of dispersion characteristics that suppress the growth of four-wave mixing, a problem with WDM (wavelength division multiplexing) systems. NZ-DSF supports high-power signals and longer distances, as well as closely spaced DWDM.

Choosing Fiber

- Install the best multimode fiber
    - OM4 - laser optimized 50/125 (best for >10G)
    - OM3 - laser optimized 50/125 (best!)
    - OM2 - 50/125
    - OM1 - 62.5/125 FDDI grade
- Include spare fibers
- Include singlemode fibers in multimode cable (hybrid)
- Include fibers in copper cables (composite - rare)

The standard multimode fiber for over 15 years had been 62.5/125 - the so-called FDDI grade fiber for it's bandwidth to support FDDI. There has been a changeover for high speed systems to 50/125 fiber for it's higher bandwidth performance with VCSELs (up to 10 Gb/s), but it cannot be mixed with 62.5/125! If you choose one fiber, all patchcords must be the same fiber! Fiber is cheap - as cheap as kit string! When specifying backbone cables, install lots of spare fibers including singlemode fibers in multimode cables - called a "hybrid" cable - for future high bandwidth applications. Sometimes it makes sense to put fibers into copper cables called a composite cable. This is becoming more common when using a combination cable (coax and UTP) for home networks that may include 2 fibers.

FRG, Chapter 5, RGPC Chapter 5, FOTM, Chapter 4,5,913, DVVC, Chapter 11
FOA Online Fiber Optic Reference Guide, Understanding Fiber Optics, The Basics: Optical Fiber, Cables

Bend Insensitive Fiber

- Normal fiber has high loss when bent
- New "bend insensitive fiber" can be bent tightly without loss - or long term harm
- Use indoors to fit fibers in small spaces

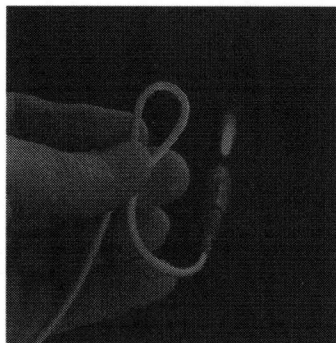

Most optical fiber manufacturers are now offering bend-insensitive fibers that can be bent tightly without much loss. This allows them to be used in close spaces like cable trays or run around the edge of a wall in a room.

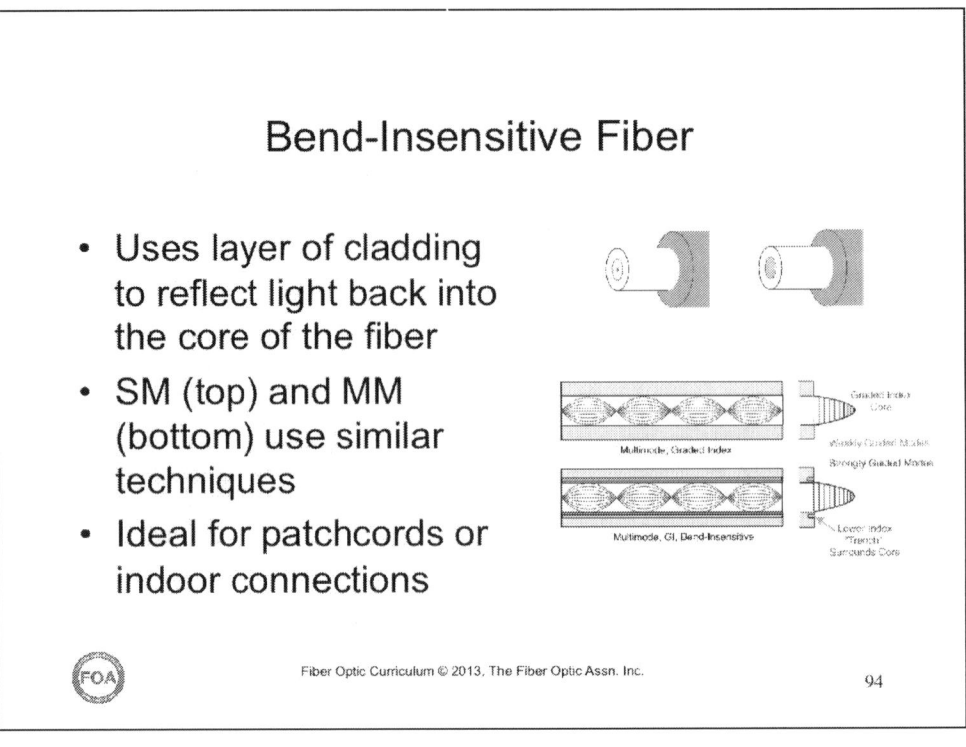

These bend-insensitive fibers – both MM and SM – use an optical ring – like a guard ring – around the core made of lower index glass to reflect light escaping the core due to stress back into the core. It's simple but very effective.

SM is used for patchcords and premises use but is compatible to other SM fibers MM B-I fiber affects modal distribution, may have high loss connecting to legacy fiber

Protecting The Fiber: Cable

- First layer of protection is the primary buffer coating of 250 μm diameter on the glass fiber
- Tight buffer fibers have secondary buffer coating of 900 μm diameter
- Cable provides strength members and jacket for protection

Because of the wide variety of conditions to which they are exposed, optical fibers have to be encased in several layers of protection. The first of these layers is the primary buffer coating, a thin protective coating made of ultraviolet curable acrylate (a plastic), which is applied to the glass fiber as it is being manufactured. This thin coating provides moisture and mechanical protection.

The next layer of protection is a buffer, that is typically extruded over this coating to further increase the strength of the single fibers. This buffer can be either a loose tube or a tight tube. The next layer is a strength member, usually an aramid fiber, that can be used for pulling the cable. Finally, the entire cable is covered by a jacket designed to withstand the environment into which the cable is going to be installed.
FRG, Chapter 6, RGPC Chapter 5, FOTM, Chapter 4,5,913, DVVC, Chapter 11, FOA Online Fiber Optic Reference Guide, Understanding Fiber Optics, The Basics: Cables
The "Cables" PPT has more information on cables and how they are installed.

Fiber Optic Cable Types

- Tight buffer (Zipcord)

- Distribution

- Loose Tube

- Tight buffer Breakout

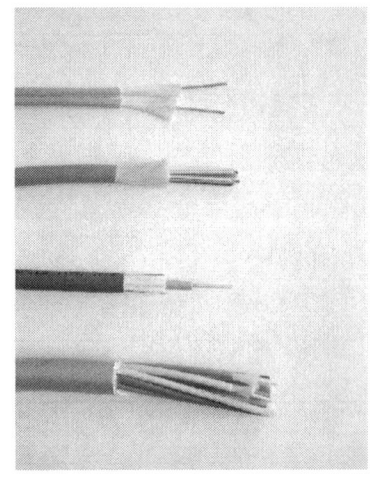

There are 4 major types of cables.

Tight buffer comes in simplex or zipcord versions.

Distribution cable has multiple 900 μm coated fibers surrounded by aramid fiber (Kevlar) strength members and a jacket.

Loose tube cable has one or more plastic tubes with 250 μm coated fibers inside the tubes, surrounded by strength members. The tubes are often filled with gels or powders to block water entry.

Breakout cable is simply a number of simplex cables in a common jacket, designed for indoor use that requires a rugged cable.

Tight buffer (a zipcord is shown), distribution and breakout cables are used indoors. Outdoors, loose tube cable is used to allow filling the cable with water-blocking materials to protect the fibers from moisture.

FRG, Chapter 6, RGPC Chapter 5, FOTM, Chapter 4,5,913, DVVC, Chapter 11

FOA Online Fiber Optic Reference Guide, Understanding Fiber Optics, The Basics: Cables

Zipcord

- Used for patchcords or short indoor runs
- Two 900 micron tight buffered fibers, color coded
- Fibers can be directly terminated
- Aramid strength members
- PVC jacket rated for flammability

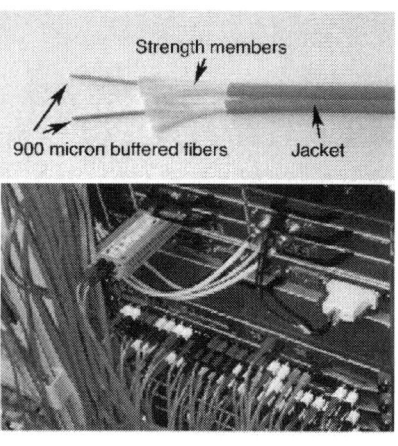

Zipcord is just two simplex cables attached by a thin web for convenience, since connections require two fibers transmitting in opposite directions

Zipcord is primarily used for patchcords or short indoor runs

It consists of two 900 micron tight buffered fibers, color coded, surrounded by aramid strength members and covered by a PVC jacket rated for flammability

Zipcord can be used for patchcords on patch panels or connecting up equipment. It can be laid in cable trays or even pulled by the strength members in conduit

FRG, Chapter 6, RGPC Chapter 5, FOTM, Chapter 4,5,913, DVVC, Chapter 11

FOA Online Fiber Optic Reference Guide, Understanding Fiber Optics, The Basics: Cables

Distribution Cable Construction

- Most popular backbone cable
- Relatively high fiber density
- Bundled 900 micron tight buffered fibers, color coded
- Fibers can be directly terminated
- Aramid strength members
- PVC jacket rated for flammability

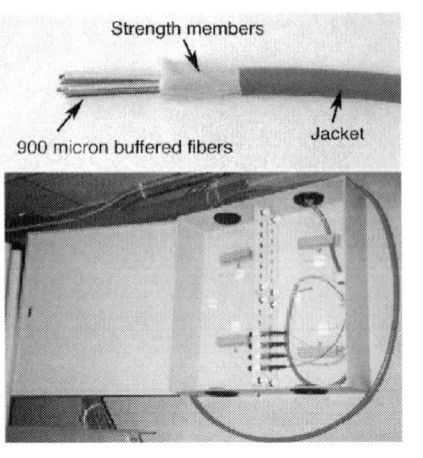

Distribution cable is the most popular backbone cable, since it offers relatively high fiber density in a small cable that is easy to install

Has many bundled 900 micron tight buffered fibers, color coded inside aramid strength members and covered by a PVC jacket rated for flammability

Each individual tight buffered fiber can be directly terminated, but terminations are not well protected like in zipcord, simplex or breakout cables, so it should be terminated inside a patch panel or wall-mounted box.

FRG, Chapter 6, RGPC Chapter 5, FOTM, Chapter 4,5,913, DVVC, Chapter 11

FOA Online Fiber Optic Reference Guide, Understanding Fiber Optics, The Basics: Cables

Breakout Cable Construction

- Bundles of simplex cables inside jacket
- Rugged cable for harsh indoor environments
- Bulky and heavy compared to distribution cable
- Directly terminate for connections to equipment

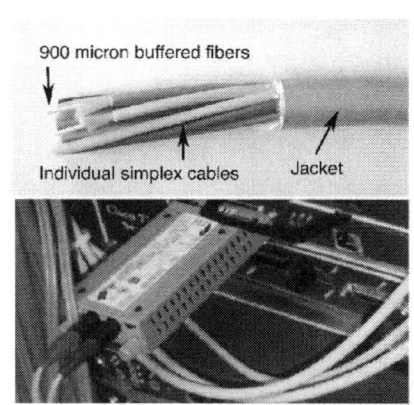

Breakout cable consists of bundles of simplex cables inside a flame-retardant jacket for use indoors. It is a very rugged cable for harsh indoor environments but is bulky and heavy compared to distribution cable

However you may directly terminate breakout cables for connections to equipment since individual fibers are protected inside individual jackets, making it very convenient to use

FRG, Chapter 6, RGPC Chapter 5, FOTM, Chapter 4,5,913, DVVC, Chapter 11

FOA Online Fiber Optic Reference Guide, Understanding Fiber Optics, The Basics: Cables

Loose Tube Cable Construction

- Fibers are loose in tubes for isolation from installation stress
- Tubes contain several individual fibers (usually up to 12)
- Tubes and cable can be filled with water-block
- Often pulled into conduit or innerduct
- Usually spliced, must use breakout kit to terminate

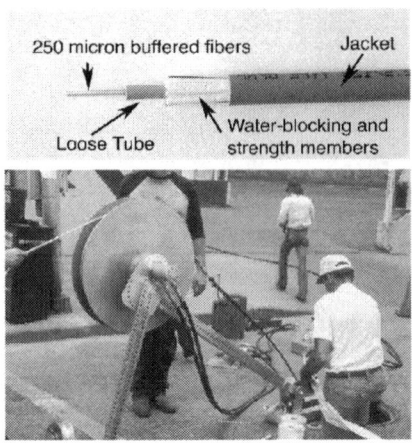

Loose tube cable is used for most outdoor installations because it has higher strength for pulling long distances or aerial installs and can provide protection from moisture or water penetration and animal penetration.

Fibers are loose in tubes for isolation from installation stress and allow the tubes and cable to be filled with water-block in gel or dry water-blocking powder. Loose tube cable contains one or more tubes which contain several individual fibers (usually up to 12). The fibers are only coated with the primary buffer coating of 250 micron diameter to keep the cable size small and are color-coded. Loose tube cables can be pulled with very high tension or suspended aerially without harming fibers. Loose tube cable is usually spliced and the splices stored in splice closures or the fibers are spliced to pigtails for termination. If directly terminated, the installer must use a breakout kit to terminate the fibers as they are too fragile to handle safely. Breakout kits use 1 mm tubing called furcation tubing to sleeve the fibers before termination

FRG, Chapter 6, RGPC Chapter 5, FOTM, Chapter 4,5,913, DVVC, Chapter 11

FOA Online Fiber Optic Reference Guide, Understanding Fiber Optics, The Basics: Cables

Armored Cable Construction

- Adds metal or dielectric armor over cable to prevent rodent damage
- Can be used in any application to prevent crushing, even indoors
- More difficult to prepare for splicing or termination
- Sometimes indoor distribution cable is armored to protect the cable from crush loads

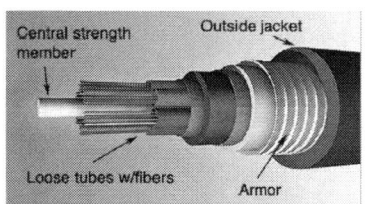

Armored cable adds metal or dielectric armor over cable, typically to prevent rodent damage in direct burial installations

Armored cable can be used in any application to prevent crushing, even indoors, for example in raised floors where there are many heavy cables already installed and potential of crushing the cable is high

Armored cable is more difficult to prepare for splicing or termination, but ripcords are included to allow slitting the armor for relatively easy removal

FRG, Chapter 6, FOTM, Chapter 4,5,913, DVVC, Chapter 11

FOA Online Fiber Optic Reference Guide, Understanding Fiber Optics, The Basics: Cables

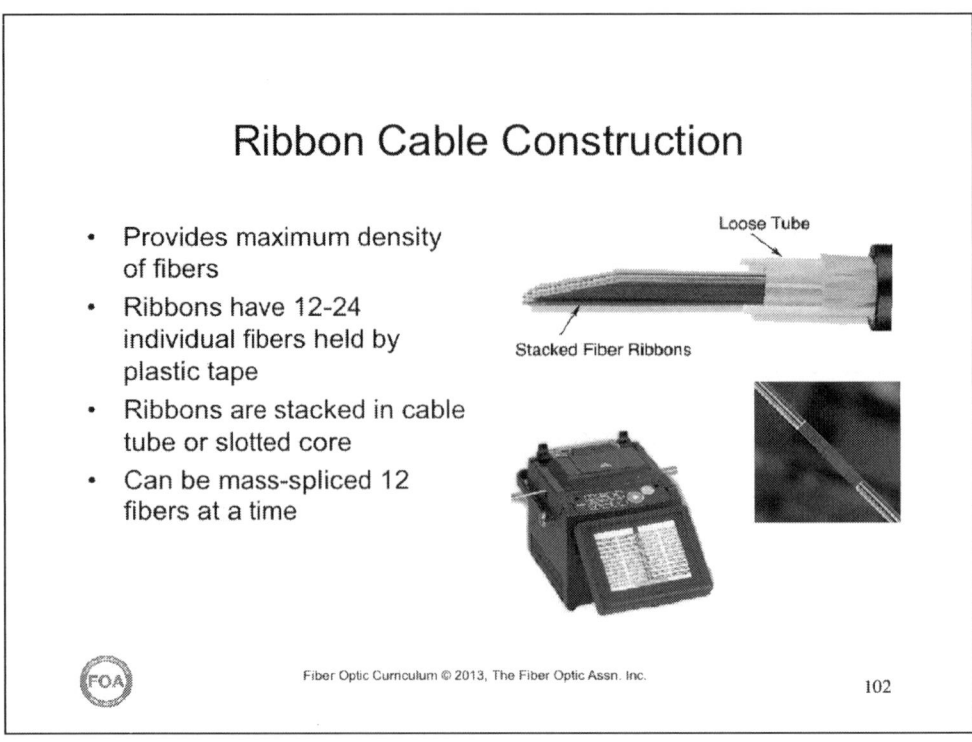

Ribbon Cable Construction

- Provides maximum density of fibers
- Ribbons have 12-24 individual fibers held by plastic tape
- Ribbons are stacked in cable tube or slotted core
- Can be mass-spliced 12 fibers at a time

Ribbon cable allows maximum density of fibers - the smallest cable with the most fibers.

Ribbons have 12-24 individual fibers held by plastic tape and ribbons are stacked in cable tubes or slotted cores.

Twelve 12-fiber ribbons can fit in a 5 m (1/4") square section and up to six of these ribbon assemblies are possible in a slotted-core cable design less than 25 mm (1") diameter. Ribbon cables have been made with over 2000 fibers.

This offers the maximum density of fibers but the cables are hard to work with. They require special tools to separate and strip the fibers and ribbon splicers to fusion splice them. Occasionally special mechanical splices using v-groove chips are used.

FRG, Chapter 6, FOTM, Chapter 4,5,913, DVVC, Chapter 11

FOA Online Fiber Optic Reference Guide, Understanding Fiber Optics, The Basics: Cables

OPGW Cable Construction

- OPGW = optical power ground wire
- Used as ground cable for high-voltage power lines
- Fiber is immune to electrical interference
- Fibers in loose tubes inside welded hermetic metal tube

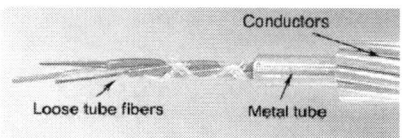

OPGW stands for "optical power ground wire."

It is used as ground cable for high-voltage power lines, made possible by the fact that fiber is immune to electrical interference

The fibers are inside plastic loose tubes which are then inside welded hermetic metal tube, covered by conductors that are also strength members. Finally, all is covered by a weather-resistant jacket.

The fiber is suspended from the power line towers then cable ends are brought to the ground to be spliced. Splice closures are mounted on the power line towers.

FRG, Chapter 6, FOTM, Chapter 4,5,913, DVVC, Chapter 11

FOA Online Fiber Optic Reference Guide, Understanding Fiber Optics, The Basics: Cables

Air - Blown Fiber
An Alternative To Cable

- Install "cable" with empty plastic tubes – indoors or OSP
- Blow special fibers into the tubes
- Allows easy installation but requires special equipment
- Requires special fibers
- Easy upgrades
- More expensive but allows flexibility

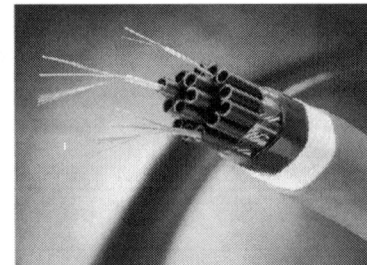

Blown Fiber - An Alternative To Cable

Instead of installing cables with fibers, you can install "cable" with open tubes. After installation, you then blow special fiber into the tubes using high pressure compressed gas. Blown fiber allows easy installation of the cable and easy later installation of the fibers, but special equipment is required for the installation, limiting it to contractors who have made significant investment into equipment and training. Blown fiber requires special fibers designed to be installed this way. They are smaller and coated with a special coating that floats better in the tubes with less friction. It can be used with multimode or singlemode fibers or a combination of the two. Cable designs can have one or several tubes. More tubes means easy upgrades or separating fibers at junctions to go in different directions, a difficulty with normal cables where tubes are not easily split except in breakout cables. Blown fiber offers easy upgrades - blow out old fibers and blow in new ones. Blown fiber installations are more expensive initially but allows flexibility for future upgrades not possible with other cable designs.

FRG, Chapter 6, RGPC Chapter 5, FOA Online Fiber Optic Reference Guide, Understanding Fiber Optics, The Basics: Cables

Fiber Optic Cables

Type	Application	#Fibers
Tight buffer	Building cable Single fiber Zipcord Breakout	1-48
Distribution	Building cable Plenum	6-144
Loose Tube	OSP Aerial Submarine	6-144+
Ribbon	OSP Aerial Submarine	72-288+

Tight buffer cable is made in three versions:
- Single fiber, usually used for patchcords
- Zipcord used as a duplex patchcord for connecting transceivers or connecting devices together
- Breakout cable, which is simply a number of single fiber cables inside a jacket used for indoor cabling where each fiber is terminated and routed directly to a connection.

Distribution cable is an indoor cable that has multiple fibers with a 900 micron buffer coating which can be terminated directly, but lacking the protection of the tight buffer cables above, must be protected by enclosure in a patch panel or box.

Loose tube cable comes in many varieties for underground, aerial or even underwater applications. It can also be armored for protection against rodents for direct burial.

Ribbon cable puts 12 or 24 fibers in ribbons and stacks the ribbons to make a small diameter very high fiber count cable. Applications are similar to loose tube designs.

FRG, Chapter 6, RGPC Chapter 5, FOTM, Chapter 4,5,913, DVVC, Chapter 11
FOA Online Fiber Optic Reference Guide, Understanding Fiber Optics, The Basics: Cables

Specifications For Fiber Optic Cable

- Installation Specifications
  - Tensile load
  - Bend radius
  - Diameter/construction
  - Temperature

- Environmental Specifications
  - Temperature
  - Long term bend radius
  - Electrical codes
  - Long term tensile load
  - Flame retardance
  - Rodent penetration
  - Water resistance
  - Crush loads
  - Abrasion resistance
  - Resistance to chemicals
  - Impact resistance
  - Vibration

Specifying the proper cable requires two major considerations:
1. How the cable will be installed.
2. What environment it will be facing after installation.
These are simply guidelines to consider when looking for a cable for any particular installation. Different manufacturers have different cable designs for applications - and maybe different designs than other manufacturers.
Therefore it is preferable to talk to several manufacturers when choosing a cable, especially in unusual situations.

FRG, Chapter 6, RGPC Chapter 5, FOTM, Chapter 4,5,913, DVVC, Chapter 11
FOA Online Fiber Optic Reference Guide, Understanding Fiber Optics, The Basics: Cables

Cable Jacket Color Codes

Fiber Type	General Use	US Military
OM1	Orange	Slate
OM2	Orange	Orange
OM3/OM4	Aqua	---
MM 100/140	Orange	Green
SM OS1/OS2	Yellow	Yellow
SM/PM	Blue	---

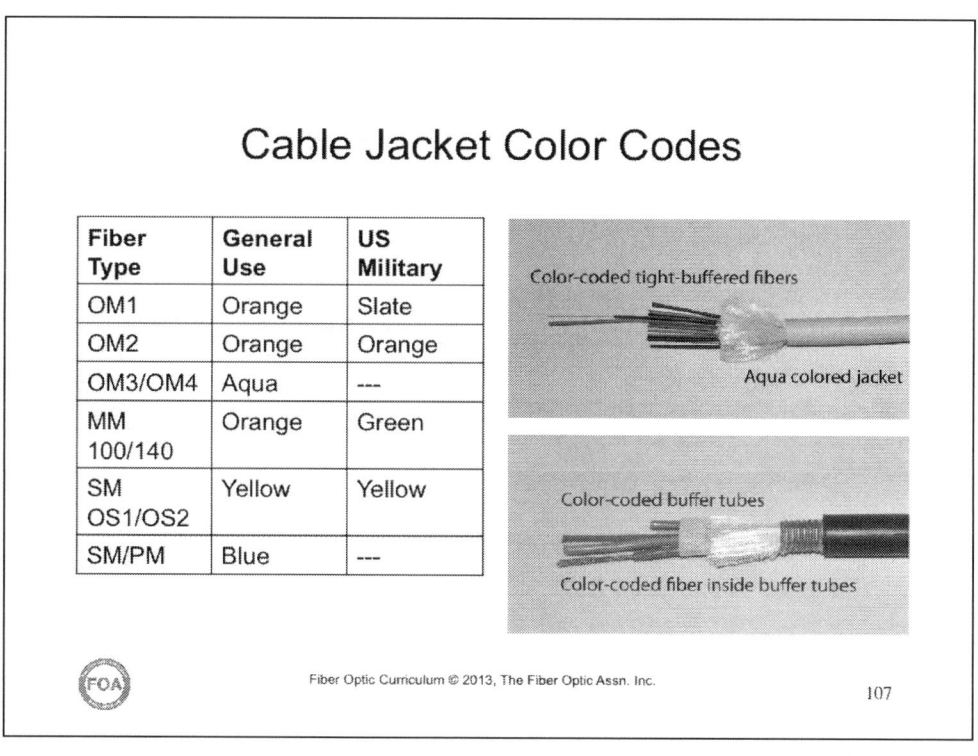

Cable jackets for indoor cables may be color-coded in the scheme given above and covered in TIA-598. Colors are optional, however, so one may find cables in any color that was specified by the buyer.

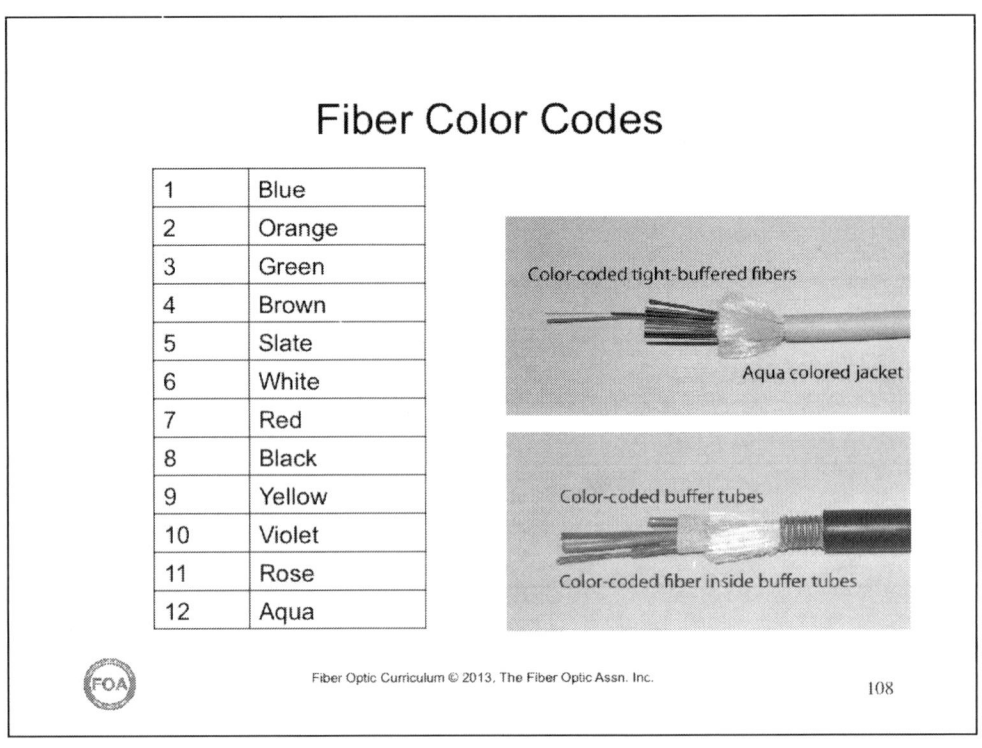

Individual fibers or buffer tubes are color-coded in this 1-12 scheme. If there are more than 12 of any item, binder tape or tracer colors on a buffer tube, for example. In a loose-tube cable, 12 color-coded buffer tubes with 12 fibers each creates a 144 fiber cable. Ribbons follow the same color codes. Since these are only guidelines, alternatives may be seen. When splicing it is normal to splice like colored fibers.

Fiber Optic Cable Selection Criteria

- Proper for the application (building, riser, plenum, aerial, direct burial, submarine, etc.)
- Enough fiber for redundancy, upgrades
- Meets environmental requirements
- Indoor meets fire codes
- Cost
- Choose hardware to fit cable needs

Choice of cables
Other factors to be considered when choosing a fiber optic cable are:
1. Current and future bandwidth requirements.
2. Acceptable attenuation rate.
3. Length of cable.
4. Cost of installation.
5. Mechanical requirements (ruggedness, flexibility, flame retardance, low smoke, cut- through resistance).
6. UL/NEC requirements.
7. Signal source (coupling efficiency, power output, receiver sensitivity).
8. Connectors and terminations.
9. Cable dimension requirements.
10. Physical environment (temperature, moisture, location).
11. Compatibility with any existing systems.

FRG, Chapter 6, RGPC Chapter 5, FOTM, Chapter 4,5,913, DVVC, Chapter 11
FOA Online Fiber Optic Reference Guide, Understanding Fiber Optics, The Basics: Cables

Choosing Indoor Cable Type

- Indoor/Premises
  - Short distances - simplex, zipcord or breakout cable
  - Longer lengths - distribution cable
  - All dielectric
  - If plenum use PVC if available
- Performance Specifications
  - Tensile load: 200-500 lbs max.
  - Temperature range: -10 to +60 °C
  - Strength members: Kevlar®
  - Jacket: UL Rated
- *Do not install cable indoors without UL or other appropriate Fire Rating!*

Breakout cable is larger and more expensive, but for short distances it offers more ruggedness and the ability to be terminated without the need for patch panels or termination boxes, saving that cost.

For most backbone cables, distribution cables have a smaller size for the number of fibers, easing pulling of the cable, and are terminated in patch panels or boxes to protect the fibers.

Remember that indoor cables must meet UL ratings!

FRG, Chapter 6, RGPC Chapter 5,7, FOTM, Chapter 4,5,913, DVVC, Chapter 11
FOA Online Fiber Optic Reference Guide, Understanding Fiber Optics, The Basics: Cables

Cable Ratings and Markings

- All premises cables must carry identification and ratings per the NEC (National Electrical Code) paragraph 770 or other local building codes. Cables without markings should never be installed indoors as they will not pass inspections!
- These ratings are:
  - OFN   optical fiber non-conductive
  - OFC   optical fiber conductive
  - OFNG or OFCG general purpose
  - OFNR or OFCR riser rated cable for vertical runs
  - OFNP or OFCP plenum rated cables for air-handling areas
  - OFN-LS low smoke density

Inspectors are not inspecting fiber for electrical safety (unless the cable is conductive),
but are inspecting for conformance with fire codes.
Outside the US, use appropriate local codes.
FRG, Chapter 6, RGPC Chapter 5,7, FOTM, Chapter 4,5,913, DVVC,Chapter 12
FOA Online Fiber Optic Reference Guide, Understanding Fiber Optics, The Basics: Cables

Choosing Outdoor Cable Type

- Outdoor
  - Loose tube
  - Water-blocked gel-filled or dry water-blocked
  - Consider ribbon for high fiber count
  - All dielectric
- Performance Specifications
  - Tensile load: 600 lbs max.
  - Strength members: fiberglass & Kevlar®
  - Temperature range -40 to +60 °C
  - Rodent resistance: armor or innerduct
  - Jacket: black polyethylene

All outdoor cables are loose tube to allow inclusion of water-blocking compounds. Most are gels but some dry water-blocking cables are available (using materials developed for disposable diapers!)
Outdoor direct buried installations will either be armored or installed in conduit to prevent rodent (or other critter) damage.
Cables pulled through conduit must be chosen for the proper pulling tension, properly lubricated and pulled with some form of limiter (breakaway swivel or tension-controlled puller).

FRG, Chapter 6, FOTM, Chapter 4,5,913, DVVC,Chapter 12
FOA Online Fiber Optic Reference Guide, Understanding Fiber Optics, The Basics: Cables

Alternate Cable Designs

- Hybrid Cable
  - Includes two fiber types, typically multimode and singlemode
  - Common in backbones - allows upgrades
- Composite Cable
  - Includes fiber and copper conductors
  - Power or signal on copper

These terms can be confusing as literature often mixes them up! These are the current TIA and ISO definitions. Adding to the confusion is the ISO has changed "hybrid" to mean fiber + conductors in some 2012 standards.

FRG, Chapter 6, FOTM, Chapter 4,5,913, DVVC, Chapter 12
FOA Online Fiber Optic Reference Guide, Understanding Fiber Optics, The Basics: Cables

Fiber Optic Connectors & Splices

- Joining fibers
- Connectors
  - Demountable terminations for fiber
  - Connect to transmitters and receivers
- Splices
  - Permanent termination of two fibers

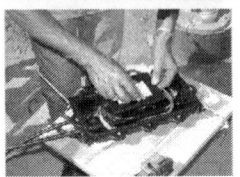

Fiber optic connectors and splices are used to join or couple two fibers together. Splices, however, are used to connect two fibers in a permanent joint. Connectors are also used to to connect fibers to transmitters or receivers, and, of course, connectors are designed to be demountable. While they share some common requirements, like low loss, high optical return loss and repeatability, connectors have the additional requirements of durability under repeated matings. Splices, meanwhile, are expected to last for many years through sometimes difficult environmental conditions, perhaps underground, underwater or suspended from aerial cables.

FRG, Chapter 7, RGPC Chapter 5, FOTM, Chapter 6,7,9, DVVC, Chapter 12, 14

FOA Online Fiber Optic Reference Guide, Understanding Fiber Optics, The Basics: Termination and Splicing

Fiber optic "Connectors" and "Splices" have their own PPTs that include detailed installation instructions for most types.

Fiber Optic Connectors & Splices

- Connectors and splices must have:
  - Low loss
  - Low reflectance
  - Mechanical strength
  - Reliability
  - Ease of use in the field

Fiber optic connectors and splices are used to join or couple two fibers together. Splices, however, are used to connect two fibers in a permanent joint. Connectors are also used to to connect fibers to transmitters or receivers, and, of course, connectors are designed to be demountable. While they share some common requirements, like low loss, high optical return loss and repeatability, connectors have the additional requirements of durability under repeated matings. Splices, meanwhile, are expected to last for many years through sometimes difficult environmental conditions, perhaps underground, underwater or suspended from aerial cables.

FRG, Chapter 7, RGPC Chapter 5, FOTM, Chapter 6,7,9, DVVC, Chapter 12, 14
FOA Online Fiber Optic Reference Guide, Understanding Fiber Optics, The Basics: Termination and Splicing

Connector & Splice Loss

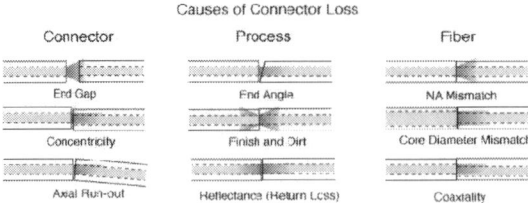

- Lowest loss requires perfect match between cores of two fibers
- Losses may be caused by imperfect connectors, fibers or processes

Connector loss is minimized when the two fiber cores are identical and perfectly aligned, the connectors or splices are properly finished and no dirt is present. Only the light that is coupled into the receiving fiber's core will propagate, so all the rest of the light becomes the connector or splice loss.

End gaps cause two problems, insertion loss and reflectance. The emerging cone of light from the connector will spill over the core of the receiving fiber and be lost. In addition, the air gap between the fibers causes a reflection when the light encounters the change in refractive index from the glass fiber to the air in the gap. The end finish of the fiber must be properly polished to minimize loss. A rough surface will scatter light and dirt can also scatter and absorb light.

Since the optical fiber is so small, typical airborne dirt can be a major source of loss. Whenever connectors are not terminated, they should be covered to protect the end of the ferrule from dirt. One should never touch the end of the ferrule, since the oils on one's skin causes the fiber to attract dirt. Before connection and testing, it is advisable to clean connectors with lint-free wipes moistened with isopropyl alcohol.

Two sources of loss are directional; mismatches in numerical aperture (NA) and core diameter caused not by the connector but the fibers being joined. Differences in these two will create connections that have different losses depending on the direction of light propagation. Light from a fiber with a larger NA will be more sensitive to angularity and end gap, so transmission from a fiber of larger NA to one of smaller NA will be higher loss than the reverse. Likewise, light from a larger fiber will have high loss coupled to a fiber of smaller diameter, while one can couple a small diameter fiber to a large diameter fiber with minimal loss, since it is much less sensitive to end gap or lateral offset.

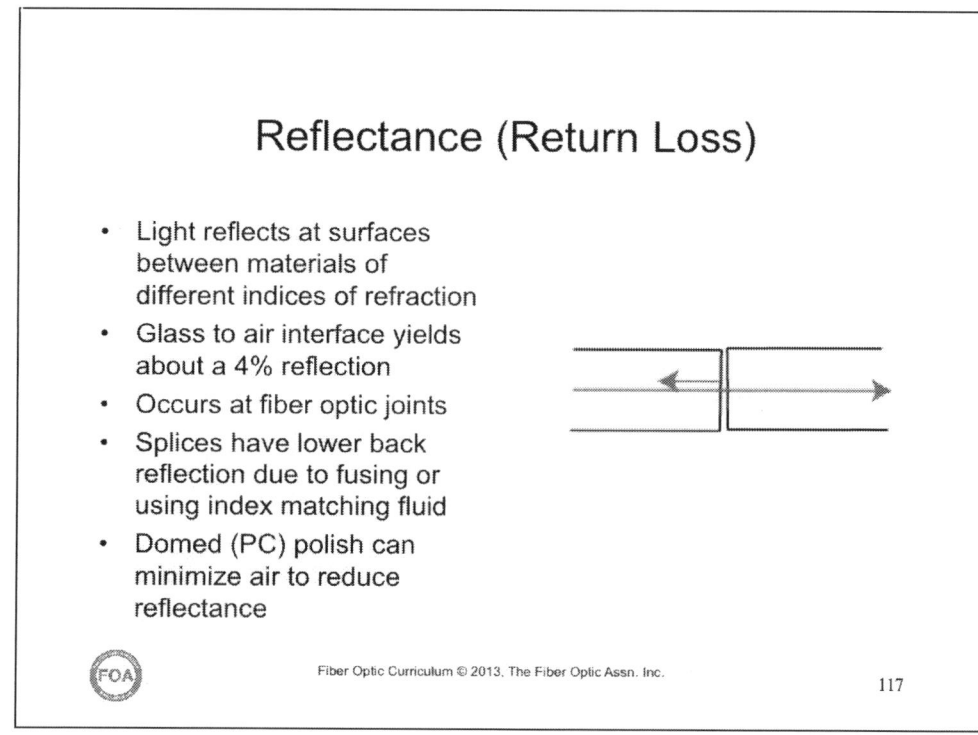

Reflectance is the term now generally used instead of optical return loss or back reflection.

Light reflects at surfaces between materials of different indices of refraction. A glass to air interface yields about a 4% reflection.

Reflectance in fiber optic cabling occurs at fiber optic joints, where connectors can have a small amount of air between dry surfaces causing reflections. Splices have lower reflectance due to the fusing of the fibers or using index matching fluid in mechanical splices.

Domed (PC or physical contact) connectors have fiber end faces can minimize air to reduce reflectance .

FRG, Chapter 7, RGPC Chapter 5, FOA Online Fiber Optic Reference Guide, Understanding Fiber Optics, The Basics: Termination and Splicing
Also see the "Virtual Hands-On" section

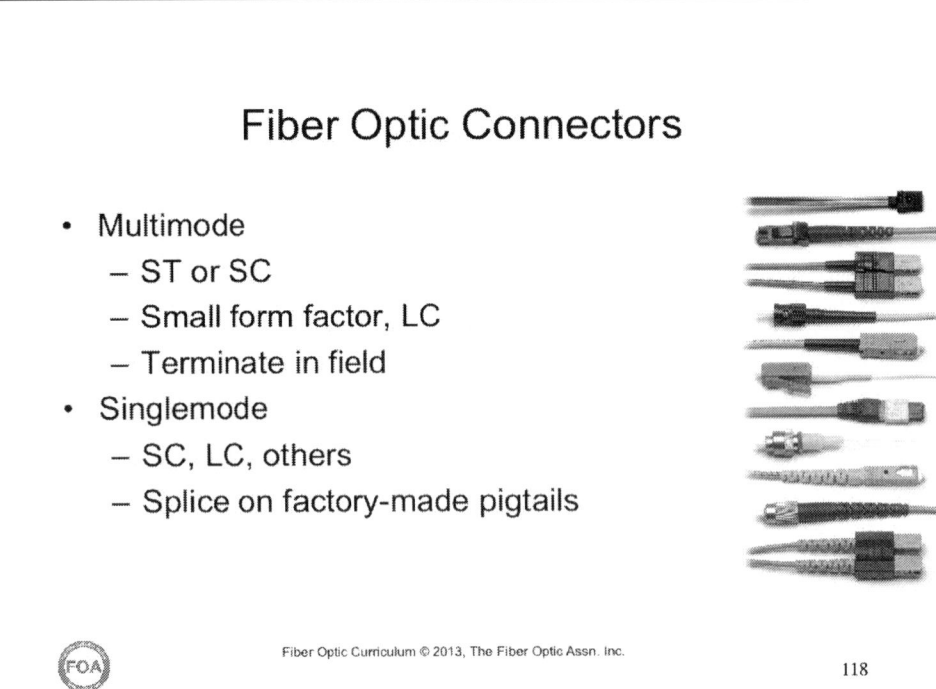

Fiber Optic Connectors

- Multimode
  - ST or SC
  - Small form factor, LC
  - Terminate in field
- Singlemode
  - SC, LC, others
  - Splice on factory-made pigtails

Since fiber optics began, over 80 different styles of connectors have been used commercially.

Most have faded from use or never became popular, so only a few connector styles dominate today's networks.

Multimode installations generally use the ST or SC connector, with a growing number of LC SFF (Small Form Factor) connectors.

LC has become the standard for transceivers at 1Gb/s and faster.

Singlemode applications use mostly SC or LCs, but many installations are still using older designs.

FRG, Chapter 7, RGPC Chapter 5, FOTM, Chapter 6,7,9, DVVC, Chapter 12, 14

FOA Online Fiber Optic Reference Guide, Understanding Fiber Optics, The Basics: Termination and Splicing

The fiber optic "Connectors" PPT includes detailed installation instructions for most types including 3 types of adhesive/polish connectors, prepolished/splice connectors and singlemode termination.

Fiber Optic Connectors

- Specifications
    - Loss
    - Repeatability
    - Environment (temp, humidity, stress, etc.)
    - Reliability
    - Back reflection
    - Ease of termination
    - Cost

Fiber Optic Curriculum © 2013, The Fiber Optic Assn. Inc.

What's important in the performance of a fiber optic connector? Of course, the most important specification for a connector is loss - the less light loss the better. But we also want the connector to be repeatable - in two ways. If we terminate a lot of connectors, we need to be assured that most have about the same loss, so we can plan on that loss for calculating the likely loss of the cable. (We'll look at power budgets later.) We also want it repeatable if we disconnect it and reconnect it many times, so we know the loss will not change when we reconnect it. Connectors must be designed to meet their specs over the environmental changes it will see. It's no problem indoors, but outdoors, temperature and humidity can change, and think about connectors on an aircraft and the vibration they must endure! Reliability means maintaining low loss over its lifetime. Back reflection is very important for Laser sources, as light reflected back can disturb the performance of the laser, plus reflected light can create optical "background noise" which confuses receivers. Ease of termination and cost probably need no further explanation.

FRG, Chapter 7, RGPC Chapter 5, FOTM, Chapter 6,7,9, DVVC, Chapter 12, 14
FOA Online Fiber Optic Reference Guide, Understanding Fiber Optics, The Basics: Termination and Splicing

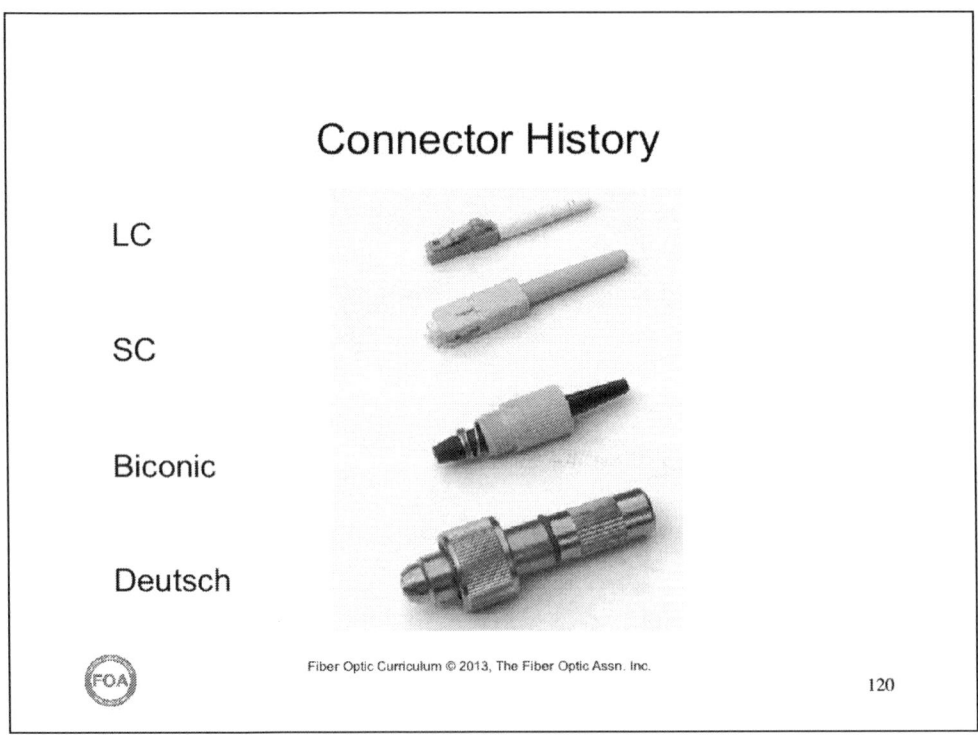

Here are four generations of fiber optic connectors, showing how their size in particular has shrunk.
On the bottom is the Deutsch 1000, one of the first commercial connectors. It held the fiber by vise-type action
and connected fibers in a plastic lens with oil in it to assist the connection.
Above it is a Biconic, AT&T's first commercial connector and the first to work with SM fiber. The Biconic ferrule is a glass-filled thermoplastic. For
The SC from NTT in Japan was one of the first to use ceramic ferrules and have very low loss, even with SM fiber. It's still widely used today.
The LC uses a very small ceramic ferrule to allow the connector to be so small, and it offers equal or perhaps even better performance than the SC.

FRG, Chapter 7, FOTM, Chapter 6,7,9, DVVC,Chapter 13, 14
FOA Online Fiber Optic Reference Guide, Understanding Fiber Optics, The Basics: Termination and Splicing

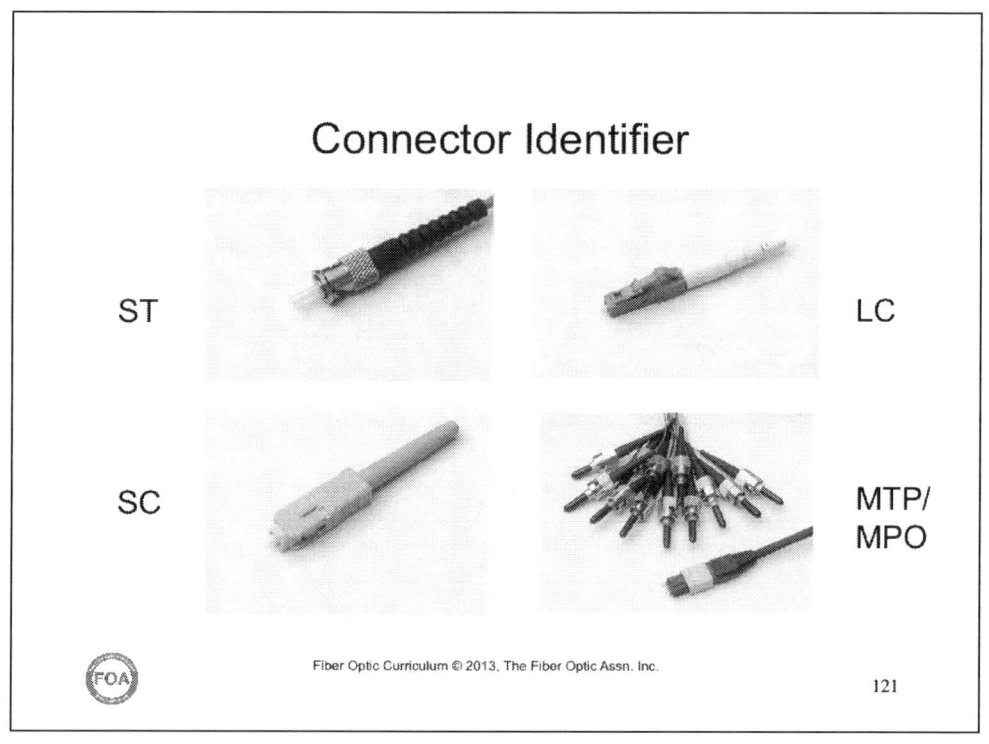

ST (an AT&T Trademark) is probably still the most popular connector for multimode networks, like most buildings and campuses. It has a bayonet mount and a long cylindrical ferrule to hold the fiber. Most ferrules are ceramic, but some are metal or plastic. And because they are spring-loaded, you have to make sure they are seated properly. If you have high loss, reconnect them to see if it makes a difference.
SC is a snap-in connector that is widely used in singlemode systems for it's excellent performance. It's a snap-in connector that latches with a simple push-pull motion. It is also available in a duplex configuration.
LC is a new connector that uses a 1.25 mm ferrule, half the size of the SC. Otherwise, it's a standard ceramic ferrule connector, easily terminated with any adhesive. Good performance, highly favored for singlemode and practically the only connector used on transceivers for gigabit/s and above.
MT is a 12 fiber connector for ribbon cable. It's main use is for preterminated cable assemblies which can be installed as complete systems to avoid field terminations.
More connectors are shown on the FOA Online Fiber Optic Reference Guide.
FRG, Chapter 7, RGPC Chapter 5, DVVC, Chapter 13, FOA Online Fiber Optic Reference Guide, Understanding Fiber Optics, The Basics: Termination and Splicing

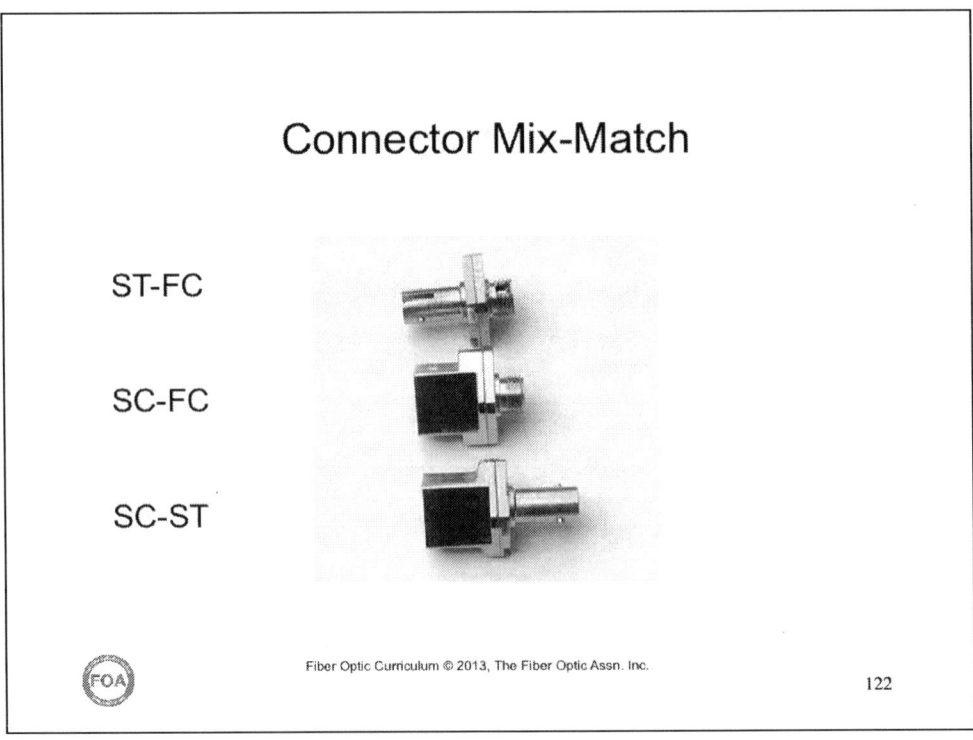

Since so many connectors use the 2.5 mm ceramic ferrule, you can cross-mate them with adapters like these. You can get adapters for ST or SC to FDDI and ESCON also.

There are some other hybrid types that claim to connect connectors with dissimilar ferrules, like SC to LC, but their alignment may not be adequate for low loss.

FRG, Chapter 7, FOTM, Chapter 6,7,9, DVVC, Chapter 13, 14
FOA Online Fiber Optic Reference Guide, Understanding Fiber Optics, The Basics: Termination and Splicing

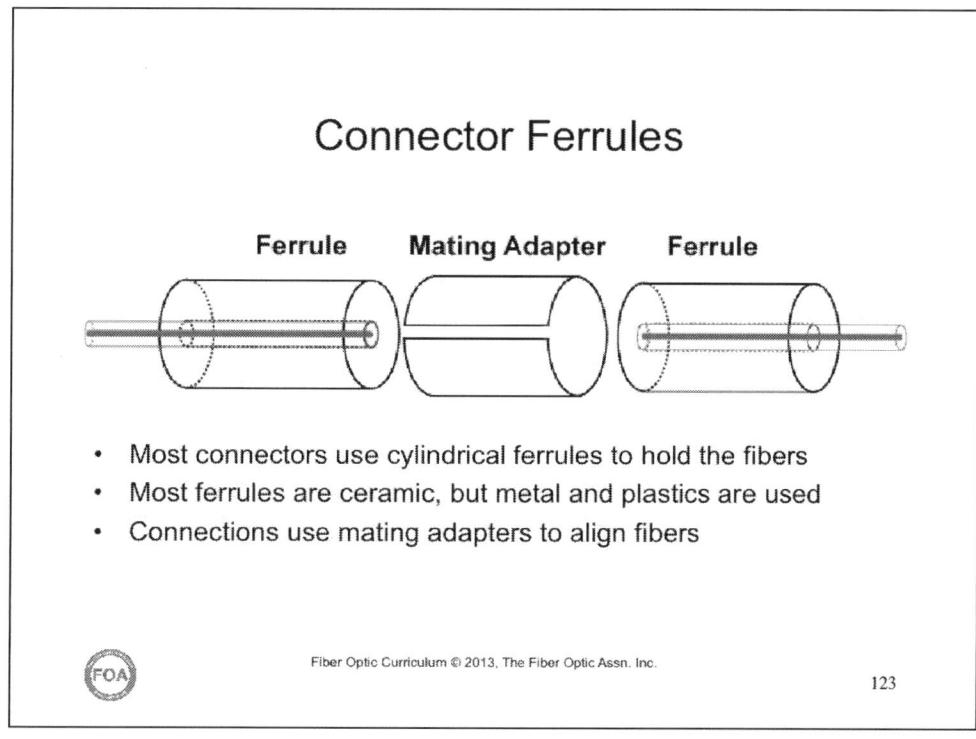

- Most connectors use cylindrical ferrules to hold the fibers
- Most ferrules are ceramic, but metal and plastics are used
- Connections use mating adapters to align fibers

Most connectors work by simply aligning the two fiber ends as accurately as possible and securing them in a fashion that is least affected by environmental factors. Note that fiber optic connectors are mainly "male" style with a protruding ferrule, since the end of the ferrule must be polished after the fiber is glued into it.

The most common method is to have a cylindrical ferrule with a fiber-sized hole in the center, in which the fiber is secured with an adhesive. Other connector techniques like expanded beam, using lenses, and alignment of bare fibers like in a splice have been tried and most have been abandoned for all but some very specialized applications.

Connectors have used metal, glass, plastic and ceramic ferrules to align the fibers accurately, but ceramic seem to be the best choice. It is the most environmentally stable material, closely matching the expansion coefficient of glass fibers. It is easy to bond to glass fiber with epoxy glues, and its hardness is perfect for a quick polish of the fiber. As volume has increased, ceramic costs have become the lowest cost material for connector ferrules.

FRG, Chapter 7, FOTM, Chapter 6,7,9, DVVC,Chapter 13, 14
FOA Online Fiber Optic Reference Guide, Understanding Fiber Optics, The Basics: Termination and Splicing

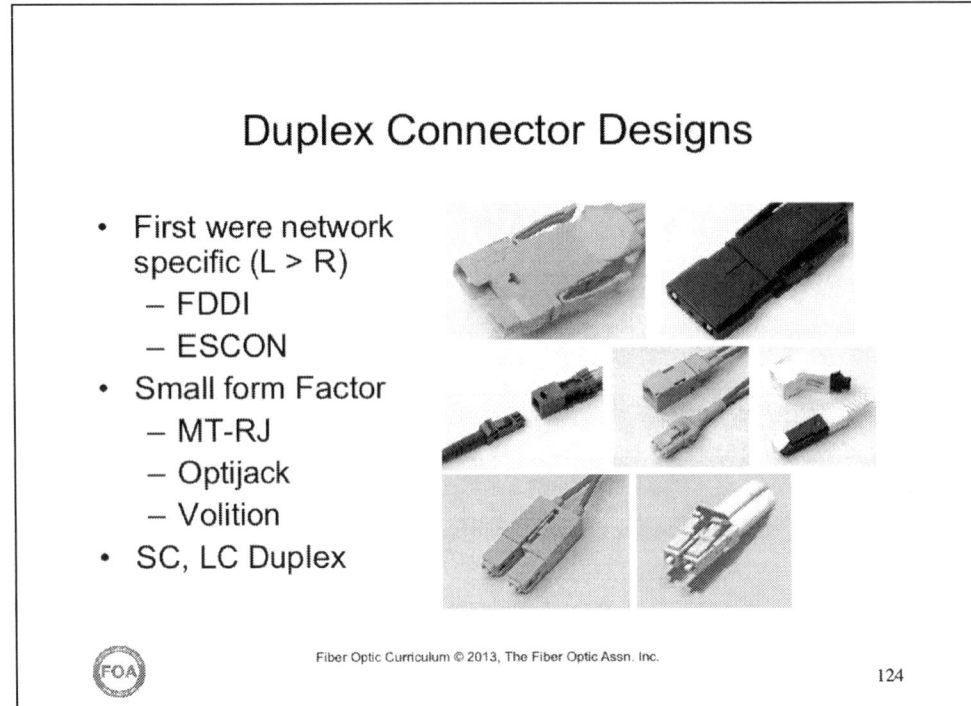

Since most fiber optic datalinks use two fibers transmitting in opposite directions, a duplex connector is an advantage, as it connects both fibers at once and maintains the polarity of the link (connecting transmitter to receiver.) The first connectors were designed as part of network standards, FDDI or Fiber Distributed Data Interface, and ESCON, the IBM peripheral network for mainframes, both introduced in the late 1980s. Both used ST/SC/FC compatible 2.5 mm ferrules in custom bodies.

Later, the competition for "small from factor" connectors in the late 1990s spawned three new and very different connectors, the MT-RJ, Panduit Optijack and 3M Volition. The MT-RJ used a molded rectangular plastic ferrule with alignment by steel pins. The Optijack used regular ST/SC ferrules but closer together to fit in a body the same size as a RJ-45 copper connector. The Volition was a real deviation, using bare fibers aligned by V-grooves, a simple mechanical splice technique. None of these made any impact on the market.

Another duplex solution was to join two regular connectors, SCs or LCs, into a duplex assembly. These are now the duplex solutions of choice.

FRG, Chapter 7, RGPC Chapter 5, FOA Online Fiber Optic Reference Guide, Understanding Fiber Optics, The Basics: Termination and Splicing

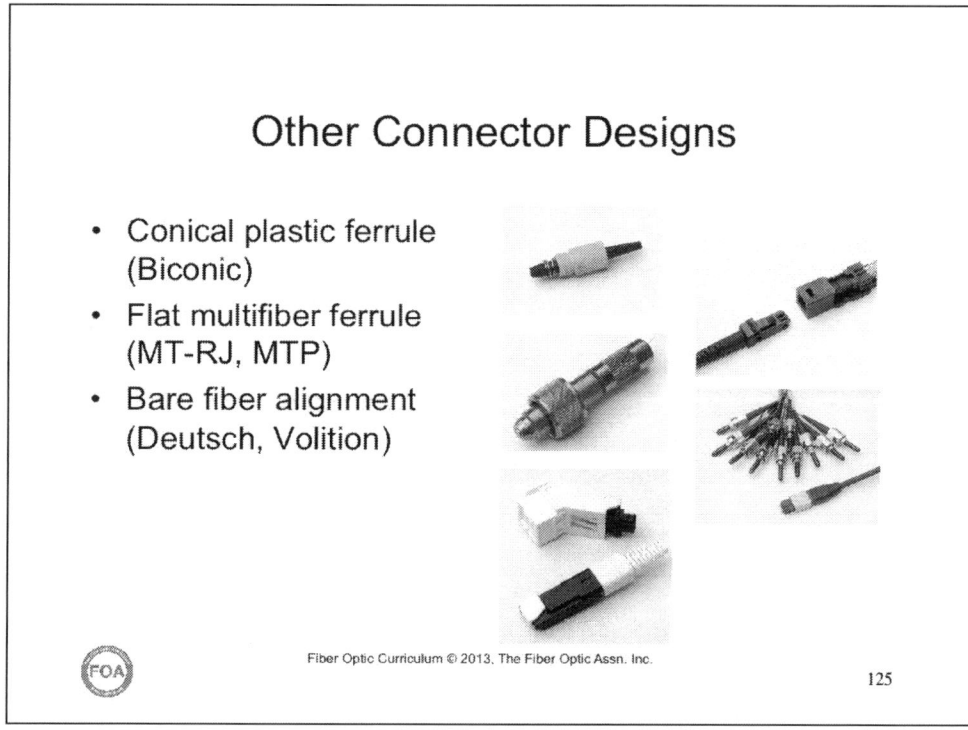

Other Connector Designs

- Conical plastic ferrule (Biconic)
- Flat multifiber ferrule (MT-RJ, MTP)
- Bare fiber alignment (Deutsch, Volition)

With over 100 unique connector designs being offered in the history of fiber optics, lots of unusual designs have been tried.

The Biconic was AT&T's first design, based on a molded plastic ferrule in a cone shape. It had to be polished carefully to an exact length measured by a gage provided in the termination kit.

The Deutsch 1000 was a bare fiber connector with the fibers mating in a lens with index matching fluid. That connector was very large and heavy.

The MT-RJ was very small, but problematic for field termination (mainly prepolished/splice type) and the alignment pins would wear out quickly. Testing was another problem.

The MTP, a 12-fiber design, has proven more reliable and is used today on many prefab cable assemblies.

The Volition was a real deviation, using bare fibers aligned by V-grooves, a simple mechanical splice technique, but was not well-received.

FRG, Chapter 7, FOA Online Fiber Optic Reference Guide, Understanding Fiber Optics, The Basics: Termination and Splicing

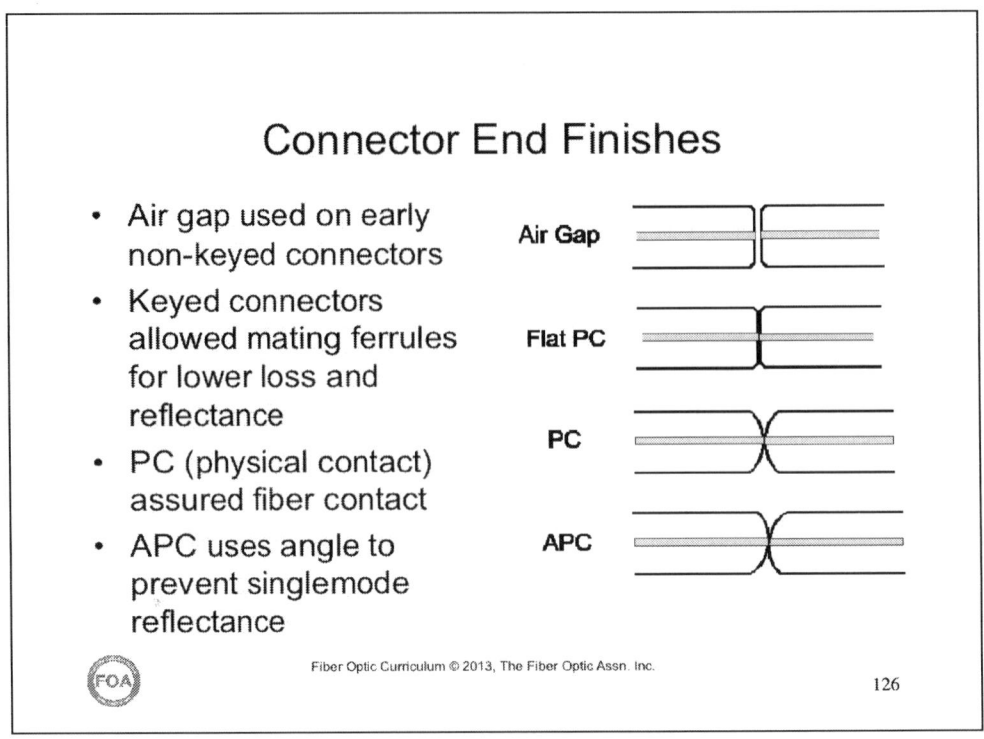

Fiber optic connectors can have several different ferrule shapes or finishes, usually referred to as polishes. Early connectors, because they did not have keyed ferrules and could rotate in mating adapters, always had an air gap between the connectors to prevent them rotating and grinding scratches into the ends of the fibers. The air gap between the fibers causes a reflection when the light encounters the change in refractive index from the glass fiber to the air in the gap. This reflection was called back reflection or optical return loss, now called reflectance, and can be a problem in laser based systems.

Connectors use a number of polishing techniques to insure physical contact of the fiber ends to minimize reflectance. Beginning with the ST and FC which had keyed ferrules, the connectors were designed to contact tightly, what we now call physical contact (PC) connectors. Reducing the air gap reduced the loss and back reflection (very important to laser-based singlemode systems), since light has a loss of about 5% (~0.25 dB) at each air gap and light is reflected back up the fiber. While air gap connectors usually had losses of 0.5 dB or more and return loss of 20 dB, PC connectors had typical losses of 0.3 dB and a return loss of 30 to 40 dB. Soon thereafter, it was determined that making the connector ferrules convex would produce an even better connection. The convex ferrule guaranteed the fiber cores were in contact. Losses were under 0.3dB and return loss 40 dB or better. The final solution for singlemode systems extremely sensitive to reflections, like CATV or high bitrate telco links, was to angle the end of the ferrule 8 degrees to create what we call an APC or angled PC connector. Then any reflected light is at an angle that is absorbed in the cladding of the fiber.

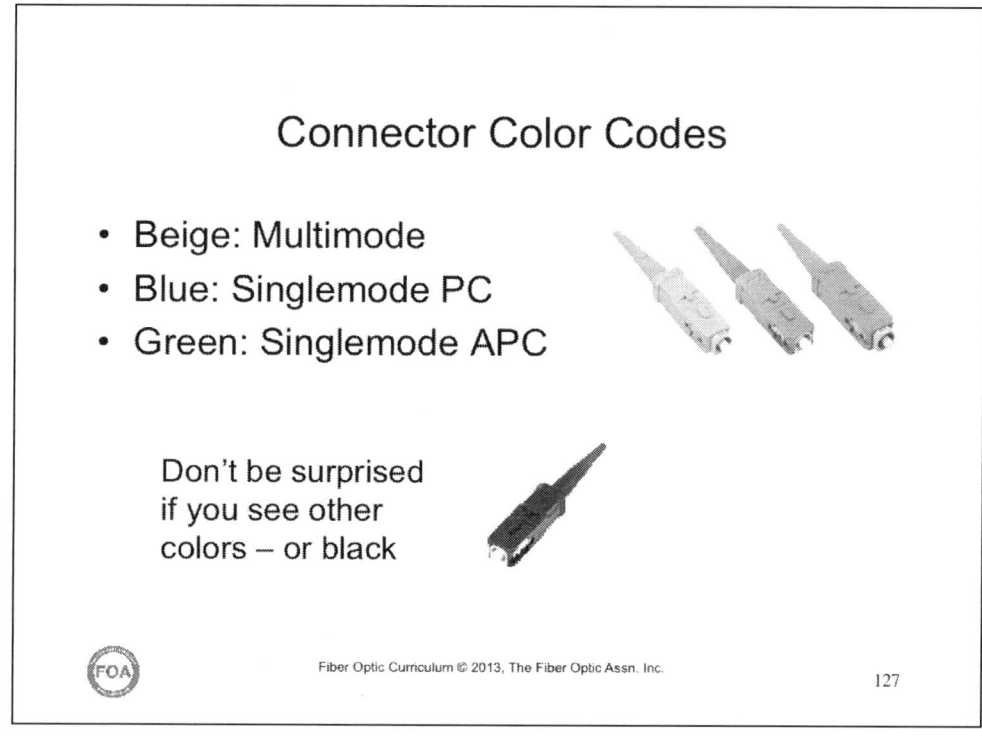

The "normal" colors for connectors are as shown, but other colors are sometimes used, especially for multimode. The thing to remember is green means APC and it CANNOT be mated with other types of connectors.

Connector Termination Processes

- Epoxy/polish
- Hot-melt (3M trademark)
- Anaerobic
- Crimp/Polish
- Crimp/cleave
- Prepolished/Splice

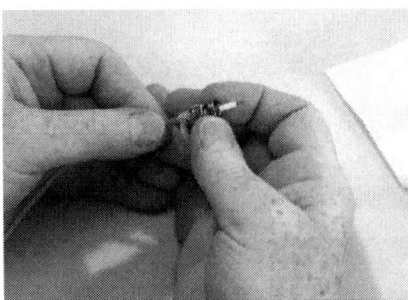

Epoxy/Polish: Most connectors are the simple "epoxy/polish" type where the fiber is glued into the connector with epoxy and the ferrule end polished with special polishing film. These provide the most reliable connection, lowest losses and lowest costs, especially if you are doing a lot of connectors. The epoxy can be allowed to set overnight or cured in an inexpensive oven in only a few minutes.

Quick Setting Adhesives: These connectors use a quick setting adhesive with a curing agent to replace the epoxy.

"Hot Melt": This is a 3M trade name for a connector that already has the epoxy (actually a heat set glue) inside the connector. You insert the connector in a special oven. In a few minutes, the glue is melted, so you remove the connector, insert the fiber, let it cool and it is ready to polish.

Crimp/Polish: Rather than glue the fiber in the connector, these connectors use a crimp on the fiber to hold it in. Expect to trade higher losses for the faster termination speed. Crimp/cleave connectors only cleave the fiber for termination - no polishing is required. Losses are higher as a result.

Prepolished/splice: Many manufacturers offer connectors that have a short stub fiber already epoxied into the ferrule and polished perfectly, so you just cleave a fiber and insert it like a splice. These connectors are very costly, you have to make a good cleave to make them low loss, and, even if you do everything correctly, you loss will be higher, because you have a connector loss plus two splice losses at every connection. Finally, they require good training and typically have lower yield in termination.

Adhesive/Polish Connector Termination

- Most adhesive/polish connectors have similar construction
- Make certain all parts are available before starting
- Slide boot and crimp sleeve on cable before stripping

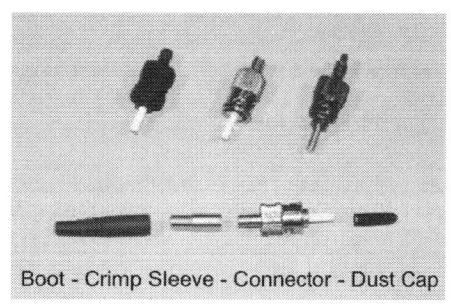

Boot - Crimp Sleeve - Connector - Dust Cap

Let's examine the process of terminating a fiber with a typical epoxy/polish connector:
Start by examining the parts of the connector you are terminating to see what parts are needed and how they are assembled.

FRG, Chapter 7, RGPC Chapter 5, FOTM, Chapter 6,7,9, DVVC,Chapter 13, 14
FOA Online Fiber Optic Reference Guide, Understanding Fiber Optics, The Basics: Termination and Splicing, Also see the "Virtual Hands-On" sections

Adhesive/Polish Connector Termination

- Stripping The Fiber
  - Strip jacket if terminating cable
  - Strip 900 micron buffer to expose glass fiber
  - Strip to proper length as shown
  - Be careful to not nick fiber
  - Cut strength members to proper length

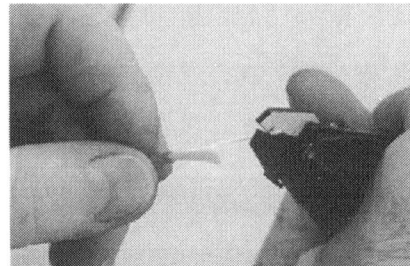

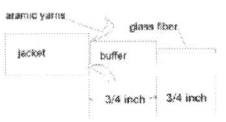

Let's examine the process of terminating a fiber with a typical epoxy/polish connector:

You will need to perform two separate operations to prepare the cable for termination. The jacket strip tool will expose the buffered fiber and strength members,

then you must carefully remove the buffer with the fiber stripper in a series of small strips.

The instructions for the connector you are using should include a drawing of the required dimensions of the prepared end of the cable ready for termination.

If it only gives dimensions, making an exact-size drawing will be very helpful.

FRG, Chapter 7, RGPC Chapter 5, FOTM, Chapter 6,7,9, DVVC,Chapter 13, 14

FOA Online Fiber Optic Reference Guide, Understanding Fiber Optics, The Basics: Termination and Splicing, Also see the "Virtual Hands-On" sections

Adhesive/Polish Connector Termination

- Applying Adhesive
  - Mix epoxy per directions
  - Fill syringe
  - Inject adhesive until bead forms on end of ferrule
  - Back needle out slightly and inject adhesive into connector body

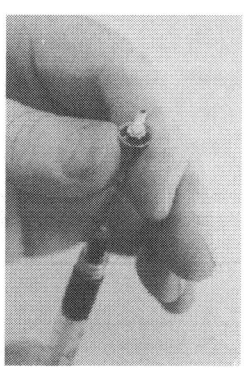

Insert the needle into the connector body as far as it will go. Lightly squeeze on the plunger until a bead of epoxy appears at the tip of the ferrule.
Having the right bead of epoxy on the end of the connector ferrule is the most important issue for getting a good finish on the end of the fiber. The bead of epoxy supports the fiber during the polishing process and makes it just about impossible to make a bad connector! The proper bead will be 1/3 to 1/2 the diameter of the ferrule of the connector.
Back the needle halfway out of the connector. Continue to gently squeeze more epoxy into the body of the connector. Stop when epoxy comes out the back of the connector body.
There are two other types of adhesive: Anaerobics are quick curing adhesives in one or two parts that set in a few minutes. Hot Melt is a 3M brand for an adhesive that is heated to melt it, the fiber is inserted, then the connector cools to set the adhesive.

FRG, Chapter 7, RGPC Chapter 5, FOTM, Chapter 6,7,9, DVVC,Chapter 13, 14, FOA Online Fiber Optic Reference Guide, Understanding Fiber Optics, The Basics: Termination and Splicing, Also see the "Virtual Hands-On" sections

Adhesive/Polish Connector Termination

- Crimping To The Cable
  - Choose proper size crimping die
  - Move crimp sleeve over connector body, capturing strength members under sleeve
  - Crimp once or twice as required

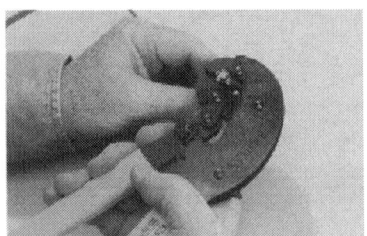

When terminating single fiber cable or zipcord, you must crimp the connector to mechanically attach it to the strength members of the cable.
This is unnecessary if you are terminating a single tight buffer fiber from a distribution cable that has no individual jacket or strength members.
Ensure the crimp die is the proper size and the aramid fiber strength members are captured under the crimp sleeve.
Some crimp sleeves require two crimps. See manufacturer's directions.

FRG, Chapter 7, RGPC Chapter 5, FOTM, Chapter 6,7,9, DVVC,Chapter 13, 14
FOA Online Fiber Optic Reference Guide, Understanding Fiber Optics, The Basics: Termination and Splicing, Also see the "Virtual Hands-On" sections

Adhesive/Polish Connector Termination

- Cleaving The Fiber
    - Cleave just above the epoxy bead
    - Lightly touch fiber with scribe
    - Pull fiber forward and slightly to the side to cleave
    - Dispose of fiber scrap carefully!

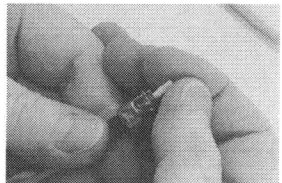

Once the epoxy has cured, the next step is to "cleave" the stub of glass protruding from the ferrule. Take the connector in one hand and the scribe in the other.
Holding the scribe very lightly, delicately give the glass 3 scratches at the point where it protrudes from the epoxy bead on the ferrule. Lay the scribe aside, and grasp the glass.
Carefully pull up and away from the scribe. The glass should break cleanly at the scribe point, but there will be a little bit left at the tip and it may be sharp!
Discard the glass fiber fragment in a safe fiber disposal bin! Fiber shards are dangerous - they can stick in your fingers or get in your eyes and cause serious injury.

FRG, Chapter 7, RGPC Chapter 5, FOTM, Chapter 6,7,9, DVVC,Chapter 13, 14
FOA Online Fiber Optic Reference Guide, Understanding Fiber Optics, The Basics: Termination and Splicing, Also see the "Virtual Hands-On" sections

Adhesive/Polish Connector Termination

- "Air Polishing"
    - Using coarse (12 µ) polishing film
    - Gently grind down the protruding fiber
    - Polish off most of the epoxy bead

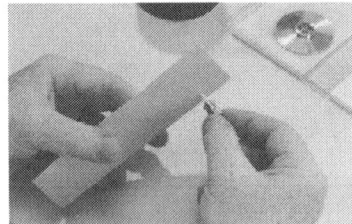

"AIr Polish" the fiber stub first with 12 micron film, holding it as shown. Polish the tip lightly for 10 to 20 seconds.
Notice the change in sound (quieter) as the burr gets filed down and the epoxy bead is removed. Remember to brush the tip lightly and do not overpolish.
Visually inspect the tip. There should be some epoxy left-just a thin film, and the glass itself will be not be smooth to the touch.
The next polish step will remove the remaining epoxy and the protruding glass fiber.

FRG, Chapter 7, RGPC Chapter 5, FOTM, Chapter 6,7,9, DVVC,Chapter 13, 14, FOA Online Fiber Optic Reference Guide, Understanding Fiber Optics, The Basics: Termination and Splicing, Also see the "Virtual Hands-On" sections

Adhesive/Polish Connector Termination

- Polishing
    - Two steps on 3 μ and 0.3 μ film or as specified by manufacturer
    - Use soft polishing surface for PC connectors
    - Place connector in puck then gently place on polishing film
    - Polish in "figure 8" pattern
    - Do not over-polish!

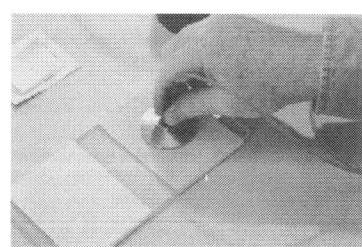

Apply sheets of 3 and 0.3 micron lapping film to the polishing plate or pad. If you are polishing PC (physical contact - or convex) ferrules, use a rubber pad between the polishing film and the plate.
Always hold the polishing puck up in your hand and then insert the connector. Gently place the puck with the connector in it on the 3 micron film which is on the polishing plate.
Remember the tip is a protruding glass end which can be easily damaged. Very lightly make 4 or 5 figure eights as you polish the tip. You'll actually feel a smoothing of the surface as the epoxy scrapes off and the ceramic surface of the ferrule meets the surface of the abrasive. Do not over-polish the tip. Wipe the ferrule tip before the final polish.
Very gently lay the puck on the 0.3 micron film. With almost no pressure, make about six figure eight strokes. Remove the tip from the puck, and clean it with an alcohol-soaked lint-free pad.
The connection is now complete, ready for visual inspection of the tip.

FRG, Chapter 7, RGPC Chapter 5, FOTM, Chapter 6,7,9, DVVC,Chapter 13, 14, FOA Online Fiber Optic Reference Guide, Understanding Fiber Optics, The Basics: Termination and Splicing, Also see the "Virtual Hands-On" sections

Adhesive/Polish Connector Termination

- Microscope Inspection
    - Magnification of 100-400X
    - Direct and angle view or lighting
    - Look for
        - Proper polish
        - Cracks
        - Scratches in fiber
        - Smooth finish

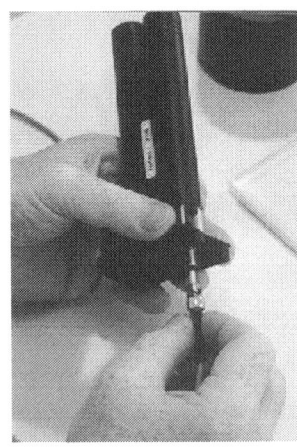

At this point, inspect the polished end of the ferrule with the microscope to see that the epoxy is completely removed and that the tip is smooth and free of scratches.

There are many inspection microscopes available with magnifications of 100X to 400X. Higher magnification may not be better, as it tends to make you more critical of scratches and imperfections. Lower magnifications work just fine.

FRG, Chapter 7, RGPC Chapter 5, FOTM, Chapter 6,7,9,17, DVVC, Chapter 12,13, 14
FOA Online Fiber Optic Reference Guide, Understanding Fiber Optics, The Basics: Termination and Splicing, Testing, Also see the "Virtual Hands-On" sections

Adhesive/Polish Connector Termination

- Microscope Inspection
  - Direct with core illuminated (top)
  - Indirect illumination or viewing at an angle (bottom)
- Ready for insertion loss testing

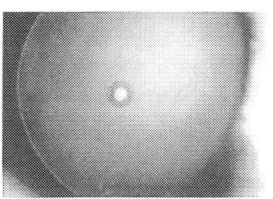
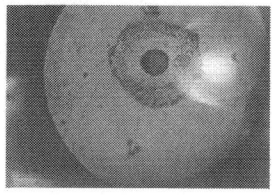

A direct view at 100 times magnification should look like this (TOP): The bright dot in the center is the core of the fiber and the darker annular ring is the cladding. On this connector, notice the dark area to the left of the core, in the cladding. This appears to be a small crack in the fiber that only affects the cladding, not the core, so it is not a problem. If the crack had been in the core, we would not have seen a round dot for the illuminated core.

You should also look at the tip under the microscope at an angle if this is possible with the microscope you are using. The angular view will highlight any surface irregularities better than the head on view. It may look like this: Now you can see some small amount of epoxy still on the end of the ferrule, which shows up as the dark, uneven ring around the fiber (the ring is caused by the convex end of the PC ferrule.) You can also see the dark area to the left of the fiber, which is the small crack we saw on the direct view, but is more obvious here. The core should be nice and smooth, an even gray color, with no big scratches. If you see large scratches, go back to the 0.3 micron film and use the polishing puck to very lightly give 1 or 2 more figure eights to remove them. The film of epoxy can be removed by polishing on the same film on the rubber polishing pad, which polishes the entire convex PC ferrule.

Anaerobic/Polish Connector Termination

- Three methods
  - Wipe fiber with adhesive before inserting into connector
  - Inject adhesive, spray accelerator on fiber at ferrule end
  - Inject adhesive, dip fiber in accelerator

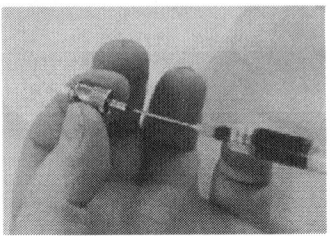

Anaerobic adhesives are used instead of epoxy for a quick termination. There are several ways that are used to apply quick curing adhesives.
1. The method we recommend uses no accelerator. The adhesive we recommend (Loctite(R) 648) is an adhesive that will cure in 3-5 minutes without an accelerator, depending on the ambient temperature. If you are making more than one termination, you do not need an accelerator at all. This process will be described without using the accelerator and then the use of the accelerator will be described.
2. Inject the adhesive into the connector with a syringe then insert the fiber in the connector. Spray an accelerator on the tip of the ferrule to make the adhesive cure at the end quickly to allow immediate polishing. After spraying the tip, residue will be left on the connector ferrule that must be cleaned. Most accelerators are highly flammable, requiring care.
3. Inject the adhesive into the connector with a syringe, dip the fiber in an accelerator solution then insert the fiber in the connector. With this method, you must work fast and make sure the fiber is inserted rapidly or the adhesive will set before the fiber is fully inserted.
Anaerobics do not leave the nice bead on the end of the ferrule, so you have to be more careful when cleaving the fiber and air polishing. Otherwise the polish process is the same.

Hot Melt/Polish Connector Termination

- Adhesive is preloaded in connector
- Heat connector to melt adhesive
- Insert fiber
- Cleave and polish as usual

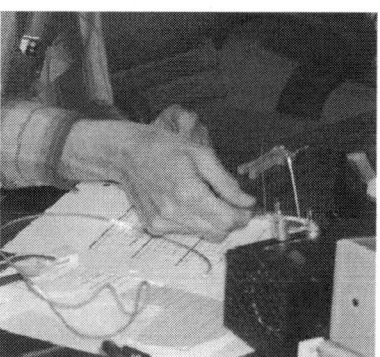

3 M Hot Melt Termination
Hot Melt connectors use a "hot melt" adhesive preloaded into the connector. The termination process involves heating up the connector until the adhesive becomes a liquid, then inserting the stripped and cleaned fiber. It is then set aside to allow the adhesive to cool and set before cleaving and polishing. The adhesive needs at least 1 minute in the oven to liquefy but after more than 10 minutes in the oven, it may not set when cooled, so the range of time in the oven is limited.
To start terminations, turn the oven on and let warm up for at least 5 minutes.
Insert a connector in the oven to let it warm up.
While waiting for the connector to heat up, strip and clean the fiber.
Remove the connector from the oven and insert the fiber. Let the connector cool to set the adhesive.
Cleave and polish as normal.
If you have a problem with the cleave/polish process, you can usually reuse the connector. If you pull the fiber back about 1 mm (1/16") you can reheat it and push it forward without problems.
Hint: Make sure you have the termination instructions for the exact connector you are using before you start! Different styles of connectors have slightly different termination processes.
Caution: The Hot Melt oven operates at twice the temperature of the epoxy curing oven - 245 - 270 degrees C. or 473 - 518 degrees F. ° C. It can cause burns if the metal parts are touched while hot. Be extremely careful with the oven!
NOTE: Paper catches fire at 451 degrees F, so don't rest anything on the oven.

Prepolished/Splice Connector Termination

- Connector has prepolished fiber stub in ferrule and mechanical splice
- Terminated by cleaving an splicing fiber
- No polishing but requires a precision cleave to get low loss

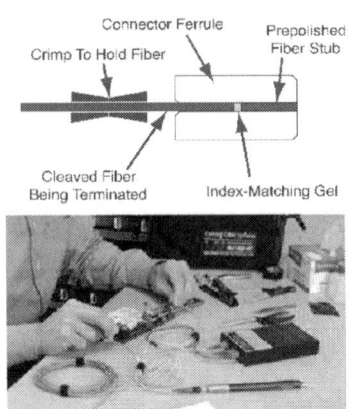

Most manufacturers now offer connectors that have a short stub fiber already epoxied into the ferrule and polished perfectly, so you just cleave a fiber and insert it like a splice.

While this technique makes termination faster, saving labor costs, it has several downsides. First tools are more complex and expensive and connectors are more costly, five to ten times as much as an epoxy/polish type. Second, you have to make a good cleave to make them low loss, and that is not always easy, especially in kits that only include a cheap cleaver (get a fusion splicer cleaver instead). Third, even if you do everything correctly, you loss will be higher, because you have a connector loss plus two splice losses at every connection. Finally, they generally have lower yield in termination.

It is highly recommended that you use a high-quality cleaver for fusion splicing when terminating these connectors.

FRG, Chapter 7, RGPC Chapter 5, DVVC, Chapter 15, FOTM, Chapter 4,5,913, FOA Online Fiber Optic Reference Guide, Understanding Fiber Optics, The Basics: Termination and Splicing, Also see the "Virtual Hands-On" section

Photo courtesy Corning Cabling Systems

Prepolished/Splice Connector Termination

- Insert connector in fixture/tool
- Strip fiber
- Cleave fiber
- Insert fiber in connector
- Cam and crimp
- Remove from fixture
- Attach boot

It's important to follow the manufacturer's process exactly when terminating prepolished/splice connectors. The Corning UniCam process is:
Insert connector in fixture
Strip fiber
Cleave fiber
Insert fiber in connector
Cam and crimp
Remove from fixture
Slide boot onto connector

Photo courtesy Corning Cabling Systems

Prepolished/Splice Connector Termination

- Use Visual Fault Locator to verify splice
- Red laser light shows splice loss
- Optimize

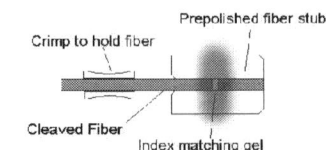

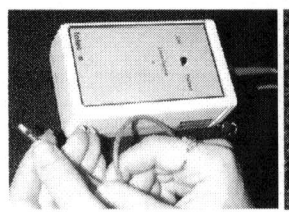
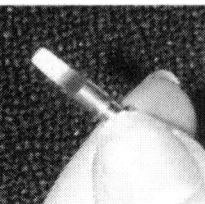

Prepolished connectors require a good cleave on the fiber to get proper termination and you must fully insert the fiber in the connector to make a good splice. Using a visible fault locator (a bright red laser coupled into the fiber) allows you to see the "loss" in the connector and work the fiber position to get a good termination.

FRG, Chapter 7, RGPC Chapter 5, DVVC, Chapter 15
FOTM, Chapter 4,5,913
FOA Online Fiber Optic Reference Guide, Understanding Fiber Optics, The Basics: Termination and Splicing, Also see the "Virtual Hands-On" section

Fusion Splice-On Connectors

- Terminate fibers by fusion splicing a connector to the bare fiber
- Connectors are already polished by machine

These connectors have a short fiber in the back that can be fusion spliced onto a fiber for termination. They offer significantly lower loss than prepolished splice connectors which include a mechanical splice. Some can even be spliced in standard fusion splicers.

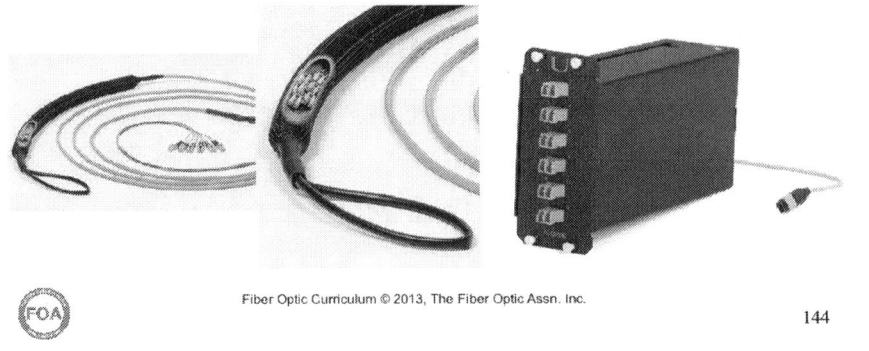

Here is a possible alternative - installing a prefabricated or pre-terminated system. You design the network on CAD, give the information to a manufacturer and they provide a complete modular system.

Some manufacturers terminate the cable in standard connectors (easier with small form factor connectors) and cover it with a pulling boot.

The downside is they require extra care in installation to avoid damaging connectors and the higher loss for multifiber connectors used in many modular systems can cause problems with the total cable plant loss.

Photos courtesy Nexans & Corning.

FRG, Chapter 7, RGPC Chapter 5, DVVC, Chapter 15, FOTM, Chapter 4,5,913
FOA Online Fiber Optic Reference Guide, Understanding Fiber Optics, The Basics: Termination and Splicing, Also see the "Virtual Hands-On" section

OSP Prefabricated Cabling Systems

- Factory terminated cables used for drop to home in FTTH
- Weather-resistant closures used on cables, poles or underground
- Saves time and cost

Many FTTH systems now use prefabricated cables for the drop to the house. Crews come into the neighborhood and install the drop closures on poles or in underground vaults and splice the fibers into the backbone fiber network that terminates in the central office or a local PON distribution hub. The tech doing the actual FTTH install merely plugs in the cables between the closure and the optical network terminal and spends the bulk of the time connecting the user to telephone, Internet and TV services.

Fiber Optic Splices

- <u>Permanent</u> terminations for fiber
- Specifications
    - Loss
    - Repeatability
    - Environment
    - Reliability
    - Back reflection
    - Ease of termination
    - Cost

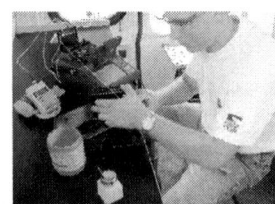

While connectors are demountable, splices are permanent connections. Splicing is only needed if the cable runs are too long for one straight pull or you need to mix a number of different types of cables (like bringing a 48 fiber cable in and splicing it to six 8 fiber cables - could you have used a breakout cable instead?)
And of course, we use splices for restoration, after the number one problem of outside plant cables, a dig-up and cut of a buried cable, usually referred to as "backhoe fade" for obvious reasons!
They may have different uses, but the basic specifications for splices are the same as for connectors.
Splices may be fusion, where the fibers are welded together using a machine which produces a splice that looks like the one shown on the left in the lower photo, or a mechanical splice, several examples of which are shown in the lower photo.

FRG, Chapter 7, DVVC, Chapter 15
FOA Online Fiber Optic Reference Guide, Understanding Fiber Optics, The Basics: Termination and Splicing
Also see the "Virtual Hands-On" section
Fiber optic "Splices" PPTs includes detailed installation instructions

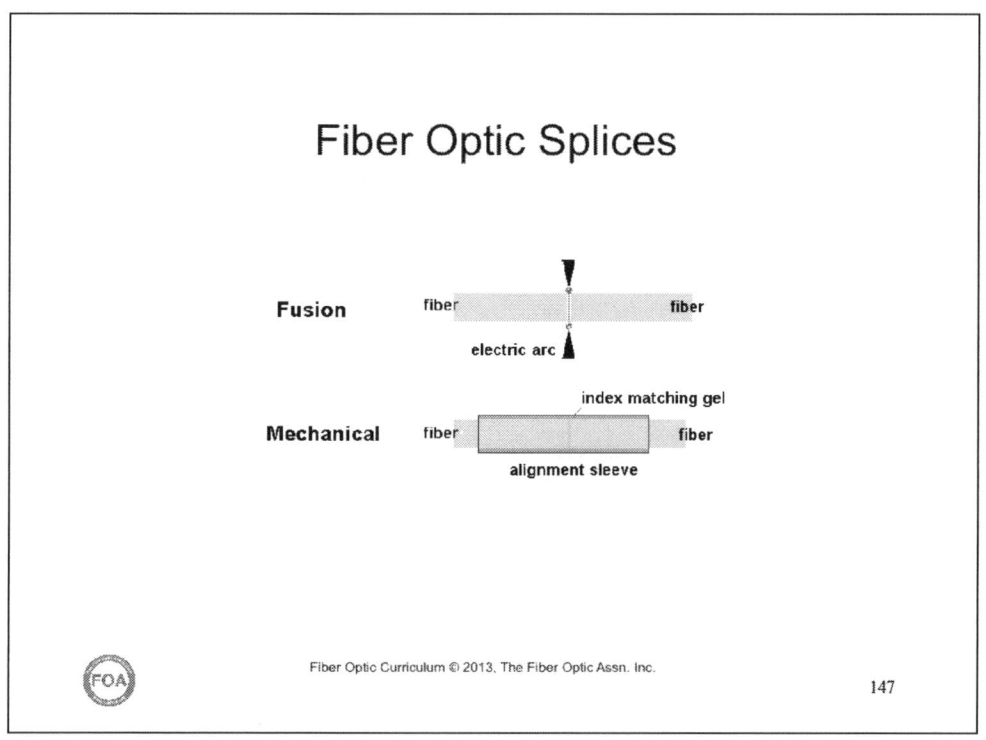

There are two types of splices, fusion and mechanical.
Fusion splicing is done by welding the two fibers together, usually with an electrical arc with an automated splicer which aligns the fibers exactly. It has the advantages of low loss, high strength, low reflectance (optical return loss) and long term reliability.
Mechanical splices use an alignment fixture to mate the fibers and either a matching gel or epoxy to minimize back reflection. Some mechanical splices use bare fibers in an alignment bushing, while others closely resemble connector ferrules without all the mounting hardware.
While fusion splicing normally uses active alignment to minimize splice loss, mechanical splicing relies on tight dimensional tolerances in the fibers to minimize loss.

FRG, Chapter 7, FOTM, Chapter 6,7,9,17, DVVC, Chapter 12,13, 14
FOA Online Fiber Optic Reference Guide, Understanding Fiber Optics, The Basics: Termination and Splicing and Fusion and Mechanical Splice pages,
Also see the "Virtual Hands-On" section

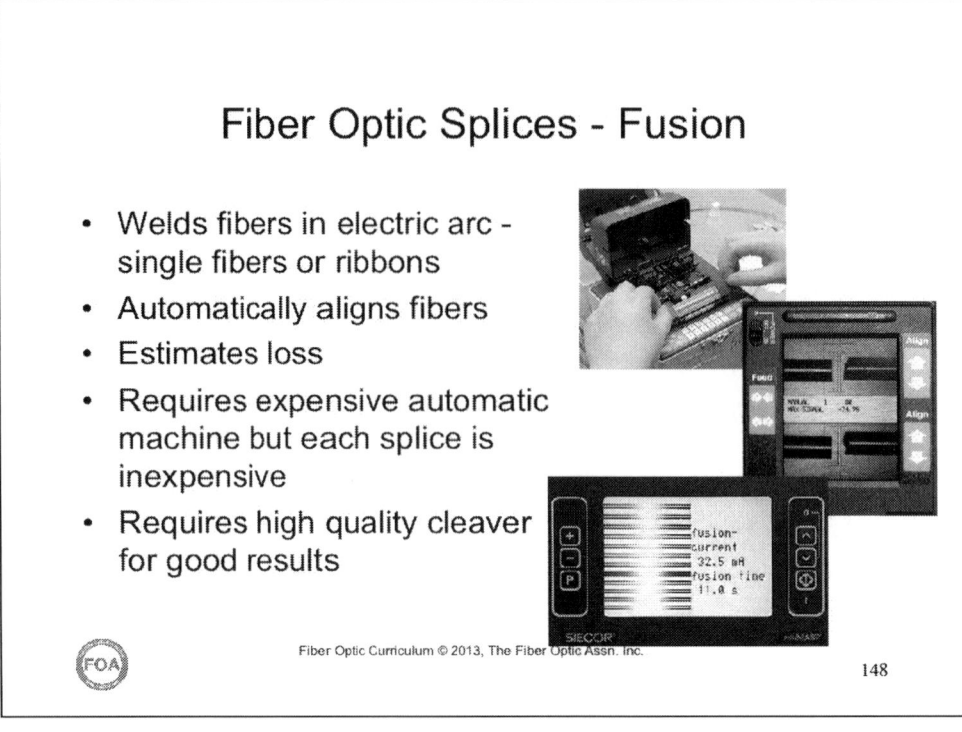

Fusion splicers are expensive, highly automated machines that do most of the work. The operator uses a high quality clever to prepare the fibers and inserts them into the jaws of the splicer. The machine automatically aligns the ends, makes the splice and even gives an estimate of the loss. The operator then places the splice in a holder which also seals it and inserts it in a splice tray.

While fusion splicers are expensive, each splice is cheap. So if you are doing lots of splices, fusion is more cost effective.

FRG, Chapter 7, FOTM, Chapter 6,7,9,17, DVVC, Chapter 12,13, 14
FOA Online Fiber Optic Reference Guide, Understanding Fiber Optics, The Basics: Termination and Splicing
Also see the "Virtual Hands-On" section

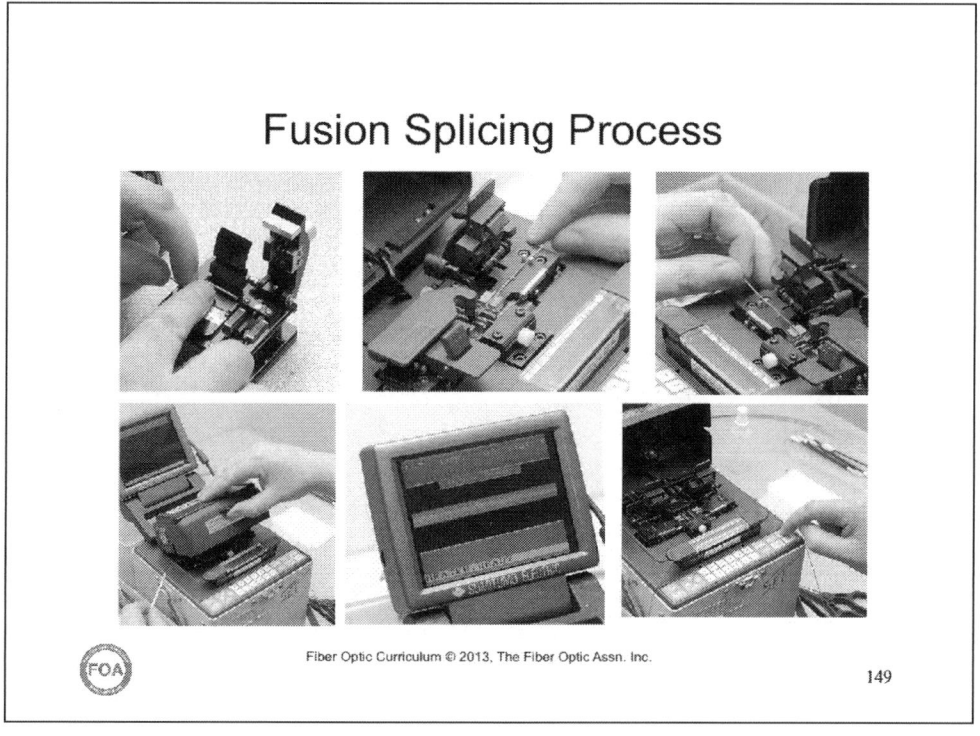

The fusion splicing process is as follows:

Strip and cleave the fiber

Place fiber in splicer properly

Repeat with second fiber

Close cover, start automated program

Splicer competes splice and estimates loss

Remove fibers and place protector over splice

Ribbon splicing works in a similar fashion. See the VHO section for both single and ribbon splicing.

FRG, Chapter 7, FOTM, Chapter 6,7,9,17, DVVC, Chapter 12,13, 14

FOA Online Fiber Optic Reference Guide, Understanding Fiber Optics, The Basics: Termination and Splicing

Also see the "Virtual Hands-On" section

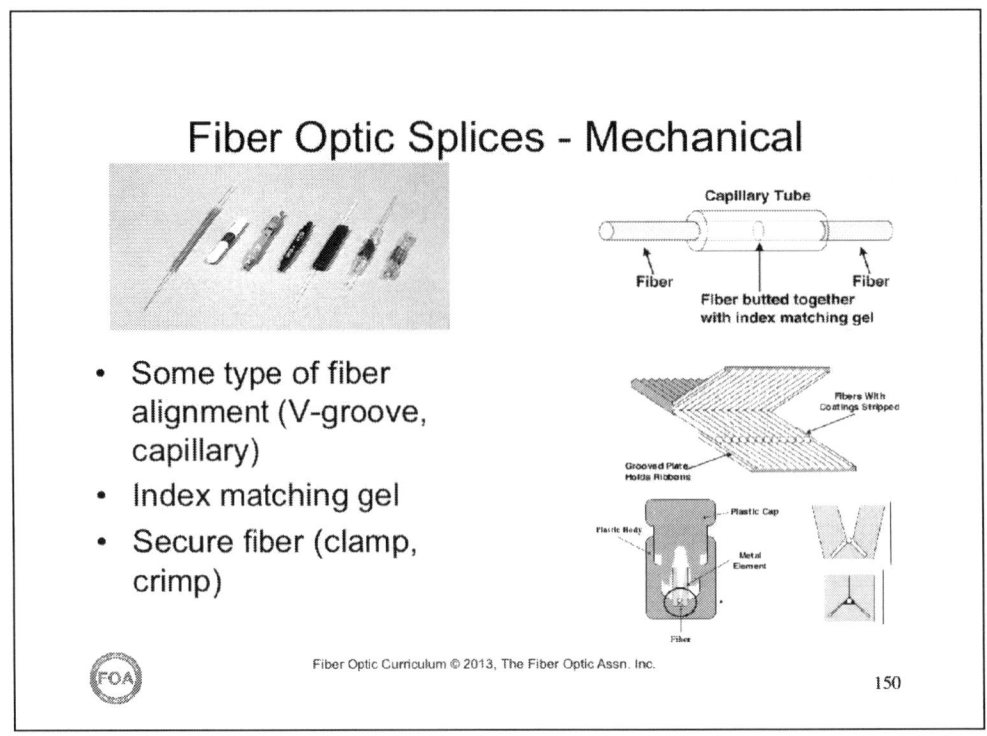

Mechanical splices have been offered in many varieties. All use some mechanical alignment fixture, v-groove, glass capillary, soft elastomeric or metal clamp v-groove, etc. and some means of securing the fibers in the splice. Mechanical splices are more common with multimode fiber but are used for singlemode restoration until fusion splicing can be done.

The three examples of alignment shown here are the capillary as used on the Ultrasplice, a ribbon V-grove splice using glass or silicon V-grooves and a 3M Fiberlok which clamps the fiber in a stamped metal element.

Mechanical splices themselves are more expensive per splice than fusion splicing which only has the cost of the splice protector, but the equipment necessary is relatively inexpensive. So if you are only making a few splices, mechanical may be the less expensive choice.

FRG, Chapter 7, FOTM, Chapter 6,7,9,17, DVVC, Chapter 12,13, 14
FOA Online Fiber Optic Reference Guide, Understanding Fiber Optics, The Basics: Termination and Splicing
Also see the "Virtual Hands-On" section

Fiber Optic Splices - Mechanical

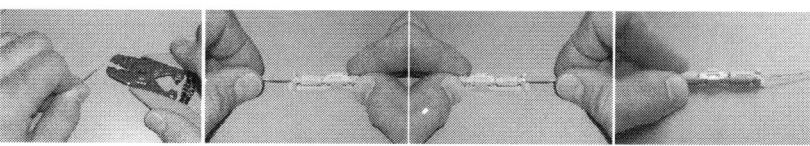

- Splicing using a mechanical splice requires stripping and cleaving the fiber
- Inserting one fiber in one end
- Insert the second fiber
- Check the alignment with a Visual Fault Locator (VFL)
- Secure the fibers

Mechanical splices, like this Ultrasplice, use a mechanical alignment fixture, a glass capillary in this case, and some means of securing the fibers in the splice, clamps secured by nuts in this case.

FRG, Chapter 7, FOTM, Chapter 6,7,9,17, DVVC, Chapter 12,13, 14
FOA Online Fiber Optic Reference Guide, Understanding Fiber Optics, The Basics: Termination and Splicing
Also see the "Virtual Hands-On" section

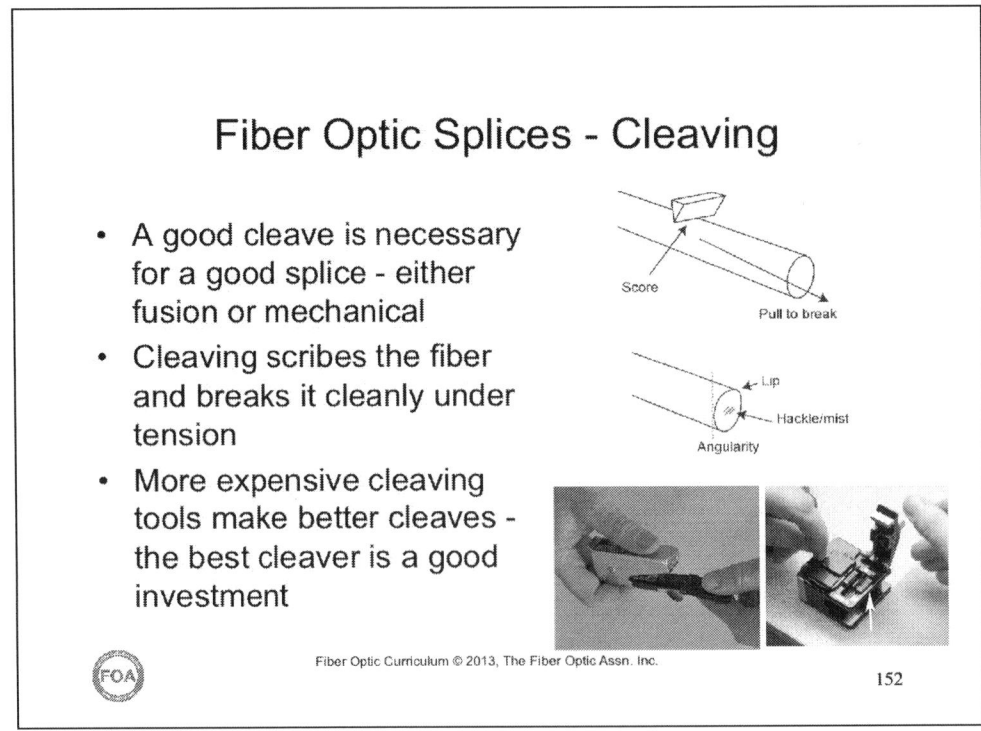

In order to get good fiber optic splices or terminations, especially when using the pre-polished connectors with internal splices, it is extremely important to cleave the fiber properly.

Cleaving is the process by which an optical fiber is "cut" or precisely broken for termination or splicing. Just like cutting glass plate, fiber is cut by scoring or scratching the surface and applying stress so the glass breaks in a smooth manner along the stress lines created by the scratch. Properly done, the fiber will cleave with a clean surface perpendicular to the length of the fiber with no protruding glass on either end (called a lip) and no surface roughness (hackle or mist.)

A cleaver is a tool that holds the fiber under low tension, scores the surface at the proper location, then applies greater tension until the fiber breaks. Good cleavers are automatic and produce consistent results, irrespective of the operator. The user need only clamp the fiber into the cleaver and operate its controls. Some cleavers, especially the handheld ones, are less automated, for example requiring operators to exert force manually for breaking the fiber, making them more dependent on operator technique and therefore less predictable.

Protecting Splices

- Completed splices are inserted in a splice tray
- Splice tray goes in a splice closure
- Incoming cables are secured to the closure
- Loose tubes on cable are secured to splice tray
- Closure is sealed to protect fibers and splices

Splices always require protection from the environment and are often outdoors. Protection for splices is provided by a splice closure which contains trays for individual splices. Completed splices are inserted in a splice tray which goes in a splice closure. Incoming cables are secured to the closure for mechanical strength and sealed. Loose tubes on the cable are secured to splice tray so the bare fibers are only exposed inside the tray. The closure is sealed to protect fibers and splices from moisture, water and anything else in the outside environment. Closures can be buried underground, supported on aerial cables or whatever means of cable installation is being spliced.

FRG, Chapter 7, FOTM, Chapter 6,7,9,17, DVVC, Chapter 12,13, 14
FOA Online Fiber Optic Reference Guide, Understanding Fiber Optics, The Basics: Termination and Splicing

Fiber Optic Testing

- Continuity testing with visual tracer/fault locator
- Visual Inspection of connectors
- Optical power
- Insertion loss with source and meter
- OTDR testing

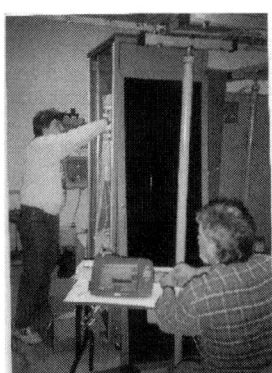

Testing fiber optic cables, connectors and splices is primarily done at the terminated phase on installed cable plants and patchcords. There are three ways of testing these cables:
Continuity testing with a visible light source - a LED or incandescent bulb in a fiber tracer or a higher power visible laser in a visual fault locator.
Microscope inspection allows finding damaged or dirty connectors.
Optical power is used to measure transmitter output and receiver input power, plus differences before and after losses.
Insertion loss simulated the way the cable will be used by a transmission system, using a source (LED or Laser at the same wavelength(s) as the system) and optical power meter, with two reference cables.
OTDR testing uses a unique property of fiber - backscatter - to create a "picture" of the fiber and find faults.

FRG, Chapter 8, FOA Online Fiber Optic Reference Guide, Understanding Fiber Optics, The Basics: Testing, RGPC Chapter 5, Also see the "Virtual Hands-On" section
Fiber optic "Testing" PPT includes detailed information on testing, including types of test equipment, tests performed and measurement accuracy.

Visual Tracing and Fault Location

- Continuity testing with visual tracer/fault locator
- Also use for verifying mechanical splices or prepolished/splice-type connectors

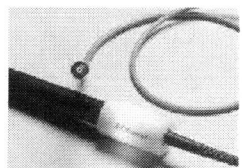 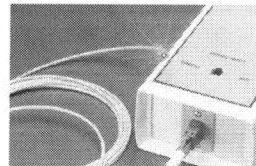 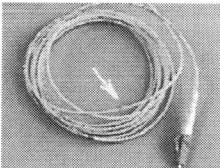

Continuity testing is done with a visible light source - a LED or incandescent bulb in a fiber tracer or a higher power visible laser in a visual fault locator.

The low-powered fiber tracer can be used to confirm that light can indeed be transmitted through the fiber and the proper connections between transmitter and receiver have been made.

The higher powered laser in a visual fault locator (VFL) can trace fibers longer distances and even find breaks. In a break, the light lost can be seen through the jacket of simplex or zipcord cable and tight buffered fibers.

Visual fault locators can also be used to optimize mechanical splices and prepolished/splice type connectors by adjusting the fibers to minimize the visible light lost.

FRG, Chapter 8, RGPC Chapter 5, FOTM, Chapter 17, DVVC, Chapter 14
FOA Online Fiber Optic Reference Guide, Understanding Fiber Optics, The Basics: Testing
Also see the "Virtual Hands-On" section

Connector Inspection With Microscope

- Visual Inspection can find connector problems
    - Polish quality
    - Dirt or other contamination
    - Scratches
- Use 100-400X magnification
- Direct and side illumination
- Eye Safety! Microscope focuses power into eye! Test for power in cable before inspection

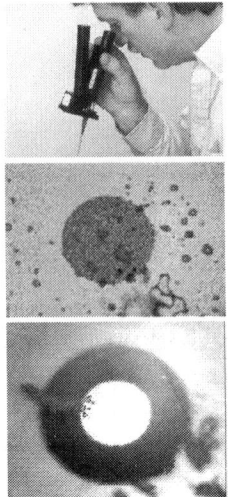

You can visually inspect the polished end of a connector ferrule with a microscope to see that the ferrule is properly polished, there are no cracks in the fiber and that the tip is smooth and free of scratches. And of course, you can see dirt and any other contamination on the end of the ferrule that can affect light transmission through the connection.

There are many inspection microscopes available with magnifications of 100X to 400X. Higher magnification may not be better, as it tends to make you more critical of scratches and imperfections. Lower magnification works just fine.

A note on eye safety: A microscope focuses all the power in the core of the fiber into eye! Some microscopes have filters to remove potentially harmful infrared light but always test for power in the fiber optic cable with a power meter before inspection.

FRG, Chapter 8, RGPC Chapter 5, FOTM, Chapter 17, DVVC, Chapter 14

FOA Online Fiber Optic Reference Guide, Understanding Fiber Optics, The Basics: Testing

Also see the "Virtual Hands-On" section

Optical Power Testing Per FOTP-95

- Most fiber optic measurements are based on optical power
- Test transmitter output or receiver input:
  - Connect power meter to test cable
    - System cable at source or receiver
    - Reference cable attached to source
  - Set meter to calibrated wavelength
  - Measure output with meter in "dBm" or watts
- Loss is measured as difference in power before and after cause of loss

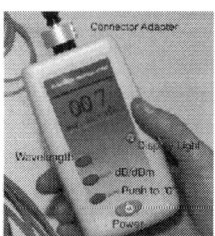
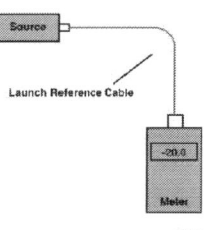

Fiber Optic Curriculum © 2013, The Fiber Optic Assn. Inc.

Measuring Optical Power

Most fiber optic measurements are based on optical power

Optical power is typically measured to check transmitter source power output at the transmitter or receiver power at its input. Optical power is measured with the power meter attached to the system cable or, when testing source output, a reference test cable. Power can be measured in "milliwatts or microwatts" which is a linear scale of power or "dBm" which is dB referenced to 1 milliwatt, which is more common.

Transmitter Power

The amount of light coupled into a fiber by a source is measured by attaching a patchcord to the source, either a known good system patchcord or a reference test cable. The cable used must have a connector that mates with the transmitter and a fiber size the same as the system cabling (50/125, 62.5/125 or SM) since the coupled power is highly dependent on the core size of the fiber. The meter connector adapter must be the same as the cable to allow connection.

Connect the meter, set the range on dBm or watts as appropriate and be sure to set the wavelength to the wavelength of the source, as the meter's calibration will be different due to the wavelength sensitivity of its detector!

Optical Power Testing Per FOTP-95

- Most fiber optic measurements are based on optical power
- Test transmitter output or receiver input:
  - Connect power meter to test cable
    - System cable at source or receiver
    - Reference cable attached to source
  - Set meter to calibrated wavelength
  - Measure output with meter in "dBm" or watts
- Loss is measured as difference in power before and after cause of loss

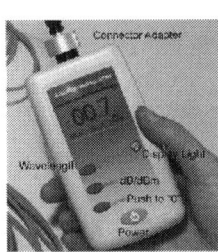
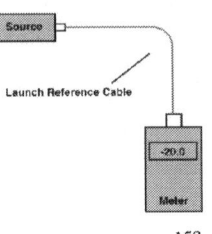

Receiver Power

Receiver power is measured by removing the cable connected to the receiver input and connecting it to the power meter.

Set the meter range on dBm or watts as appropriate and be sure to set the wavelength to the wavelength of the source, as the meter's calibration will be different due to the wavelength sensitivity of its detector!

Measure the power and record the results.

Loss is measured as difference in power before and after cause of loss, which is discussed in detail later.

FRG, Chapter 8, FOTM, Chapter 17, DVVC, Chapter 14

FOA Online Fiber Optic Reference Guide, Understanding Fiber Optics, The Basics: Testing

Also see the "Virtual Hands-On" section

Understanding Measurements in "dB"

- Loss is measured in "dB" or decibels
- dB is a Logarithmic scale: dB=10 log (power ratio)
  - 10 dB = 10X
  - 0 dB = 1X
  - 3 dB = 2X
  - -10 dB = 0.1X
- Power is measured in dBm which is dB referenced to 1 mw
  - 0 dBm = 1 mw
  - -10 dBm = 0.1 mw = 100μw

Fiber Optic Curriculum © 2013, The Fiber Optic Assn. Inc.

dB is a measure of optical power on a log scale, simplifying measurements over a wide dynamic range. Fiber optics typically uses power levels from +20 to -40 dBm, a range of 1,000,000 to 1! But that translates to 60 dB, an easier number to deal with.

Absolute power is measured in dBm or dB referenced to 1 mw. Positive dBm means the power is greater than 1 mw, while negative numbers mean the power level is less than 1 mw.

A nice thing about dB is loss is easily measured by subtracting the reference level for "0" dB from the measured value of the loss. That is, if you measure -20 dBm from the end of the reference cable, then -22 dBm when testing cables, the cable loss is 2 dB.

FRG, Chapter 8, RGPC Chapter 5, FOTM, Chapter 17, DVVC, Chapter 14
FOA Online Fiber Optic Reference Guide, Understanding Fiber Optics, The Basics: Testing
Also see the "Virtual Hands-On" section

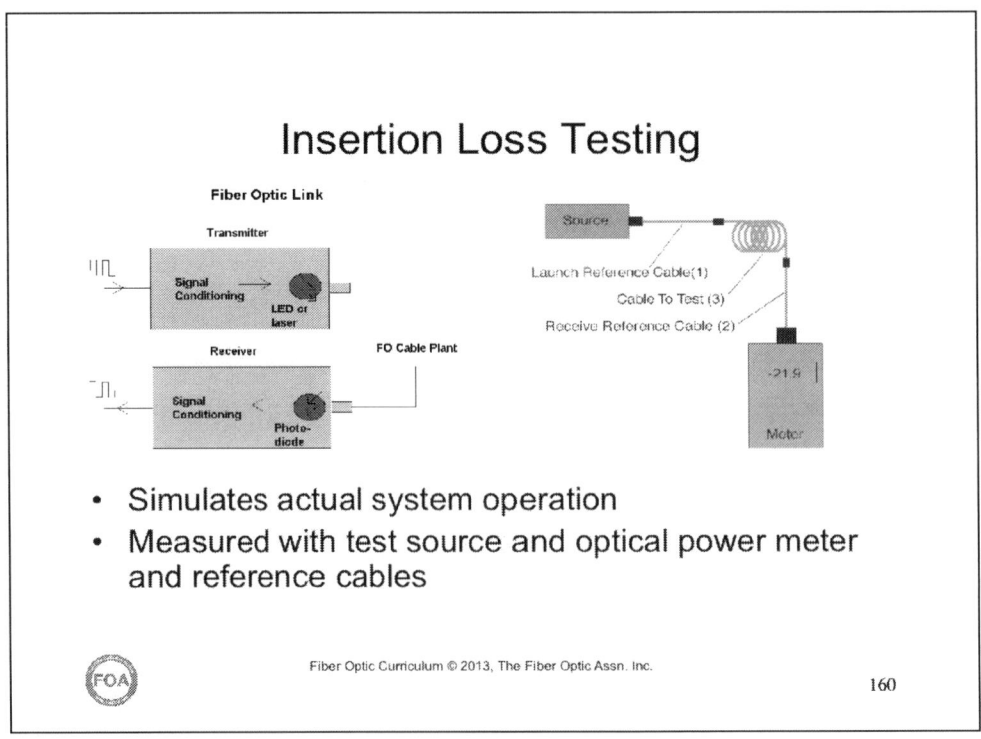

Insertion loss testing simulates the way the cable will be used by the systems operating over it. A source, similar to the system source is used for inserting light into the cable under test. A meter is used to measure the source output and the loss when the cable under test is added.

A double-ended test like this measures the loss of the fiber and connectors on both ends, plus anything in the middle.

The source should match the system source in type (LED or laser) and wavelength (850 or 1300 nm for LEDs and 850, 1310 or 1550 nm for lasers.)

The power meter needs to be calibrated to NIST (standards US national standards labs) and be able to measure at appropriate wavelengths (850, 1310 or 1550 nm.)

Reference cables provide the test conditions for the loss test. They mate to the connectors on each end of the cable under test to measure the loss of those connectors. The reference cables are critical to making good measurements. They must mate with the cable under test, so connectors must match or mating adapters be available, and the fiber must be the same type (MM or SM) and core diameter.

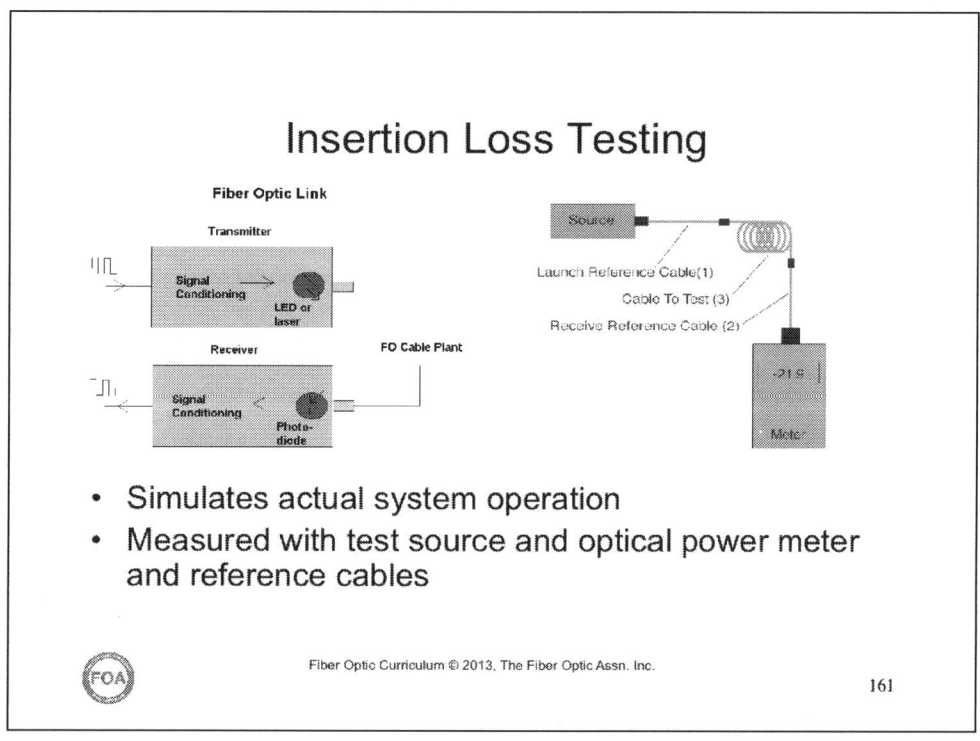

One makes the measurement by calibrating the output of the source and storing this measurement as "0 dB" loss reference. The attach the cable to test and receive reference cable and meter, then measure the loss. The loss will be a negative number. Most standards call for measuring the "0 dB" reference at the end of the launch cable.

Alternative methods of setting the "0 dB" reference include using both launch and receive cables or both those cables and a third reference cable. These methods are used with some types of connectors not compatible with direct connection to a power meter. The measured loss is reduced by one connector loss value with two reference cables and two connector loss values with three reference cables. The method used for referencing should be disclosed with the cable loss data.

Another test uses only a launch reference cable and the cable under test. This method allows testing a single cable from each end to find out if either connector is bad.

FRG, Chapter 8, RGPC Chapter 5, FOA Online Fiber Optic Reference Guide, Understanding Fiber Optics, The Basics: Testing

Also see the "Virtual Hands-On" section ad the FOA Test Standards

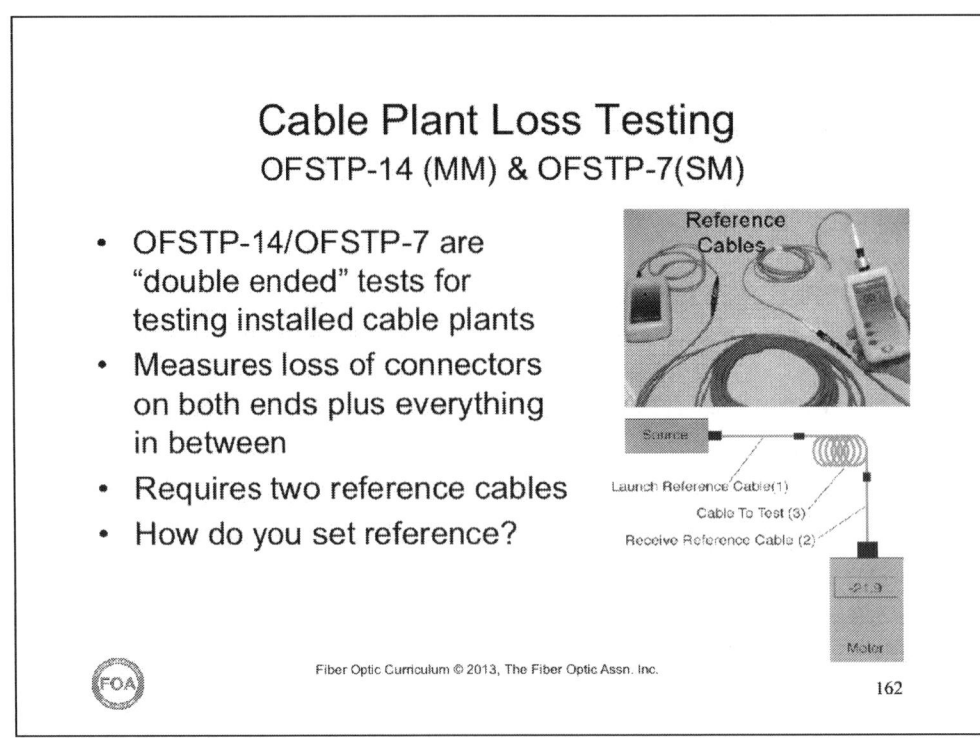

OFSTP-14 and OFSTP-7, double ended testing

OFSTP-14/OFSTP-7 are used for testing installed and terminated cable plants, where we want to test the connectors on each end and everything in between. So we use a meter and source with two reference cables - one on each end. Different standards exist for multimode and singlemode fibers due to the requirements for modal power control in multimode fiber.

The big issue with this test method is how one sets the 0 dB reference.

FRG, Chapter 8, RGPC Chapter 5, FOA Online Fiber Optic Reference Guide, Understanding Fiber Optics, The Basics: Testing

Also see the FOA "1 page" Standards for details on these tests

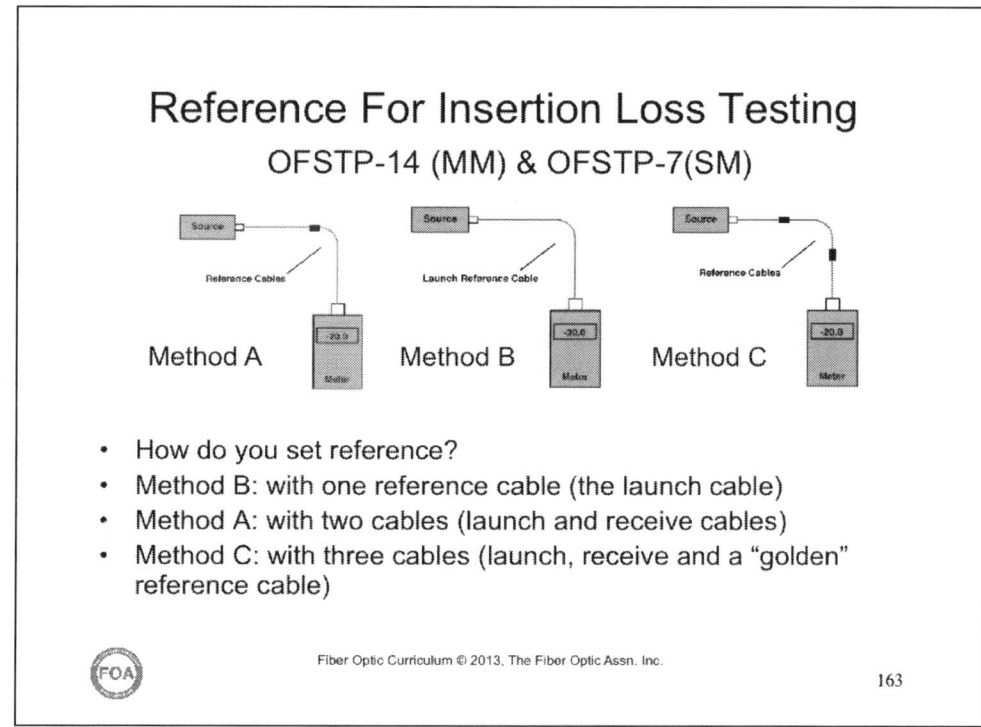

OFSTP-14/OFSTP-7 offers three options on how one sets the 0 dB reference with 3 options for reference cables. These used to be called Methods A, B and C but that terminology is being dropped in standards.

Method B with one reference cable (the launch cable)

This method sets the "0 dB reference" with the power meter measuring the output of the launch cable directly, so that no connector loss is included when setting the reference. Then when testing a cable with both launch and receive cables, the loss includes the loss of both connectors on the cable under test and the loss of all the components in between.

Method A with two cables (launch and receive cables)

This method sets the "0 dB reference" with the launch cable mated to the receive cable, so that one mated connector loss is included when setting the reference. Then when testing a cable with both launch and receive cables, the loss includes the loss of connectors on the cable under test and the loss of all the components in between, less the loss of the mated connectors included in the reference.

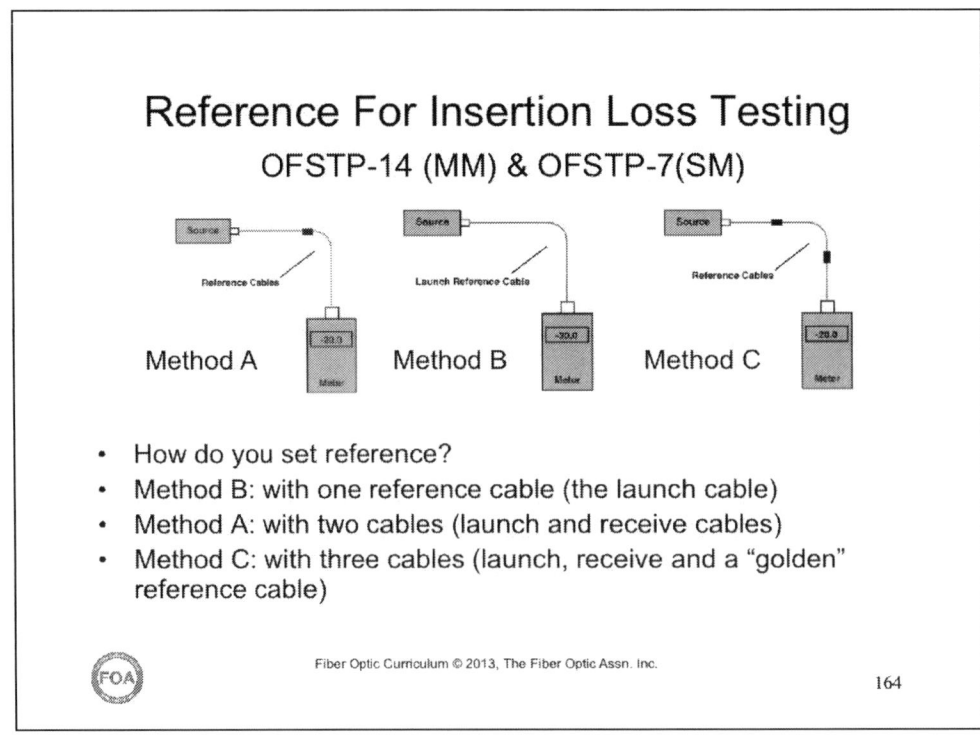

OFSTP-14/OFSTP-7 offers three options on how one sets the 0 dB reference.

Method C: with three cables (launch, receive and a "golden" reference cables)

This method sets the "0 dB reference" with the launch cable and the receive cable, plus a "golden" reference cable mated to them, so that two mated connector losses and any fiber loss in the third cable are included when setting the reference. Then when testing a cable with both launch and receive cables, the loss includes the loss of connectors on the cable under test and the loss of all the components in between, less the loss of the mated connectors included in the reference.

What is the reason for three different methods? It's determined by the compatibility of the power meter and source with the connectors on the cable plant, and whether the connectors are normal ferrule-type connectors that use mating adapters or plug and jack type connectors. Read "5 Different Ways To Test" on the Reference website for a complete explanation.

FRG, Chapter 8, RGPC Chapter 5, FOA Online Fiber Optic Reference Guide, Understanding Fiber Optics, The Basics: Testing

Reference For Insertion Loss Testing
OFSTP-14 (MM) & OFSTP-7(SM)

Method A — Reference Cables (two cables to meter)
Method B — Launch Reference Cable (one cable to meter)
Method C — Reference Cables (three cables to meter)

- How do you set reference?
- Method B: with one reference cable (the launch cable)
- Method A: with two cables (launch and receive cables)
- Method C: with three cables (launch, receive and a "golden" reference cable)

OFSTP-14/OFSTP-7 offers three options on how one sets the 0 dB reference.

What is the reason for three different methods? It's determined by the compatibility of the power meter and source with the connectors on the cable plant, and whether the connectors are normal ferrule-type connectors that use mating adapters or plug and jack type connectors.

The 1-cable method works when the connectors on the cable plant are compatible to the connectors on the test equipment.

The 2-cable method works when the connectors on the cable plant are not compatible to the connectors on the test equipment, but can be mated with mating adapters.

The 3-cable method works when the connectors on the cable plant are not compatible to the connectors on the test equipment and are "male/female" or "plug/jack" types that cannot be randomly mated.

Read "5 Different Ways To Test" on the Reference website for a complete explanation.

FRG, Chapter 8, RGPC Chapter 5, FOA Online Fiber Optic Reference Guide, Understanding Fiber Optics, The Basics: Testing

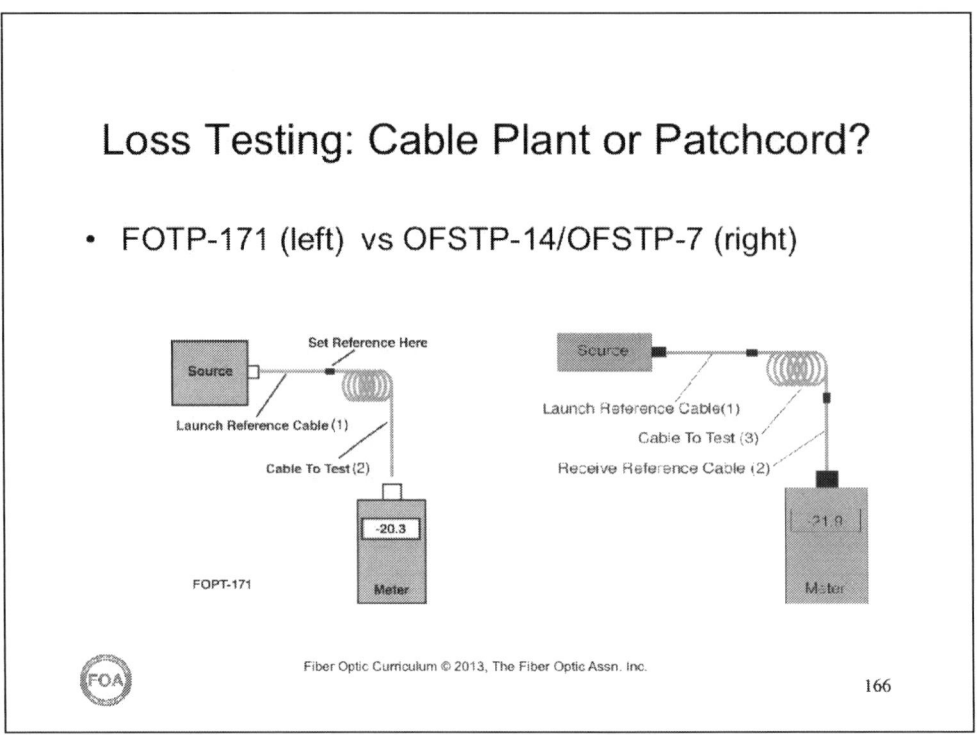

There are really two methods of insertion loss testing

So far we have talked about testing installed and terminated cable plants, where we want to test the connectors on each end and everything in between. So we use a meter and source with two reference cables - one on each end. This test is defined by a standard OFSTP-14 (OFSTP = optical fiber standard test procedure) for multimode and OFSTP-7 for singlemode.

Another test, FOTP-171, uses only a launch reference cable and the cable under test and is sometimes called a "single-ended" test. This method allows testing a single cable like a patchcord from each end separately to help find out if either connector is bad.

FRG, Chapter 8, RGPC Chapter 5, FOTM, Chapter 17, DVVC, Chapter 14

FOA Online Fiber Optic Reference Guide, Understanding Fiber Optics, The Basics: Testing

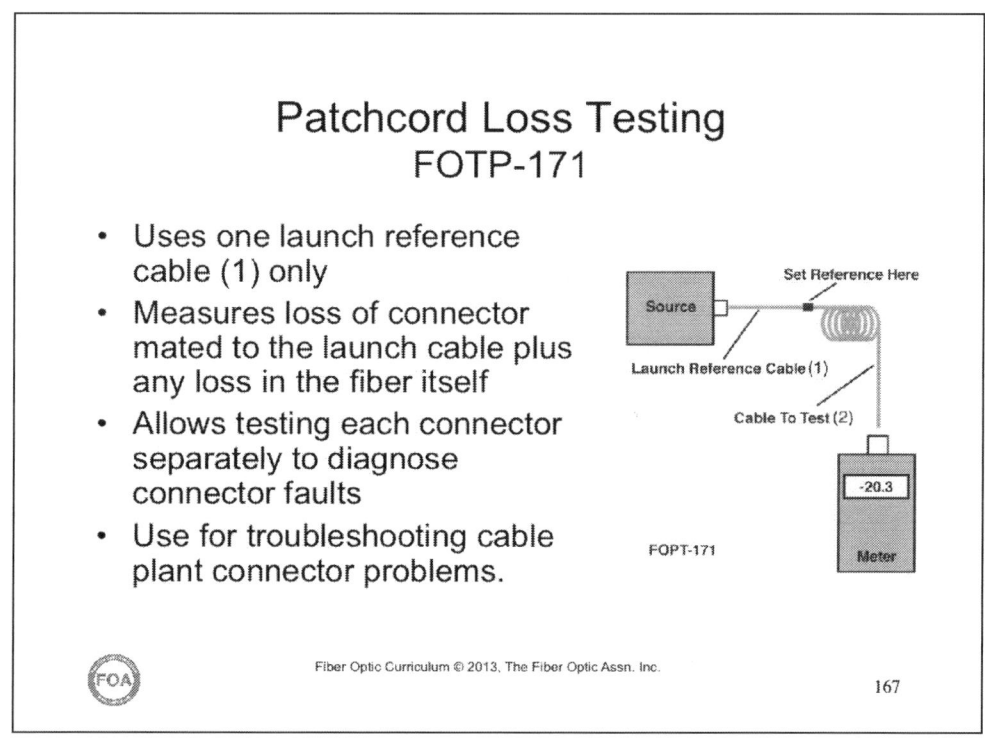

FOTP-171 or single-ended testing

A FOTP-171 test uses only a single launch reference cable to test the cable. This method allows testing a single cable from either end to find out if one connector is bad. It's main use is testing patchcords to insure both connectors are good, but it can also be used to troubleshoot installed cables where one connector is suspected of being bad.

The 0 dB loss reference is made by connecting the power meter to the output of the launch cable and measuring the power output. The cable under test is connected to the launch cable and the meter. The loss measured is only the loss of the mated connectors and any loss of the fiber in the cable, usually very small when testing patchcords this way.

The fact that the connector on the launch cable and the cable under test are mated directly to the meter, with it's large detector, means that the connection loss to the meter is calibrated out of the loss test, allowing testing of only the connector mated to the launch cable.

See also "Patchcord or Single Cable Testing" on the Reference Website

FRG, Chapter 8, RGPC Chapter 5, FOA Online Fiber Optic Reference Guide, Understanding Fiber Optics, The Basics: Testing

Issues For Loss Testing

- Measurement accuracy depends on:
    - Quality and condition of reference cables
    - Modal distribution in multimode fiber
    - Proper setting of "0 dB" reference
    - Cleanliness of reference cables
    - Stability of source and meter

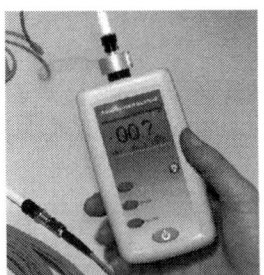

Insertion loss measurement accuracy depends on a number of factors that need consideration by any fiber optic tech:

First, it is important to be confident of the quality and condition of reference cables. The do not need to be special cables, just good quality patchcords with low loss connectors (certainly under 0.5 dB, preferably under 0.3 dB, tested single ended per FOTP-171 against each other.)

One should consider modal distribution in multimode fiber. Most standards call for a source of calibrated output with a mandrel wrap on the launch cable. This subject is covered in detail on the FOA website on the page Modal Effects on Multimode Fiber Loss Measurements.

The calibration of the source output when setting the 0 dB reference is very important. The method of setting the reference must be documented as it affects the loss measured and the value used will affect all measurements. It's a good idea to recheck the reference level occasionally to ensure the source has not changed.

The cleanliness of reference cables is vitally important. Dirt on the connectors when setting the reference that's cleaned off later can cause loss measurements to be lower or even read as a gain. Setting the reference with clean cables that get dirty over time will cause a systematic increase in loss.

Issues For Loss Testing

- Measurement accuracy depends on:
    - Quality and condition of reference cables
    - Modal distribution in multimode fiber
    - Proper setting of "0 dB" reference
    - Cleanliness of reference cables
    - Stability of source and meter

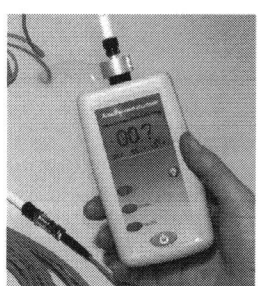

Insertion loss measurement accuracy depends on a number of factors that need consideration by any fiber optic tech:

Needless to say, the stability of the meter and source is important since if either changes, the 0 dB reference will change and all loss measurement will be in error. If you don't know if your equipment is stable, connect your source to a power meter with a reference cable and let it run for a while. And check it with a good battery and a discharged one to see if the battery level affects the power output. Always make certain that your batteries are good before beginning testing!

FRG, Chapter 8, RGPC Chapter 5, FOA Online Fiber Optic Reference Guide, Understanding Fiber Optics, The Basics: Testing

OTDR Testing

- Makes indirect measurement using fiber backscatter
- Takes "snapshot" of fiber
- Tests from one end of cable
- Requires trained operator to interpret measurements
- Lots of setup parameters
- Doesn't match insertion loss

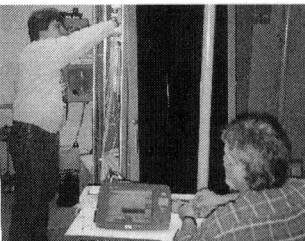
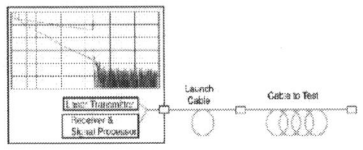

Fiber Optic Curriculum © 2013, The Fiber Optic Assn. Inc.

Unlike sources and power meters which measure the loss of the fiber optic cable plant directly, testing just like the fiber is used for transmission of data, the OTDR works indirectly. It uses backscattered light of the fiber to imply loss (remember that scattering is the major cause of loss in the fiber.) The OTDR works like RADAR, sending a high power laser light pulse down the fiber and looking for return signals from backscattered light in the fiber itself or reflected light from connector or splice interfaces.

The OTDR test is an indirect test and will not generally correlate with insertion loss testing. However, it is useful to confirm splice losses and find faults in fibers, like breaks or severe stress losses such as from too tight bends.

Most problems with fiber optic testing are caused by improper use of OTDRs, either on short cable plants where OTDR testing is not appropriate or by use by inadequately trained personnel.

FRG, Chapter 8, RGPC Chapter 5, FOA Online Fiber Optic Reference Guide, Understanding Fiber Optics, The Basics: Testing
Also see the "Virtual Hands-On" section
Fiber optic "Testing" PPT includes detailed information on OTDRs, including types of tests performed and measurement accuracy.

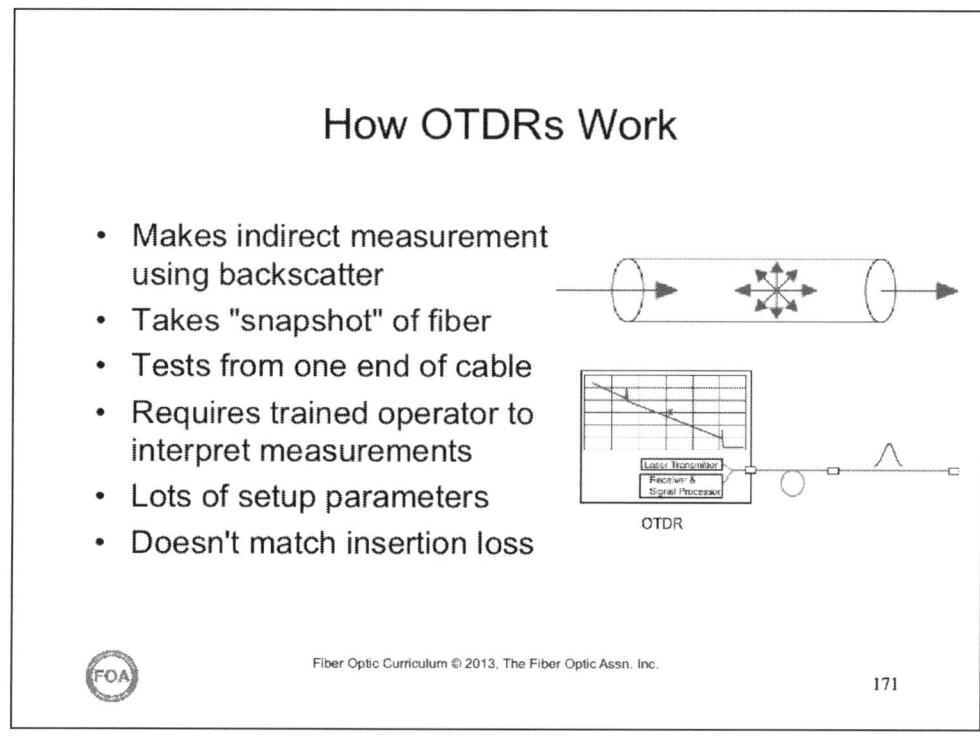

The OTDR works like RADAR, sending a high power laser light pulse down the fiber that is scattered in all directions including a small amount back toward the instrument itself. The OTDR receives the backscattered light and converts it into a display. It also receives reflected light from connector or splice reflectance. Only a small amount of light is scattered back toward the OTDR, but with sensitive receivers and signal averaging, it is possible to make measurements over relatively long distances.

At any point in time, the light the OTDR sees is the light scattered from the pulse passing through a section of the fiber. The test pulse is attenuated by the fiber and connector or splice losses as it travels down the fiber, so the returned signal is lower as the pulse goes further. The attenuation is seen by the OTDR which processes the data.

Since it is possible to calibrate the speed of the pulse as it passes down the fiber by knowing the time it takes and the speed of light in the fiber, the OTDR can measure time, calculate the pulse position in the fiber and correlate what it sees in backscattered light with an actual location in the fiber.

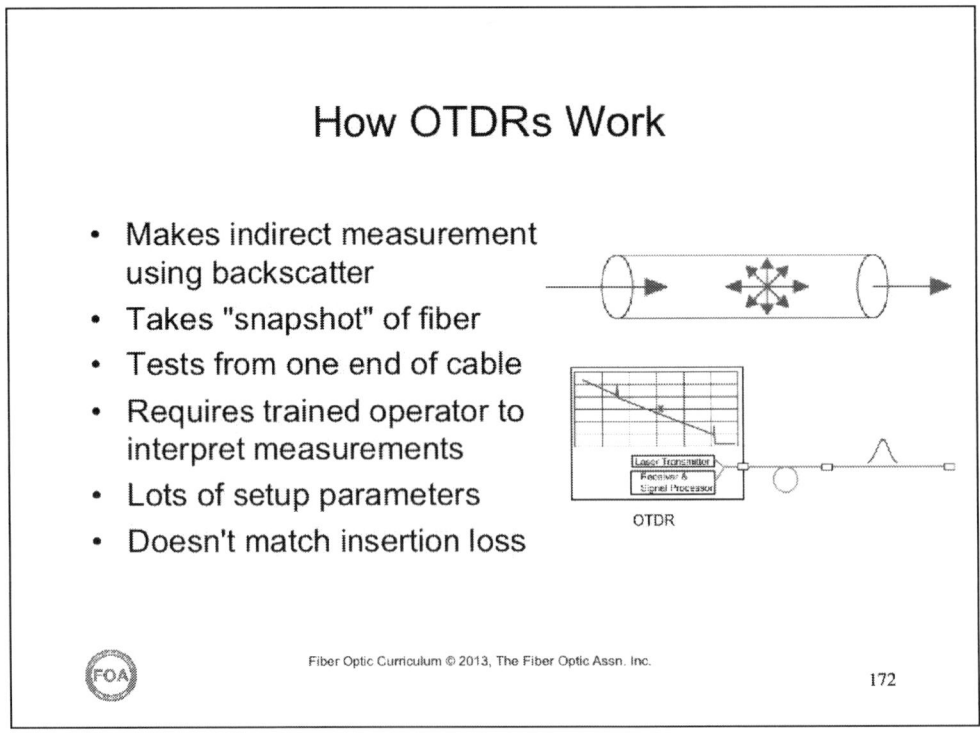

Thus the OTDR can create a display of the amount of backscattered light at any point in the fiber. Since the pulse is attenuated in the fiber as it passes along the fiber and suffers loss in connectors and splices, the amount of power in the test pulse decreases as it passes along the fiber in the cable plant under test. The portion of the light being backscattered will be reduced accordingly, producing a picture of the loss occurring in the fiber. Some calculations are necessary to convert this information into a display, since the process occurs twice, once going out from the OTDR and once on the return path from the scattering at the test pulse. The final OTDR display is dB on the Y-axis and distance on the X-axis.

FRG, Chapter 8, RGPC Chapter 5, FOTM, Chapter 17, DVVC, Chapter 14

FOA Online Fiber Optic Reference Guide, Understanding Fiber Optics, The Basics: Testing

Also see the "Virtual Hands-On" section and the FOA YouTube videos on OTDRs.

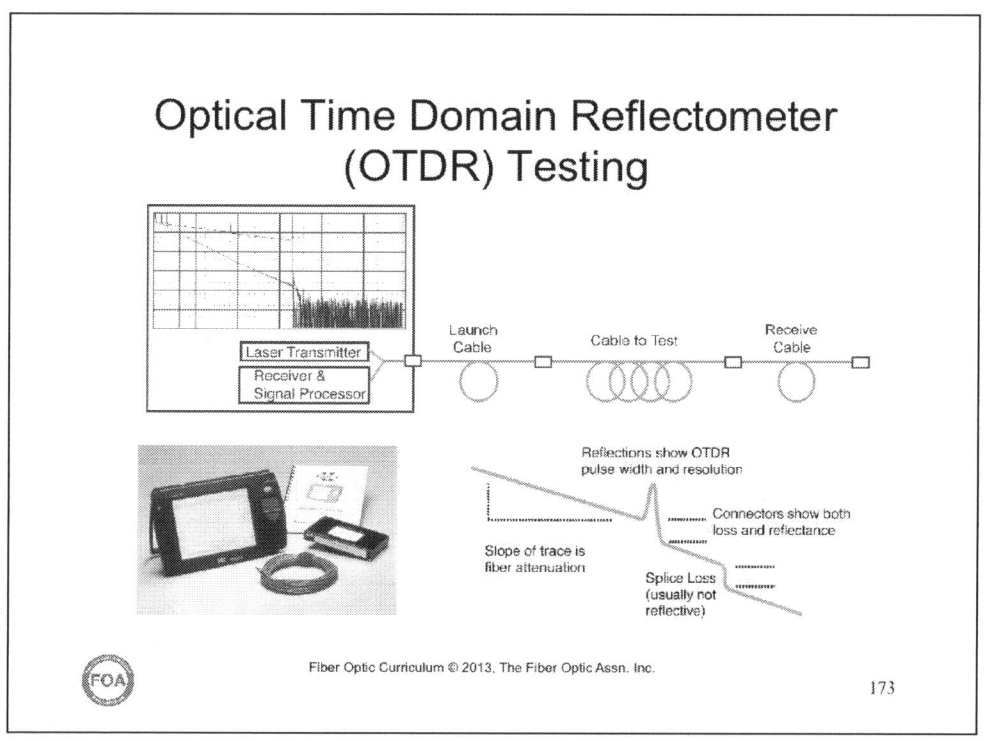

Unlike sources and power meters which measure the loss of the fiber optic cable plant directly, the OTDR works indirectly. It uses backscattered light of the fiber to imply loss (remember that scattering is the major cause of loss in the fiber.) The OTDR works like RADAR, sending a high power laser light pulse down the fiber and looking for return signals from backscattered light in the fiber itself or reflected light from connector or splice interfaces. At any point in time, the light the OTDR sees is the light scattered from the pulse passing through a region of the fiber.

FOTM, Chapter 6,7,9,17, DVVC, Chapter 12,13, 14 - Also Lennie for more on OTDRs

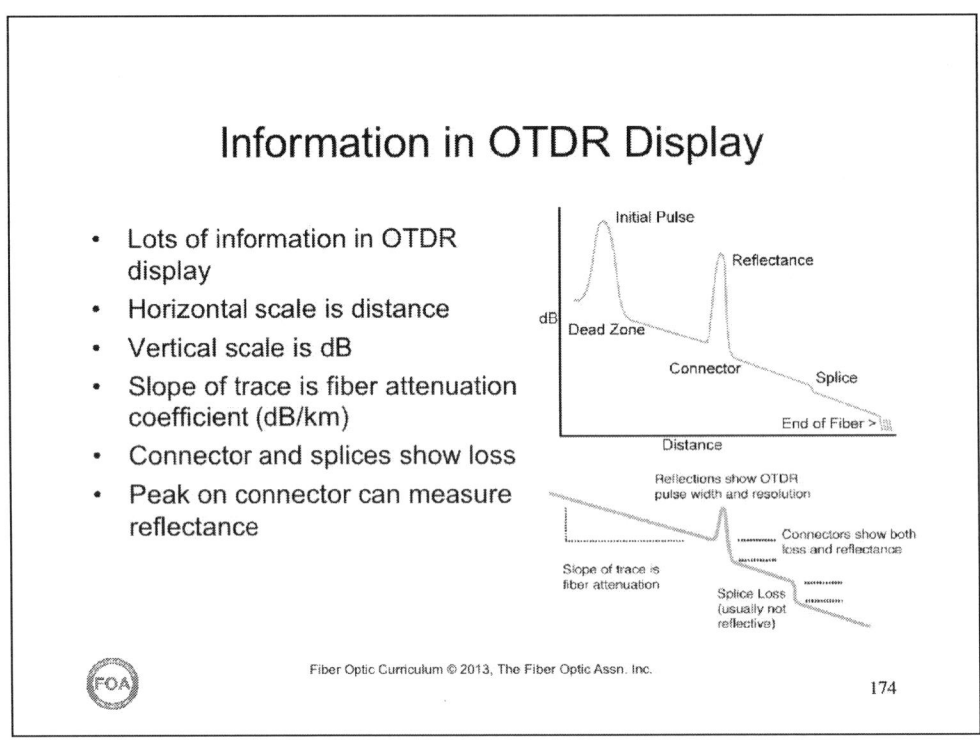

There is a lot of information in an OTDR display.

The slope of the fiber trace shows the attenuation coefficient of the fiber and is calibrated in dB/km (or sometimes kilofeet for the metric-challenged) by the OTDR. In order to measure fiber attenuation, you need a fairly long length of fiber with no distortions on either end from the OTDR resolution or overloading due to large reflections. If the fiber looks nonlinear at either end, especially near a reflective event like a connector, avoid that section when measuring loss.

Understanding how to interpret OTDR traces requires lots of training and practice, and misinterpreting traces can be very expensive if good cables are rejected or bad ones accepted.

FRG, Chapter 8, RGPC Chapter 5, FOTM, Chapter 17, DVVC, Chapter 14

FOA Online Fiber Optic Reference Guide, Understanding Fiber Optics, The Basics: Testing

Also see the "Virtual Hands-On" section

Information in OTDR Display

- OTDR trace has lots of information for the knowledgeable user
- Attenuation: dB loss per fiber length, dB/km (top)
- Loss: loss of power at event in dB (middle)
- Reflectance: power level of reflected pulse, dB
- Autotest may not be trustworthy

Fiber Optic Curriculum © 2013, The Fiber Optic Assn. Inc.

The slope of the fiber trace shows the attenuation coefficient of the fiber and is calibrated in dB/km (or sometimes kilofeet for the metric-challenged) by the OTDR. In order to measure fiber attenuation, you need a fairly long length of fiber with no distortions on either end from the OTDR resolution or overloading due to large reflections. If the fiber looks nonlinear at either end, especially near a reflective event like a connector, avoid that section when measuring loss.

Connectors and splices are called "events" in OTDR jargon. Both should show a loss, but connectors and mechanical splices will also show a reflective peak so you can distinguish them from fusion splices.

Also, the height of a reflective peak will indicate the amount of reflection at the event, unless it is so large that it saturates the OTDR receiver. Then peak will have a flat top and tail on the far end, indicating the receiver was overloaded.

The width of the peak shows the distance resolution of the OTDR, or how close it can detect events.

Understanding how to interpret OTDR traces requires lots of training and practice, and misinterpreting traces can be very expensive if good cables are rejected or bad ones accepted.

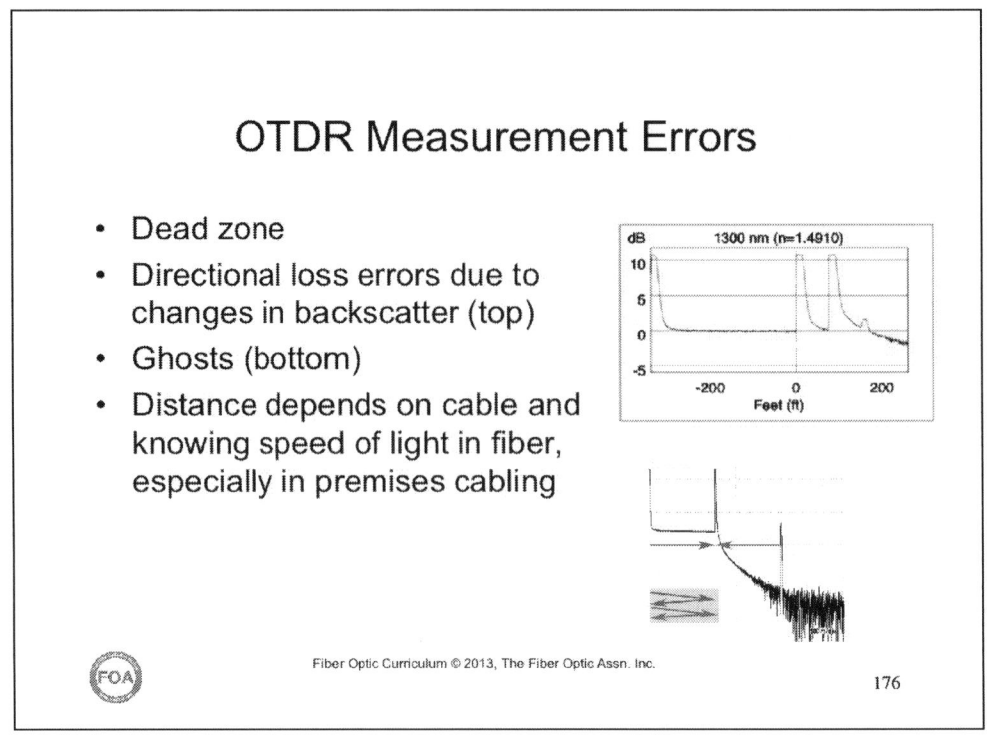

OTDR Measurement Errors

- Dead zone
- Directional loss errors due to changes in backscatter (top)
- Ghosts (bottom)
- Distance depends on cable and knowing speed of light in fiber, especially in premises cabling

The large initial pulse of the OTDR causes recovery problems that limits the ability of the OTDR to see anything near it, even for high resolution instruments like the one shown here. That is caused by the high-powered test pulse reflecting off the OTDR connector and overloading the OTDR receiver. The recovery of the receiver causes the "dead zone" near the OTDR. To avoid problems caused by the dead zone, always use a launch cable of sufficient length when testing cables.

Ghosts are causes by reflective events bouncing back and forth in a cable. Short cables with highly reflective connectors can show several ghosts. They can be detected by noting the reflective peaks are at multiples of the same distance.

The limited distance resolution of the OTDR makes it very hard to use in a LAN or building environment where cables are usually only a few hundred meters long. The OTDR has a great deal of difficulty resolving features in the short cables of a LAN and is likely to show "ghosts" from reflections at connectors, more often than not simply confusing the user.

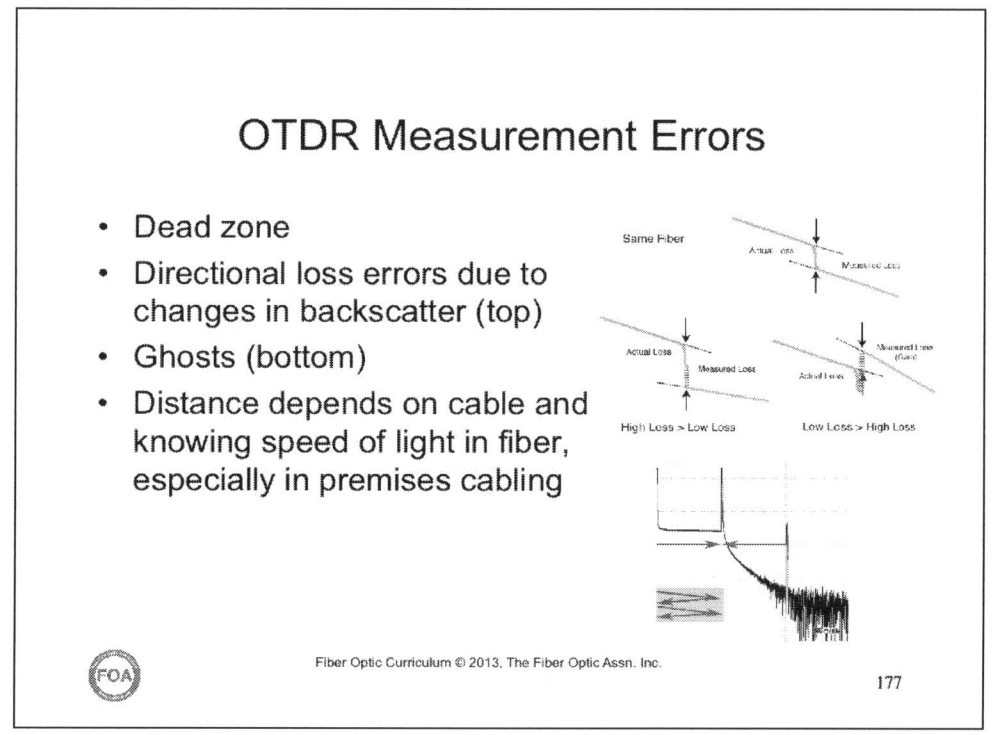

OTDR Measurement Errors

- Dead zone
- Directional loss errors due to changes in backscatter (top)
- Ghosts (bottom)
- Distance depends on cable and knowing speed of light in fiber, especially in premises cabling

Since the OTDR uses backscatter light to make measurements, it's dependent on the consistency of the backscatter. But scattering is the largest cause of loss in the fiber and various fibers have different losses - and different backscatter coefficients. When measuring connectors of splices, the loss measured will be higher going from a low loss fiber to a high loss one and lower in the other direction. The only way to overcome this error is to take data in both directions and average the measurement. OTDR distance measurements are often wrong because of two factors. Distance is calculated from the speed of light in the fiber (NVP) which may not be known or may vary over many fibers in a link and the length of the fiber is longer than the cable, a design feature of cable to prevent stress on the fiber. If a reel of fiber is available, it can be calibrated; otherwise assume the cable is 1-2% shorter than the fiber.

The Reference Guide section on OTDRs has much more detailed explanations of these issues.

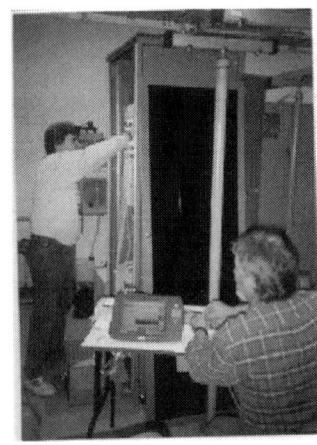

Specialized Fiber Optic Testing

- Mostly long distance outside plant testing
- Reflectance
- Chromatic Dispersion
- Polarization Mode Dispersion
- DWDM, Spectral Attenuation

These are a number of tests that are typically done only on high bitrate and/or long distance networks.

FOA Online Fiber Optic Reference Guide: Testing

Optical Reflectance Testing

- Reflectance is connection test
- Called ORL-Optical Return Loss - in installed cable plant but includes backscatter
- Test with meter and source or OCWR (optical continuous wave reflectometer)
- Test with OTDR

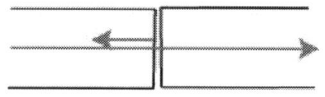

Fiber Optic Curriculum © 2013, The Fiber Optic Assn. Inc.

Optical Reflectance (Return Loss) in Connectors

If you have ever looked at a fiber optic connector on an OTDR, you are familiar with the characteristic spike that shows where a connector is. That spike is a measure of the reflectance or optical return loss of the connector, or the amount of light that is reflected back up the fiber by light reflecting off the interface of the polished end surface of the connector and air. It is called fresnel reflection and is caused by the light going through the change in index of refraction at the interface between the fiber (n=1.5) and air (n=1). For most systems, that spike is just one component of the connector's loss, representing as much as 0.3 dB loss (two air/glass interfaces at 4% reflection each), the minimum loss for non-contacting connectors without index-matching fluid.

In high-bit rate singlemode systems, that reflection can be a major source of bit-error rate problems. The reflected light can interfere with the laser diode and can be a source of noise by multipath reflectance in short links.

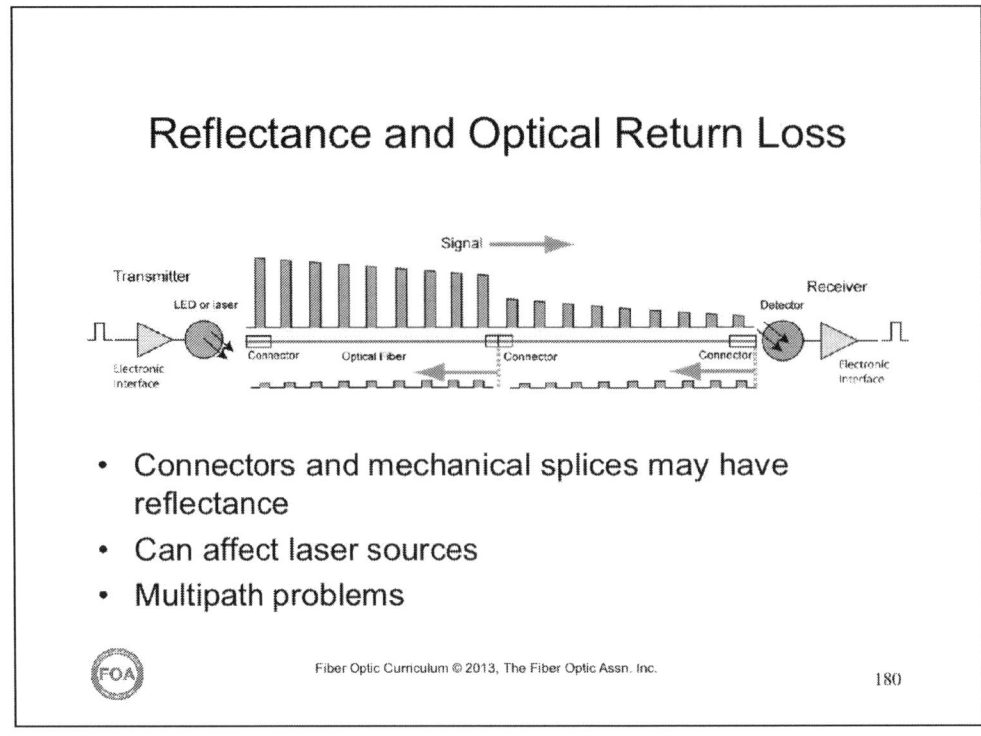

Reflectance occurs at optical interfaces where glass and air mix. Connectors are the major source of reflectance in a fiber link, while splices, especially fusion splices, as permanent joints are designed to minimize reflections. Some lasers are sensitive to reflected light and all systems may suffer from optical multipath interference which degrades S/N.

State-of-the-art connectors will have a return loss of about 40-60 dB, or about one-ten thousandth to one millionth of the light is reflected back towards the source. Measurements setups need to be carefully controlled to get valid data. The test connector being used to test other connectors or jumper cables must be kept clean and periodically repolished to insure as perfect a surface finish as possible. Purists will note that measurements of Pout ignore the fresnel reflection from the end of the test cable fiber and perhaps even the window of the detector, which can add a few percent to the errors.

FOA Online Fiber Optic Reference Guide: Testing

Reflectance Testing - FOTP-107

- Uses laser source, meter and 1X2 coupler
- Source needs high power for wide dynamic range (up to 60 dB)
- Coupler needs calibration for split ratio
- Terminate end of cable in alcohol, mineral oil or index matching fluid
- Large uncertainty

Measuring reflectance per standard test procedure EIA FOTP-107 is straightforward, but requires the setup shown in the diagram. This test setup can be used with a bare fiber output into which a connector pair is installed or with a connectorized output for testing jumpers.

The coupler split ratio must be calibrated to know how much of the return signal goes to the power meter and how much is diverted to the source side of the coupler to calculate the total amount of back reflection. Due to the dynamic range required to measure return losses of -25 to -60 dB, a high power laser source is necessary.

To measure return loss, measure the amount of power transmitted to the end of the cable (P^{out}) and the power reflected back up through the coupler test port (P^{back}) with a fiber optic power meter. To calibrate out any crosstalk in the coupler or the back reflections of any intermediate connectors or splices, dip the connector end being tested in an index matching fluid (alcohol works well and isn't messy to clean up) and record the power at the coupler test port (P^{zero}). If the coupler split ratio is R^{split} (the fraction of the light that goes to the measurement port when transmitting in the back direction), the return loss is:

ORL = P^{back} - P^{out} + R^{split} (all in dB)

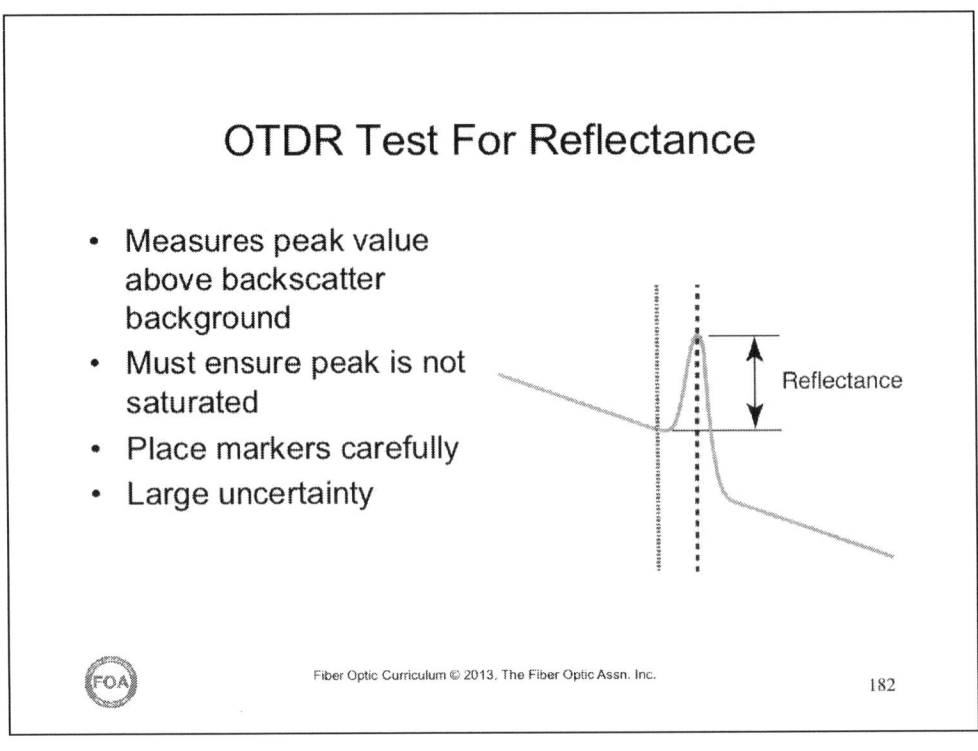

The OTDR is often programmed to measure return loss or reflectance from a connector or splice (usually a mechanical splice.) This is a complicated process involving the baseline of the OTDR, backscatter level and power in the reflected peak. Like all backscatter measurements, it has a fairly high measurement uncertainty, but has the advantage of showing where reflective events are located so they can be corrected if necessary.

FOA Online Fiber Optic Reference Guide: Testing

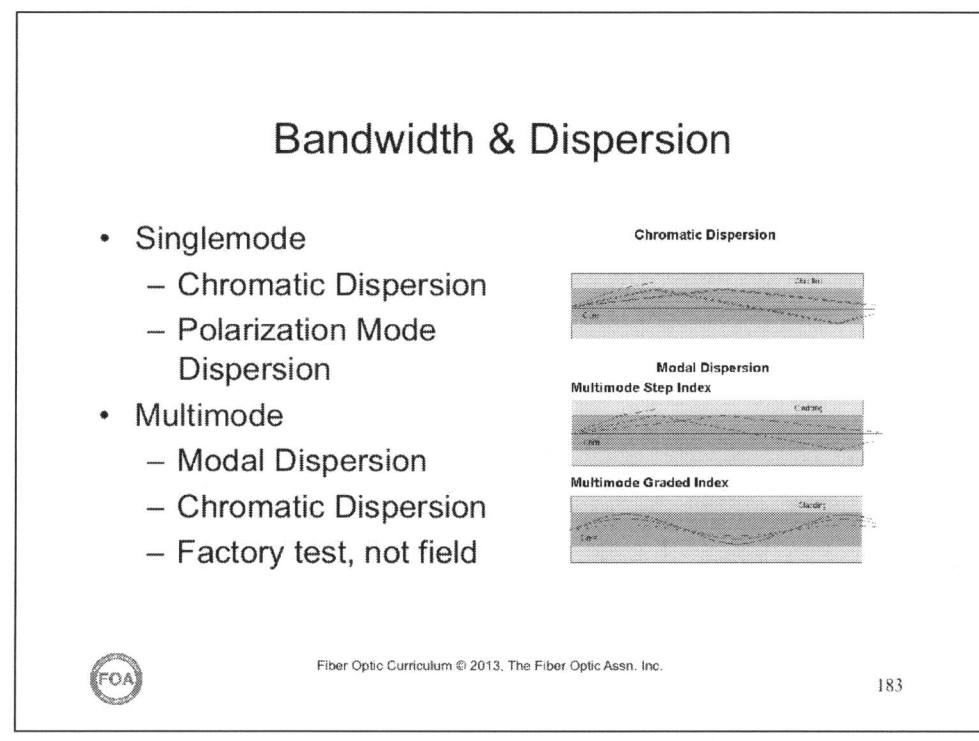

Bandwidth and Dispersion

Some people have the impression that fiber has infinite bandwidth, but it's not true. In fact, the distance fiber can carry network signals depends as much on bandwidth as loss - sometimes more.

There are several factors that affect the bandwidth of singlemode fiber, but the two major ones for singlemode fiber are chromatic dispersion, of the fact that light of different colors travels at different speeds in glass (the definition of index of refraction) and polarization mode dispersion, caused by the varying speeds of planes of polarization. Equipment, expensive and complicated) are available to test these factors for long SM links, but it's beyond the scope of this presentation.

In multimode fiber, you have chromatic dispersion for the same reasons as in SM fiber, but you also have modal dispersion, caused by the different path lengths light follows in the larger core. While these factors are tested in the lab by fiber manufacturers, field testing is not done. However, bandwidth testers for MM fiber may become available in the near future due to the high bandwidth requirements of networks like 10 GbE.

FOA Online Fiber Optic Reference Guide: Testing

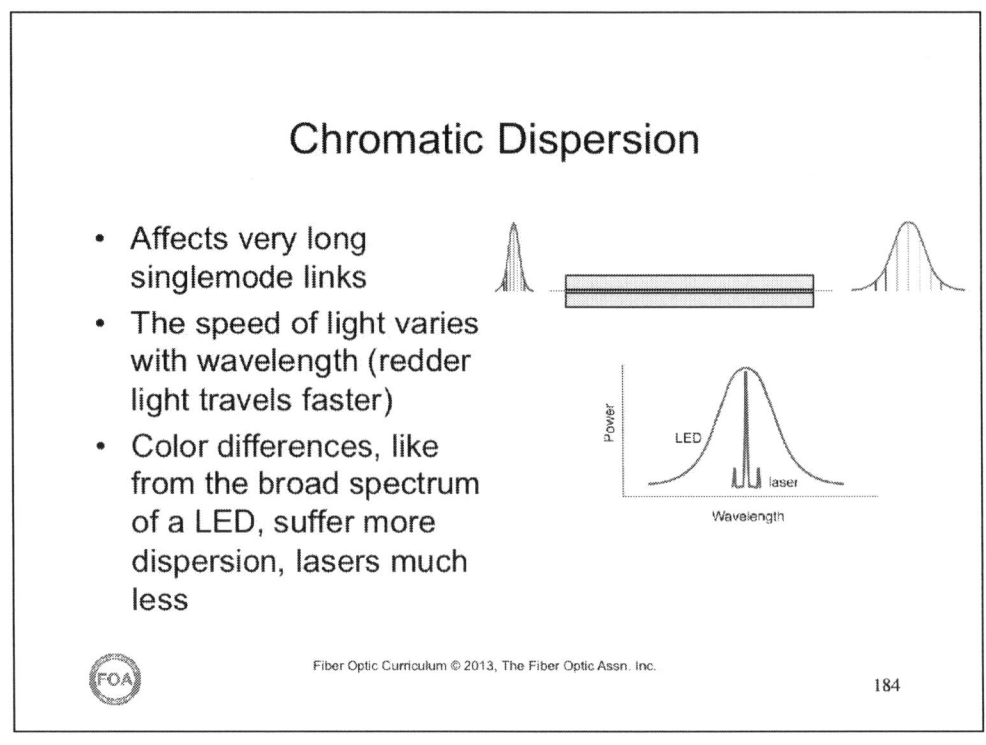

The second factor in fiber bandwidth is chromatic dispersion. Remember a prism spreads out the spectrum of incident light since the light travels at different speeds according to its color and is therefore refracted at different angles. The usual way of stating this is the index of refraction of the glass is wavelength dependent. Thus a carefully manufactured graded index multimode fiber can only be optimized for a single wavelength, usually near 1300 nm, and light of other colors will suffer from chromatic dispersion. Even light in the same mode will be dispersed if it is of different wavelengths.

Chromatic dispersion is a bigger problem with LEDs, which have broad spectral outputs (their output light is comprised of many wavelengths of light), unlike lasers which concentrate most of their light in a narrow spectral range. Chromatic dispersion occurs with LEDs because much of the power is away from the zero dispersion wavelength of the fiber. High speed systems, based on broad output LEDs, suffer intense chromatic dispersion, about equal to the modal dispersion.

FRG Chapter 5, RGPC Chapter 5, FOA Online Fiber Optic Reference Guide, Understanding Fiber Optics, Optical Fiber

Polarization Mode Dispersion (PMD)

- Affects long singlemode links
- The speed of light varies with polarization
- Depends on fiber ovality, wavelength and stress on fiber
- Can vary with temperature or even wind on aerial cable
- Small effect but can be important on long fibers at 40-100 Gb/s

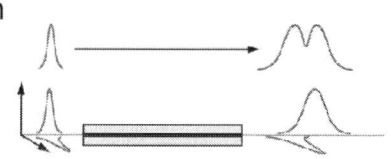

Another factor in fiber bandwidth is polarization mode dispersion. Polarization mode dispersion (PMD) is a bit more complex. Polarization is a phenomenon of light traveling in a medium as a wave with components at right angles. Some materials, like a glass optical fiber, have a different index of refraction for each of those components of the light wave, which is called birefringence. A different index of refraction means light travels at a different speed, so in the simplest visualization, PMD in fiber looks like the drawing below, where each component of the polarized light travels at a different speed, causing dispersion. The magnitude of PMD in a fiber is expressed as this difference, which is known as the differential group delay (DGD) and called Δτ(delta Tau). PMD is generally tested for fibers during manufacture or when being cabled. In the field, it is common to test PMD on newly installed fibers which are intended for operation at high speeds, generally above 2.5 Gb/s or when upgrading fibers installed some time in the past. Since PMD varies over time, a single test becomes an average and tests at a later time may be done for comparison. There are a number of commonly used test methods for PMD, some of which are limited to the manufacturing environment, while others can be used in the field. Essentially, all the test instruments have a source which can vary the polarization of the test signal and a measurement unit that can analyze polarization changes.

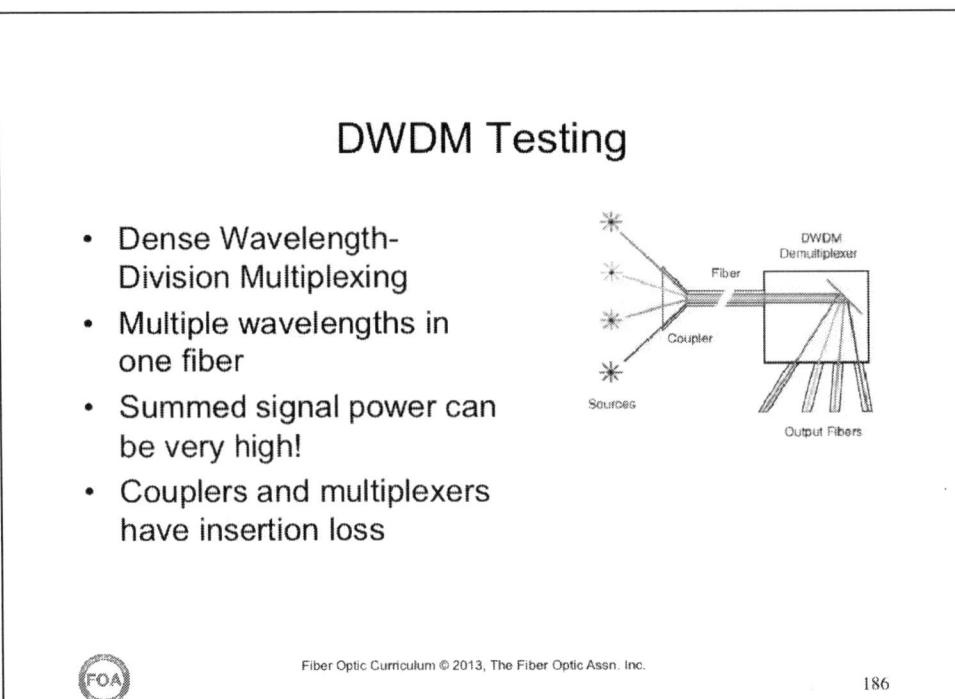

DWDM or Dense Wavelength-Division Multiplexing creates a whole different situation for testing. With multiple wavelengths in one fiber, it may require a power meter with wavelength selectivity if testing a fiber carrying multiple signals. It will also probably require high power capability, since not only are multiple sources using the fiber, but they are generally amplified to high levels to allow very long distance links.

All couplers and DWDM multiplexers have significant insertion loss which may need to be tested.

A proper treatment of this subject is beyond the scope of this presentation. A FTTH presentation will cover some of the issues of DWDM and PON (passive optic network) testing.

FOA Online Fiber Optic Reference Guide: Testing

Spectral Attenuation

- Wavelength division multiplexing systems use wavelengths from 1260 to 1675 nm
- May require testing over whole wavelength range
- Uses broad sources to cover wavelength range

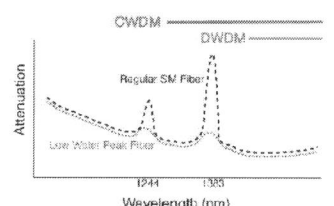

With the development of low water peak fibers, the possibility of transmission from 1260 to 1675 nm has been considered. This results from careful manufacturing of the fiber to reduce the water in the fiber (in the form of OH- ions) that causes higher spectral attenuation at around 1244 and 1383 nm. Systems using coarse wavelength division multiplexing (CWDM) use lasers at 20 nm increments over this range.

Since one may want to use available fibers †of unknown spectral attenuation for CWDM which uses lasers from 1260 to 1670 nm in 20 nm windows, it becomes necessary to test for spectral attenuation to verify the usability. At the water peaks, legacy fibers may have attenuation coefficients around 2 dB/km while low water peak fibers may be as low as 0.4 dB/km. Testing spectral attenuation is done per TIA/EIA-455-61 or IEC 61300-3-7 with broadband sources like LEDs and a spectrum analyzer on the receiving end of the fiber. Calibration is done with a short fiber length, the the instrument calculates the spectral attenuation on a long length being tested. The measurement of spectral attenuation uses instruments similar to those used for CD testing by the phase shift method, so some instruments do both measurements at one time.

FOA Online Fiber Optic Reference Guide, Testing Long Links

Specialized Test Equipment

- Reflectance/ORL, CD, PMD and SA have special test equipment designed to make tests
- All have multiple methods of making test
- See FOA Online Reference Guide for details

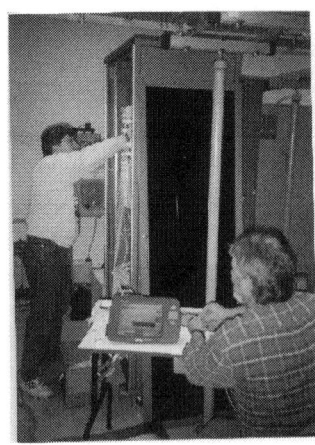

Specialized Test Equipment

Most of these tests require specialized test equipment. Most also have several methods to make the tests. See the review articles in the FOA Online Fiber Optic Reference Guide for more details.

FOA Online Fiber Optic Reference Guide: Testing

Fiber Optic Network Design

- Determine communications needs
- Determine routing and cable plant requirements
- Check power budget
- Choose components
- Create installation plan

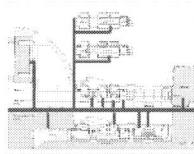
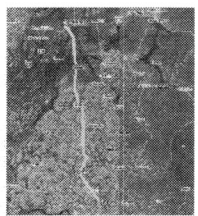

What is fiber optic network design? Fiber optic network design refers to the specialized processes leading to a successful installation and operation of a fiber optic network. It includes determining the type of communication system(s) which will be carried over the network, the geographic layout (premises, campus, outside plant (OSP, etc.) and routing, the transmission equipment required and the fiber network over which it will operate. Next we have to consider requirements for permits, easements, permissions and inspections. When you know the communications equipment and routing, you can calculate a power budget to confirm the system will work once it is installed. Once we get to that stage, we can consider actual component selection, placement, installation practices, testing, troubleshooting and network equipment installation and startup. Finally, we have to consider documentation, maintenance and planning for restoration in event of an outage.

FRG, Chapter 9, RGPC Chapter 5,7, FOA Online Fiber Optic Reference Guide, Understanding Fiber Optics, The Basics: Design

This topic is covered in detail in the "Design.ppt"

Fiber optic "Design" PPT includes detailed information on designing fiber optic networks and loss budgets.

The Design Process
And Writing Specifications For Cable Plants

- Specify route
- Specify network equipment or communication signals
- Specify components, e.g. fiber/cable type and connectors
- User should have specifications for max loss based on loss budget calculations for testing
- Other standard specs needed to create SOW (Statement of Work), RFP (Request for Proposal) and RFQ (Request for Quote)

Writing Specifications For Cable Plants

It's probably impossible to cover every possible issue in a design specification document, but here are some reminders to include:

Specify route

Specify network equipment or communication signals

Specify fiber type and connectors

User may specify connector termination type if preferred, e.g. epoxy/polish, prepolished/splice, fusion-spliced pigtails for SM

User may specify cable and hardware types, but should allow for alternate suggestions. Vendors may be able to offer alternatives that can save cost or enhance performance or reliability.

User should have specification for max loss based on loss budget calculations and reflectance if important

Other standard specs - the "boilerplate" put in every spec!

FRG, Chapter 9, Online Reference Guide, Basics, Design

Design Tech Bulletin

FOA Tech Topics: Users' Guide

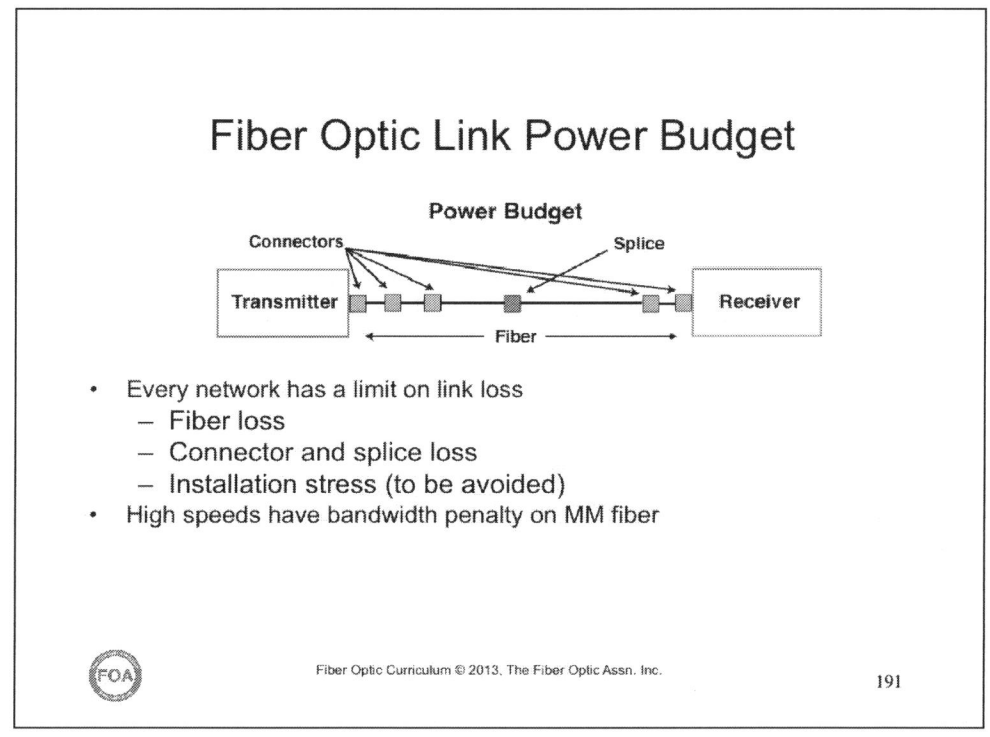

After a fiber optic cable plant is installed, it may be used with a number of different types of fiber optic networks. Computer networks, telephone signals, video links, and even audio can be sent on the installed fibers. Each network type has a requirement for the performance of the fiber optic cable link. Most simply specify the maximum loss in the link that can be tolerated, a function of component specifications and installation quality. Others also specify the bandwidth performance of the fiber which is determined by the specifications of the fiber chosen.

Every fiber optic link has a maximum loss of a cable plant over which it can work. That loss is determined by the output power of the transmitter coupled into the fiber and the sensitivity of the receiver, all expressed in dBm, and the difference between is the maximum loss in dB. The loss of the fiber optic cable (in dB) it uses must be less than that maximum loss for proper operation.

While every link installed must meet some maximum loss to allow operation of the network intended to use it, different networks may have different link margins. Therefore we use a different approach. The loss of the link is considered acceptable if it is less than standard maximum values calculated from the characteristics of the link installation.

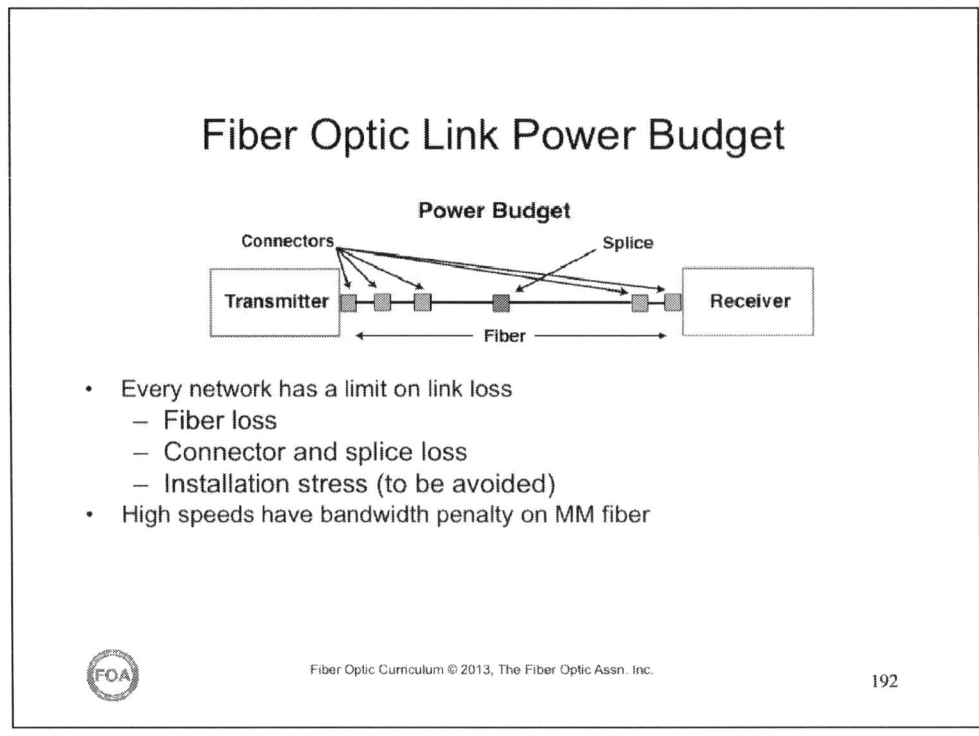

What causes the losses in the fiber optic cable? First the fiber itself. The next loss factor is terminations. Splices are common in singlemode but rare in multimode networks Singlemode fiber is usually spliced with a fusion splicer which welds the two fibers together in an electric arc, with much lower losses.

The final loss factor is stress in installation. Fiber optic cable pulled with too much tension may be damaged. Each time you make a bend with a fiber optic cable, you put some stress in the fiber which can cause loss. Even cable ties tightened on the cable can cause loss. Stress loss should be zero!

The drawings here illustrate the example in the textbook.

Here is a link. The transmitter couples a certain amount of power into the fiber in the cable plant. As the light is transmitted down the fiber, it is attenuated by the attenuation of the fiber and the loss in connectors and splices. In this link, the cable plant has 5 connections and a splice, plus the length of the fiber to cause loss.

FRG, Chapter 9, RGPC Chapter 5,7, FOTM, Chapter 10, DVVC, Chapter 11,

FOA Tech Topics: Loss Budgets

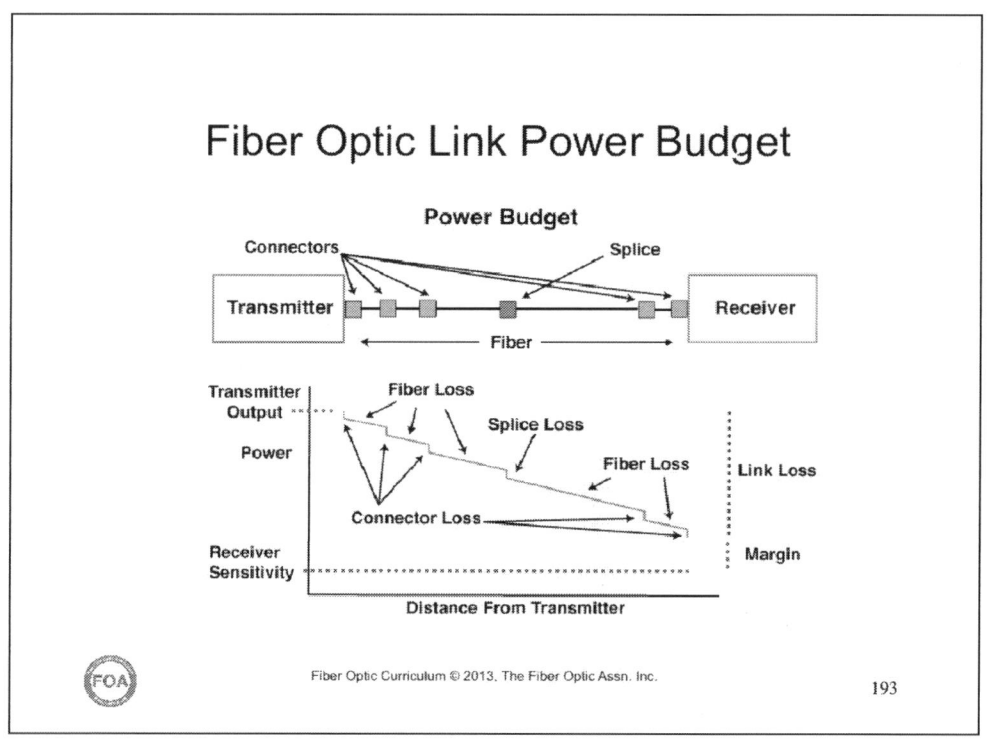

The graph below the link diagram shows the actual amount of light in the fiber along the length, directly corresponding to the link diagram above it. This diagram looks like an OTDR plot, since it is similar to what the OTDR measures. If you are not familiar with OTDRs, we will cover them in the testing sections.

But look at the diagram closely. The power goes down as the light goes down the fiber, reduced by the attenuation of the fiber and the losses in connectors and splices. By convention, we include the loss of the connectors on the end of the cable plant, since when we test connectors, we do so by mating them to another reference connector.

The power level starts at the transmitter output, coupled into the fiber, shown at the top of the X-axis of the graph. After the loss of the cable plant, it is reduced by the amount of the loss. In order for the link to work properly, the power at the receiver must be higher than the receiver sensitivity, shown at the bottom of the X-axis of the graph. The amount by which the receiver power exceeds the receiver sensitivity is the margin of the link.

FRG, Chapter 9, RGPC Chapter 5,7, FOTM, Chapter 10, DVVC, Chapter 11, FOA Tech Topics: Loss Budgets

Fiber Optic Installations

Outside Plant or Premises ?

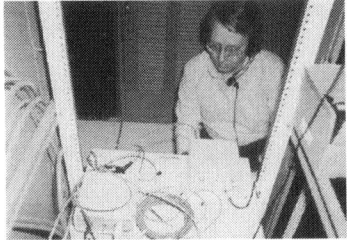

"Fiber optics" is not all the same. "Outside plant" refers tp fiber optics as used outdoors in telephone networks or CATV. "Premises" fiber optics is used in buildings and on campuses.

Outside Plant: Telephone companies, CATV and the Internet all use lots of fiber optics, most of which is outside buildings. It hangs from poles, is buried underground, pulled through conduit or is even submerged underwater. Most of it goes relatively long distances, from a few thousand feet to hundreds of miles, over what we call "singlemode" fiber.

Premises Cabling: By contrast, premises cabling involves cables installed in buildings for LANs or security systems. It involves short lengths, rarely longer than a few hundred to two thousand feet, of mostly "multimode" fiber.

Both these applications are unique in the components they use, the installation methods and the testing procedures, but they share many of the basic principles we learn in this course.

Whether the installation is outside plant or premises is very important to the installer of fiber optic cabling systems.

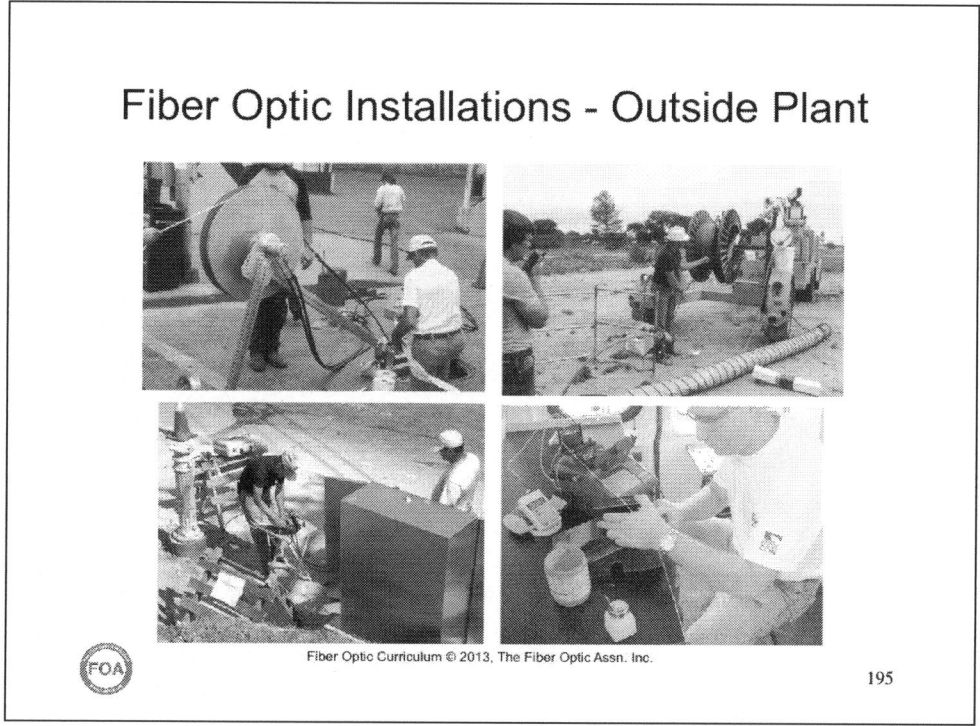

Outside plant installations are almost all singlemode fiber, and cables often have very high fiber counts. Cable designs are optimized for resisting moisture and rodent damage. Installation requires special pullers or plows, and even trailers to carry giant spools of cable. Long distances mean cables are spliced together, since cables are not made longer than about 4 km (2.5 miles), and most splices are by fusion splicing. Connectors (SC, ST or FC styles) on factory made pigtails are spliced onto the end of the cable. After installation, every fiber and every splice is tested with an OTDR. The installer usually has a temperature controlled van or trailer for splicing and/or a bucket truck. Investments in fusion splicers and OTDRs can add up to over $100,000 alone.

Outside plant installations require more hardware (and more investment in the tools and test equipment.) Pullers, splicers, OTDRs and even splicing vans are the tools of the trade for OSP contractors.

FRG, Chapter 10, FOTM, Chapter 9,12,13,15, DVVC, Chapter 11, 15
FOA Online Fiber Optic Reference Guide, Understanding Fiber Optics, The Basics: Basic overview, Installation
See also the FOA PPT presentation on Fiber To The Home/Premises (FTTX)

Cable Installation - OSP Buried

- Know the install method
- Know limits in tension and bend radius
- Attach pulling eyes properly
- Despool by rolling off the spool
- Figure 8 for midspan pulls

CALL BEFORE YOU DIG: Dial 811

Cable Installation - OSP Buried
Know the installation method - direct buried, conduit or innerduct, aerial, etc. and have an experienced crew leading the install. This is not a time for inexperienced people learning on the job. Bring along some new personnel as helpers so they can learn from the experienced ones.
Know limits in tension and bend radius for the cable you are installing.
Attach pulling eyes properly to the strength members and jacket.
Despool cable by rolling it off the spool, not pulling off the sides of the spool, as that will put a twist in the cable and perhaps kink it.
Figure 8 the cable on the ground for midspan pulls to avoid putting a twist in the cable.

The biggest cause of fiber optic network failure (and equally for other buried utilities) is "backhoe fade!" Never dig until you know what is underground where you plan to dig! A new nationwide service is available: dial 811 to get information on buried utilities before you dig! See http://www.commongroundalliance.com/ for more information.

FRG, Chapter 10, FOTM, Chapter 9,12,13,15, DVVC, Chapter 11, 15
FOA Online Fiber Optic Reference Guide, Understanding Fiber Optics, The Basics: Basic overview, Installation

Cable Installation - Microtrenching

- Cuts a narrow groove in roadways or sidewalks
- Inserts small duct to blow in small cables or fibers
- Covers groove to finish the job

CALL BEFORE YOU DIG: Dial 811

Cable Installation – Microtrenching

Microtrenching is becoming popular in metropolitan areas because it disrupts traffic less and leaves less of a mess on roadways.

The biggest cause of fiber optic network failure (and equally for other buried utilities) is "backhoe fade!" Never dig until you know what is underground where you plan to dig! A new nationwide service is available: dial 811 to get information on buried utilities before you dig! See http://www.commongroundalliance.com/ for more information.

FRG, Chapter 10, FOTM, Chapter 9,12,13,15, DVVC, Chapter 11, 15
FOA Online Fiber Optic Reference Guide, Understanding Fiber Optics, The Basics: Basic overview, Installation

Cable Pulling - OSP

- Use powered capstans for applying tension on long pulls through conduit or innerduct
- Use automated tension control
- Apply lubricant as needed

Cable Pulling - OSP
Use powered capstans for applying tension on long pulls through conduit or innerduct to control tension properly.
Use automated tension control equipment available with the capstans.
Plan for lubrication on conduit pulls. See the American Polywater video (www.polywater.com)

FRG, Chapter 10, FOTM, Chapter 9,12,13,15, DVVC, Chapter 11, 15
FOA Online Fiber Optic Reference Guide, Understanding Fiber Optics, The Basics: Basic overview, Installation

Cable Installation - OSP Aerial

- Aerial cable can be self supporting (ADSS), supported by a messenger or, as used by many electrical utilities, inside the optical power ground wire

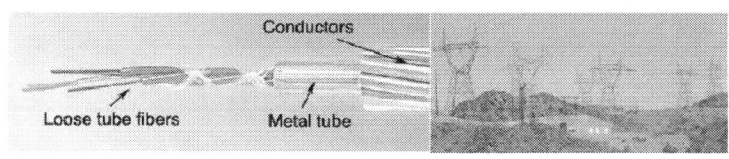

Aerial cable can be self-supporting (ADSS), supported by a messenger or, as used by many electrical utilities, inside the optical power ground wire. Cable manufacturers should be consulted for specific design and installation instructions for their cable designs.

FRG, Chapter 10, FOTM, Chapter 9,12,13,15, DVVC, Chapter 11, 15
FOA Online Fiber Optic Reference Guide, Understanding Fiber Optics, The Basics: Basic overview, Installation

Cable Installation - Submarine

- Beside transoceanic links, includes river and lake crossings
- Requires special cables and appropriate equipment - like boats
- Sometimes trench into bottom to prevent snagging
- Special safety considerations

Submarine/Underwater Cable

Transoceanic links require giant ships and long cables stored in special reels on the ship. Most times a complete link is prepared and installed "hot" - transmitting data" so the condition can be monitored during installation. If anything fails, it can be more easily pulled up and repaired at that time than after the whole cable is installed.

Crossings of lakes and rivers are simpler, but it's a good idea to trench for the cable to bury it and reduce the chances of it being snagged.

Most underwater installs will require special permits. And safety is more complicated!

OSP: Chapter 10

Fiber To The Home
FTTH PON (Passive Optical Network) Network

The latest application for fiber is direct connection to the home, providing virtually unlimited bandwidth, limited only by the electronics delivering services. FTTH involves OSP installation to the curb, drops into the subscriber premises and then requires a home that can deliver the services to telephones, TVs and computers.

FRG, Chapter 10, FOTM, Chapter 9,12,13,15, DVVC, Chapter 11, 15
FOA Online Fiber Optic Reference Guide, Understanding Fiber Optics, The Basics: Basic overview, Installation
See also the FOA PPT presentation on Fiber To The Home/Premises (FTTX)

Premises cabling is mostly multimode in short lengths, rarely longer than a few hundred feet, with 2 to 48 fibers per cable typically. Some users install hybrid cable with both multimode and singlemode fibers. Splicing is practically unknown in premises applications. Most connectors are SC or ST style. Termination is by installing connectors directly on the ends of the fibers, primarily using adhesive technology. Testing is done my a source and meter, but every installer has a flashlight type tracer to check fiber continuity and connection.
Unlike the outside plant technician, the premises cabling installer (who is often also installing the power cable and Cat 5 for LANs too!) probably has an investment of less than $2,000 in tools and test equipment.
Premises applications usually mean lots of cables - both copper and fiber - terminated in telecom rooms.

FRG, Chapter 10, RGPC Chapter 5,8, FOTM, Chapter 9,12,13,15, DVVC, Chapter 11, 15
FOA Online Fiber Optic Reference Guide, Understanding Fiber Optics, The Basics: Basic overview, Installation
See also the FOA Reference Guide: Premises Cabling

Fiber Optic Installations - Premises

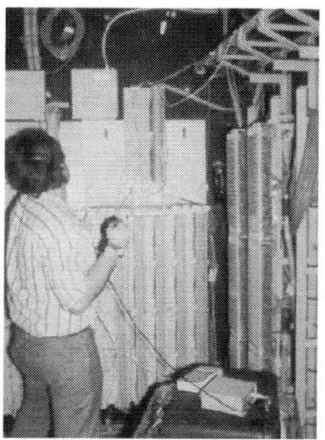
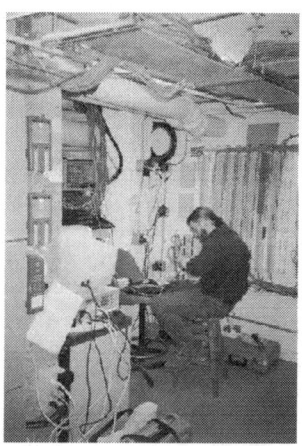

Premises installers need only a termination kit for attaching connectors and a simple test kit for their installations. Working in crowded telecom closets or communications rooms is the norm.

FRG, Chapter 10, RGPC Chapter 5,8, FOTM, Chapter 9,12,13,15, DVVC, Chapter 11, 15
FOA Online Fiber Optic Reference Guide, Understanding Fiber Optics, The Basics: Basic overview
See also the FOA Reference Guide: Premises Cabling

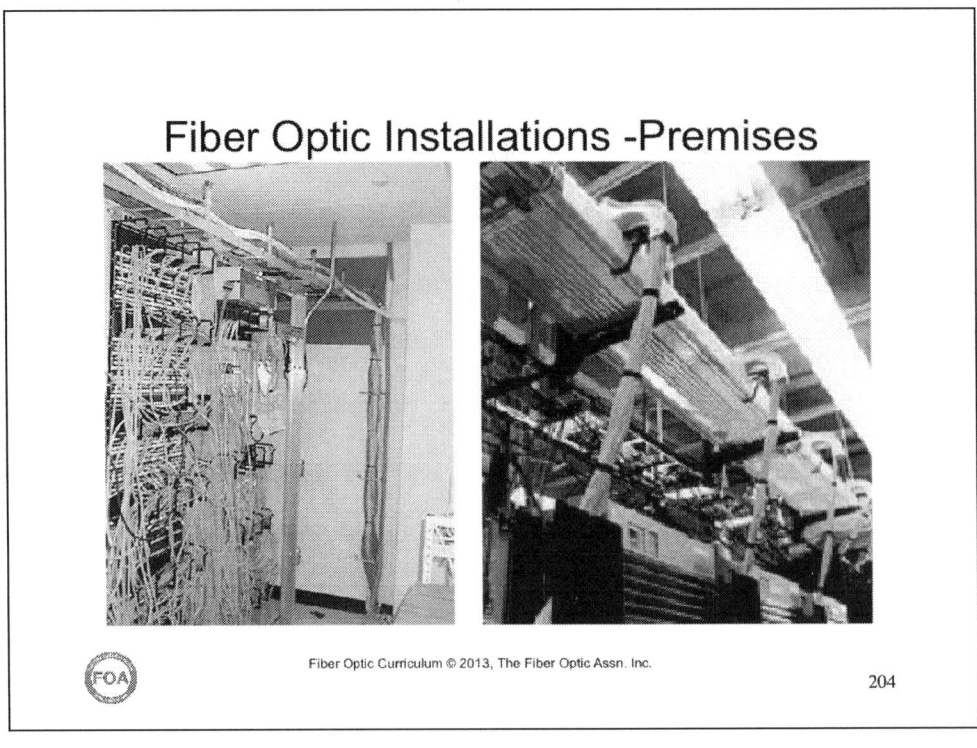

Premises applications usually mean lots of cables - both copper and fiber - run inside the building in conduit, cable trays or proper hangers and terminated in telecom rooms.

FRG, Chapter 10, RGPC Chapter 5,8, FOTM, Chapter 9,12,13,15, DVVC, Chapter 11, 15

FOA Online Fiber Optic Reference Guide, Understanding Fiber Optics, The Basics: Basic overview

See also the FOA Reference Guide: Premises Cabling

Premises Installation

- Cable may be suspended, placed in cable trays or pulled in conduit or fire-rated innerduct
- All cable must meet fire codes
- Mixed with copper cables, fiber should be run on top or suspended below cable trays

Premises Installation

Cable may be suspended, placed in cable trays or pulled in conduit or fire-rated innerduct

All cable must meet fire codes and all installation practices must meet local building and fire codes.

Mixed with copper cables, fiber should be run on top or suspended below cable trays

FRG, Chapter 10, RGPC Chapter 5,8, FOTM, Chapter 9,12,13,15, DVVC, Chapter 11, 15

FOA Online Fiber Optic Reference Guide, Understanding Fiber Optics, The Basics: Basic overview

See also the FOA Reference Guide: Premises Cabling

Premises Installation - Codes

- All cable and cable installations must meet building and fire codes
- All penetrations of fire-rated walls must be firestopped

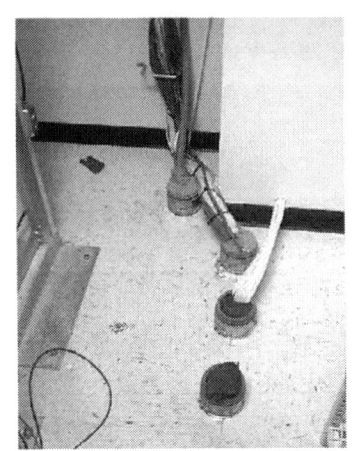

Premises Installation - Codes
All cable must meet fire codes - look for NEC ratings and testing on the cable jacket
All penetrations of fire-rated walls or floors must be firestopped

FRG, Chapter 10, RGPC Chapter 5,8, FOTM, Chapter 9,12,13,15, DVVC, Chapter 11, 15
FOA Online Fiber Optic Reference Guide, Understanding Fiber Optics, The Basics: Basic overview
See also the FOA Reference Guide: Premises Cabling

Fiber Optic Network Installation

- Pre-Installation:
  - Design complete
  - Plans complete
  - Components ordered
  - Coordination with others done, including permits and inspectors
  - Schedule reviewed
  - Site prepared
  - Test plan completed
  - Documentation ready
  - Safety rules posted
  - Components received and secured

Pre-Installation

No installation should begin until there is a complete design, all equipment and components have been chosen, the cable routing is determined and any permits or coordination with other groups is ready. Cable documentation should be started before installation so the installation is properly documented and ready for labeling and recording test data. Documentation will facilitate installation, allow planning for upgrades and provide data needed for restoration.

Components must be ordered and delivered to the job site before installation can begin. Relevant personnel who will be affected by the install, for example those located in the installation area or who may lose communications services, must be notified. If the installation takes more than one day, arrange security to guard the equipment and components left on the construction site.

FRG, Chapter 10, RGPC Chapter 5,8, FOTM, Chapter 9,12,13,15, DVVC, Chapter 11, 15

FOA Online Fiber Optic Reference Guide, Understanding Fiber Optics, The Basics: Basic overview

See also the FOA Reference Guide: Premises Cabling

Fiber Optic Network Installation

- During The Installation:
  - Inspect workmanship at every step
  - Daily review of process, progress, test data
  - Immediate notification and solution of problems, shortages, etc.

- After completion of cable plant installation:
  - Inspect workmanship
  - Review test data on cable plant
  - Set up and test communications system
  - Update documentation

During The Installation Inspect all installation workmanship during the installation itself so any problems can be identified and solved before they become major issues. Daily supervisors and installers should review processes, progress on the job and test data. All affected personnel should receive immediate notification of problems and solutions, shortages, etc. Be careful when installing cables to avoid stress, hazards that may snag cables and kink them or installing cables where heavier cables may be placed on top of them. Bundling cables for neatness is fine, but be careful using cable ties. Tightening them can put harmful stress on the fibers (or pairs in UTP copper cables), so hand tighten them and cut off the excess length. Even better, use soft "hook and loop" ties that can be reopened to move cables.

FRG, Chapter 10, RGPC Chapter 5,8, FOTM, Chapter 9,12,13,15, DVVC, Chapter 11, 15

FOA Online Fiber Optic Reference Guide, Understanding Fiber Optics, The Basics: Basic overview

See also the FOA Reference Guide: Premises Cabling

Myths of Fiber Optics

- Light from the fiber will harm eyes
- Fiber is extremely hard to work with
- Fiber is fragile
- Fiber is expensive
- You need expensive installation and test equipment

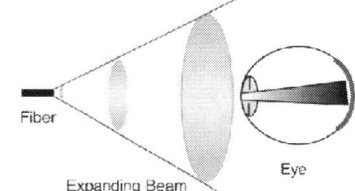

Most fiber optic sources, especially LEDs used with multimode fiber are generally too low in power to cause any eye damage. Some laser transmitters used in gigabit LANs, telecom and CATV systems have higher power and extended exposure could be harmful. Microscopes focus all the light into the eye and can increase the hazard unless they have an infrared filter for protection. So better safe than sorry. NEVER LOOK INTO THE END OF THE FIBER. It's invisible infrared light, so you eye probably can't see it under any circumstances! Check with a power meter before inspecting it.

Fiber is no harder to install, splice or terminate than copper wire. It takes some training, practice and patience, but so does copper.

Fragile? What is a fiberglass boat reinforced with?

Today, fiber is cheaper than kite string or fishing line. Connectors are getting cheaper too. And all the while, copper components are getting more expensive as they try to keep up with fiber for new high bitrate networks.

And a good fiber test set is under $1000 while a copper tester will run $6000 or more.

FRG: Chapter 1, FOTM, Chapter 2, DVVC, Chapter 11
FOA Online Fiber Optic Reference Guide, Understanding Fiber Optics, The Basics: Basic Overview

Safety Rules

- Read and follow rules in lab manual
- Wear safety glasses
- Dispose of fiber scraps carefully
- Work on dark surface to help spot fiber scraps
- Be careful with chemicals
- No eating or drinking

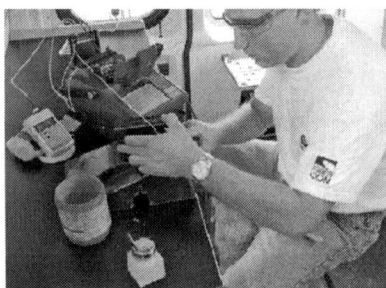

See lab manual for more safety rules

The lab manual has several pages of rules for safety in fiber optic labs. Each student should be familiar with them and follow them carefully. Instructors must follow them too!

FRG, Chapter 10, RGPC Chapter 8, FOA Online Fiber Optic Reference Guide, Installation, Safety Procedures, also in all Instructor and Student Manuals

Preparing For The FOA CFOT Exam

- Study the CFOT reference texts - *The FOA Reference Guides or the FOA Online Reference Guide* and answer all the quizzes
- Study the *FOA Installation Tech Bulletin or NECA/FOA-301 Installation Standard*
- Read supplemental topics on the FOA *Online Reference Guide - there is an online study guide for CFOT!*
- Review this presentation

FRG, FOTM, FOA Online Fiber Optic Reference Guide, Understanding Fiber Optics, The Basics: Plus CFOT Study Guide, linked on Contents Page

Don't forget the FOA YouTube Lectures also!

End

Made in the USA
Charleston, SC
08 March 2017